COACHING THE TIKI TAKA STYLE OF PLAY

WRITTEN BY
JED C. DAVIES

PUBLISHED BY

COACHING THE TIKI TAKA STYLE OF PLAY

First Published November 2013 by SoccerTutor.com

Info@soccertutor.com | www.SoccerTutor.com

UK: 0208 1234 007 | **US:** (305) 767 4443 | **ROTW:** +44 208 1234 007
ISBN: 978-0-9576705-4-9

Author
Jed C. Davies © 2013

Edited by
Alex Fitzgerald - SoccerTutor.com

Cover Design by
Alex Macrides, Think Out Of The Box Ltd.
Email: design@thinkootb.com Tel: +44 (0) 208 144 3550

Diagrams
Diagram designs by SoccerTutor.com. All the diagrams in this book have been created using SoccerTutor.com Tactics Manager Software available from **www.SoccerTutor.com**

Note: While every effort has been made to ensure the technical accuracy of the content of this book, neither the author nor publishers can accept any responsibility for any injury or loss sustained as a result of the use of this material.

MEET THE AUTHOR

JED DAVIES

He is the assistant manager and head of analysis for Oxford University Centaurs and has worked with various youth players throughout Europe. Davies has studied the methods used at FC Barcelona, Liverpool FC, Swansea FC, Villarreal CF, AFC Ajax and a number of teams developing a particular fascination with the possession based philosophies in football as a way of controlling and winning games. Tiki-taka football is a style of football popularised by Spain and Barcelona during the decade ending 2010 and is part of a philosophy in football that has existed right from the game's very beginnings: a way of controlling the game through possession and positional systems.

Jed Davies has been fortunate enough to speak in great lengths with a number of coaches who work at the clubs who currently advocate the possession-based philosophy and in doing so, has developed a clear understanding of what the tiki-taka philosophy is and how it can be developed through purpose designed training sessions.

A train of thought has been developed that football that is played in this way is developed through it's 'form': positional systems, attitudes to building up possession etc. Davies therefore has proposed that football tactics should be designed around the dictum "form follows process", a way of perfect football within an adaptive structure where the structure and positional system is the agent of change, rather than the players themselves.

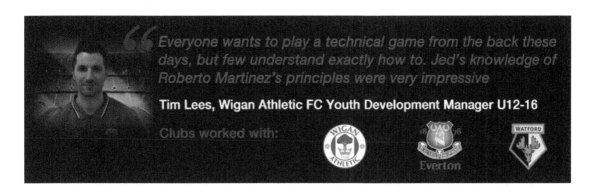

" Everyone wants to play a technical game from the back these days, but few understand exactly how to. Jed's knowledge of Roberto Martinez's principles were very impressive

Tim Lees, Wigan Athletic FC Youth Development Manager U12-16

Clubs worked with:

FOREWORD *by Jonathan Wilson*

In 1872, England travelled north to face Scotland at the West of Scotland Cricket Ground in Partick and football was changed forever. That was the first true international fixture and it led to a revolution in the tactics of the game, the repercussions of which are still being felt today.

At the time, the game was based on dribbling, not the slaloming gambetas of south America, but on head down charging, with strength and power being preferred over technique or skill.

The Scotland team, all of whom were based at the Queen's Park club, looked at England's players, realised they were over a stone heavier per man and decided they had to try something new. In the days leading up to the game, somebody suggested passing to keep the ball away from the English, so they would not be able to dominate the encounter and using charging game with their superior weight advantage. Scotland did so, and achieved a 0-0 draw that was seen as a major success; and so the passing game was born. Possession from the very start was conceived as a defensive tool.

Slowly the advantages of passing began to be recognised throughout Britain and by the end of the century the pure dribbling game had all but disappeared.

It was still Scotland though, and Queen's Park in particular, that was recognised as the centre of passing. R.S. McColl (nicknamed 'Toffee Bob' because of the chain of newsagents he established with his brother) grew up in that tradition.

In 1901, McColl headed south for Newcastle United, who at the time were recognised as a robust, direct side. He soon changed that, persuading his teammates to adopt a passing game that brought three league titles and an FA Cup before the war.

The right back in that side was Peter McWilliam who, in 1912, became manager of Tottenham. There he began to instil the same passing principles in both the first team and the youth sides. He even bought the local non-league side Northfleet Town to use as a nursery side. Although McWilliam was lured away by Middlesbrough in 1927, he returned in 1938 to

reap the benefits of the **pass and move** style he had established, inheriting a side that included Arthur Rowe, Bill Nicholson and Vic Buckingham.

All 3 of these players would go on to have great success as managers but it was Buckingham who was to carry McWilliam's philosophy abroad. He went first to Ajax, where he paved the way for Rinus Michels and gave a debut to Johan Cruyff, and then Barcelona, where again he was succeeded by Michels who was soon joined by Cruyff. Michels added pressing to the pass and move approach and so established what we know today as the Ajax and Barcelona style. It's surely no coincidence that the two Englishmen to have managed Barcelona since Buckingham also have direct links back to McWilliam: Terry Venables spent three years under Nicholson at White Hart Lane, while Bobby Robson learned the game under Buckingham at West Bromwich Albion.

It was Cruyff of course who gave Pep Guardiola his debut.

McColl → McWilliam → Buckingham → Michels → Cruyff → Guardiola

We can trace the very origins of passing football to the modern Barcelona in 6 simple steps over 14 decades.

Jonathan Wilson

Author of 'Inverting the Pyramid: A History In Football Tactics'

INTRODUCTION

For many years, grassroots football has suffered from improper football coaching and has all too often placed too much emphasis on the physical side of football, even throughout youth football competitions. While attitudes may have undergone a paradigm shift at the elite levels of the game in recent years, the remainder of football steps out onto the football field without the appropriate measures of tactical information or the technical ability to fulfil such requirements.

It is the aim of this book to provide the foundations for you to succeed as a football coach, analyst or player. Through a detailed account of the theory behind Barcelona's development model and an analysis of training methods used at Barcelona, Liverpool, Swansea and others advocating control in football through a possession based philosophy, this book provides you with a number of different training methods that support the theory presented.

As a coach, it is necessary to understand the rationale behind your actions and planned activities, so that you can act as an educator and create the appropriate environment for such an education to take place. Equally important is the mutual understanding that all of us should strive to be experts of the game and therefore, as coaches we should accept that we are the perpetual apprentice of the game itself.

The paramount truth is that without an environment that allows creativity to flourish and become unbound, we would not see the same jet-heeled Lionel Messi dribbling through a sea of bodies and yet within Messi's same skill-set is the ability to play the simple pass; that special pass before the assisting pass, the pass that nobody remembers.

This book consists of 4 parts. The first explores the existing development theory related to the training methodologies presented in part 2: "50 Practices to Coach the Tiki Taka Style of Play."

Part 2 puts forward 50 selected practices, each recorded first hand by the author.

Part 3 uncovers the historical influences on the modern day 'control-through-possession' philosophy

and then attempts to break the pertinent philosophy into its simplest components for a multi-dimensional understanding of the game. This part of the book draws emphasis on the view that tactical solutions should derive from the 'form follows process' way of thinking, a philosophy of football whereby the players play within an adaptive set of structures or forms.

As a means of ensuring the book's practical relevance, the fourth and final part delves deep into the tactical theory that supports the training methodology and theory presented in the first 3 parts. The concluding chapters offer professional advice and suggested solutions to a number of reoccurring tactical problems that possession based teams face on a game to game basis.

All in all, I hope that this book will make a significant contribution towards improving the standards of coaching at all levels in football and offer an invaluable insight into the beliefs of those who have successfully implemented such an approach to playing football.

The most important message that I would like to portray to coaches is that they should never instinctively follow the lessons of this book; this book instead represents a conscious emulation of football's genius frozen in a moment and is information that is valid to football of this era.

Finally I would like to acknowledge those who have personally responded to my many emails, given up hours of their time or invited me to observe training methods and learn from their knowledge and experience of the possession based game:

Liverpool Football Club and all the staff at Melwood, Brendan Rodgers (Liverpool FC), Chris Davies (Liverpool FC), Gary Kleiban (Barcelona-USA), Brian Kleiban (Barcelona-USA), Anthony Hudson (the world's youngest ever UEFA Pro License coach, Bahrain U23 Manager and ex-Tottenham Hotspur coach), Tim Lees (Youth Development Manager U12- 16 at Wigan Athletic FC and someone who has studied the methods of Paco Jemez at Rayo Vallecano), Jon Collins (former Reading FC, currently researching a PhD in Spanish training methodology and manager

of Oxford University Centaurs), Gareth Richards (a British coach who has studied at Barcelona), José Reis (professional football coach and ex-student of Vitor Frade, an expert on Tactical Periodisation) , Alex Covelo Lafita (ex-Barcelona player and Espanyol coach), Carles Cuadrat Xiques (ex-La Masia student of ten years and former coach of Barcelona), Albert Capellas Herms (Vitesse Assistant Manager and excoach of Barcelona), Juan Luis Delgado Bordonau (highly qualified coach with coaching experience at Villarreal and Valencia), Isaac Garcia (Barcelona coach), Patrick Williams (Bristol Inner City Football Advanced Development Centre), Jonathan Wilson (author of many great books related to football tactics and history), English FA tutors and highly respected coaches Peter Amos, Jon Murphy and Ian Tincknell.

I would also like to thank all of those who have given up many hours of their time to enable me to complete this book and contributed with their own expertise and who without them, this book may have never been published:

Translators Anna Marin Estarellas (Catalan and Spanish) and Camilo Arias Arias (Spanish); the limitlessly talented artist Nazar Stefanovic, who I am sure you will agree is truly distinctive and one of a kind with his artistic technique; Ben Ryan and Katie Rutledge, for your continued support that has come in so many forms over the years; Bethany Campbell- Boseley and Jon Trew who have given more hours than imaginable to edit each and every page; George Pallecaros and his editor Alex Fitzgerald at SoccerTutor.com who have provided me with the platform to publish my book and illustrate the pages with explanatory diagrams through their excellent Tactics Manager software, which I now use on a daily basis.

I would like to thank Bethany Campbell-Boseley once again for finding it within herself to not only accept losing me while I researched, wrote and rewrote the pages of this book but to support me through each and every page. You never once complained for the lost time we could have shared and for that, I am eternally grateful.

Lastly, I would like to acknowledge those who have written about the subjects within this book before me; all of whom have been included in the referencing and should be considered compulsive reading for anyone passionate about their related area of expertise.

It has taken two years of hard work and I hope that each and every person involved in this book has found it just as satisfying and eye-opening as I did. Thank you for your endurance.

Jed C. Davies

June 2013

CONTENTS

©SoccerTutor.com   *Coaching The Tiki Taka Style Of Play*

PART 3: INFLUENTIAL FIGURES: THE EVOLUTION OF TIKI TAKA 108

PART 4: TIKI TAKA TACTICAL THEORY 143

PART 1

THE TIKI TAKA DEVELOPMENT THEORY

1. THE IMPORTANCE OF SMALL SIDED GAMES FOR TECHNICAL DEVELOPMENT

Research and Studies

"We won, but so what? When (s)he touched the ball three times today. Our responsibility is DEVELOPMENT. So we must play 4 v 4 and 7 v 7 with plenty of time and space – to learn combinations, skills, awareness, and smartness."
Rinus Michels[1]

In our frenetic desire to win, we sometimes forget to celebrate the success of progress and the long-term view of development.

The purpose of this chapter is to isolate small sided and proportionately scaled games as a means of developing the appropriate technical ability and in turn, providing developing players with the technical ability to successfully train (training to train) and thereafter become educated tactically as footballers (training to play).

One of the immediate shifts required that this book suggests is that of a change of perception to particular aspects in football. Technique, for example, is often thought of as the manner of how we handle the football, isolated from many of the important concepts of football, such as the insight in the game and decision making.

Nonetheless, as with many of the concepts covered in this book, technique cannot be isolated in such a way; without the game insight, a player with good technique may not be as effective in a match situation.

In football, the principle criteria for a good pass, cross or shot is measured by the outcome. A good pass for example, is measured on whether the ball arrives at the receiving player in *"the right position, at the correct moment and with the desired speed."[2]*

The technique used to make the pass itself is less about developing the *'ideal technique'* but the *'functional technique.'[3]* Through small sided games, there is little doubt that the elements that make up functional technique are honed and improved on hour by hour.

Former Scottish FA Technical Director Andy Roxburg (now Technical Director for UEFA) spearheaded the movement towards small sided games as the best means of development in youth football (under 12). The principles of the move towards small sided games was based on sound educational and developmental evidence.

"There is little to be gained, and much to be lost, by attempting to force young players into the full game before they are physiologically, bio-mechanically and cognitively ready for the activity. One of the fundamental goals of teaching is to ensure that every player has a high level of success. Therefore we need to assess the development of readiness of the players in each age group."
David Hemery[4]

An independent consultation paper by Grant Small of the University of Abertay Dundee (January 2006)[5] conducted a study with the help of Falkirk Football Club and Motherwell Football Club amongst others to analyse data and compare the benefits of the 4 v 4, 7 v 7 and 11 v 11 games for under 12 football players.

1   Thomas Turner, Ph.D. (2012). Small-sided Games. Ohio: Ohio Youth Soccer Association North. 10.
2   Verheijen, R. (2011). Function Football Technique. Available: http://worldfootballacademy.com/course-programme/football-techniquetraining/. Last accessed 16 August 2013

3   Ibid.
4   Gumbrecht, H.U (2006). In Praise of Athletic Beauty. Cambridge: Harvard University Press.
5   Small, G (2006). Small-Sided Games Study Of Young Football Players In Scotland. university of Abertay Dundee: Independent Consultant Paper

The study showed that players have 3.9 times more touches of the ball in 4 v 4 compared to 11 vs 11 football and twice as many as in 7 v 7.

Similarly, another study from the English FA shows that children touch the ball up to five times more in the 4 v 4 format compared to the 11 v 11 format.

"The differences are considerable as well when the 7 v 7 is compared to the full 11 v 11 game where players touch the ball on average 50% more often."[6]

English FA and FIFA Study

The results showed that during an 11 v 11 game, the ball is out of play for 34.62% of the time and players on average have 0.60 touches per minute. In a 5 v 5 game, the ball is out play for only 1.78% of the time and players take, on average, 2.73 touches per minute.[7]

Other research[8] shows the study of two similar duration 8 v 8 and 4 v 4 game segments resulted in the average number of passes being 135% more in the 4 v 4 game, the average number of scoring attempts increased by 260%, the number of goals shot up by 500%, the number of 1 v 1 encounters rose by 225% and the number of dribbling skills (tricks) increased by 280%.

Manchester United Study

This demonstrated that players in the smaller 4 v 4 games (compared to 8 v 8) made an average of 585 more passes, 481 more scoring attempts, scored 301 more goals, encountered 525 more 1 v 1 scenarios and 436 more dribbling skills (all assuming the duration of the two games are to be equal). The impact was not only on outfield players, as the technical skills performed by the goalkeeper increased by 200-400% as well.

We can conclude that the smaller sided games offer a variety of benefits in the opportunity of improving ones functional and ideal technique.

The smaller games of 4 v 4 resulted in players to play with heart rates of approximately 8-10 beats per minute lower than the 8 v 8 games. Rick Fenoglio argues that the lower heart rate enables a higher concentration in technical development due to the decreased short term fatigue and ability for players to concentrate at a higher level, appropriate for a higher intensity in increasing a player's technical abilities.

Salmela (1995, p.62) suggests for effective learning, an athlete must involve all four components of their development: *"Physical, technical, tactical and mental."[9]*

In a game where players are working at a higher heart rate, short-term fatigue limited the ability for players to concentrate and consequently develop technically, tactically or mentally.

The benefits of small sided games are not only beneficial for technical development but also aid the mental development for the players in preparation for the adult game through the repeated decision making experience that takes place at a rate that is comfortable for the players to maintain a high concentration level.

The decision making and mental abilities are vital in increasing the ability to visualise the options available to a player and to then make a split second decision to see the best solution to the problem he faces.

"In roughly 10 seconds, Paul Scholes will see a hundred alternatives and then make his choices that will draw on his place."
Mick Critchell[10]

"In soccer, all playing actions are made up of a complex combination of perception skills, decision making and execution of technical skills. They all contribute to the success or ball loss. Coaching therefore has to focus on their improvement."

Research on Decision Making
(Manchester United, 2003; Insight, 2004; Winter, 2005)

This has concluded that the ability of children to make decisions in a difficult and ever changing environment is influenced by their developmental age, their exposure to the situation and the complexity of the situation.

---

6   Ibid.

7   Academic research carried out by FA and FIFA research department

8   Fengolio, N (2003). The Manchester United 4 vs. 4 Pilot Scheme For Under-9s: Part II The Analysis. Manchester: Independent Consultant Paper.

9   Small, G (2006). Small-Sided Games Study Of Young Football Players In Scotland. university of Abertay Dundee: Independent Consultant Paper

10   Critchell, M (2011). The Blizzard Magazine issue 3. Sunderland: A19. 99.

A child's capacity to make decisions is limited at an early age, so by limiting the number of players playing in a small sided game, this enables players to feel more comfortable to make decisions and through the process of possession play and decision making in passing options, there is an encouragement of both ideal and functional technical development.

Consequently, getting the correct size of the pitch is important. On a full sized pitch, players with a lower ability spend much of the game running without touching the ball.

Without the direct interaction with the ball or combination play of any kind, the moments of opportunity to develop as players are few and far between.

Research by Kevin McGreskin and Chris Carling[11]

This has offered evidence that a player spends 98.3% of the game in an 11 v 11 (full sized pitch) without the ball. This equates to an average of 53 seconds of the match spent on the ball. In no circumstances can this aid development in young or learning players of any kind.

Thus, it is important that the size of the field should be appropriate for both ability and age.

"We need to teach small sided games which are appropriate for the age and ability of each child."
Mick Critchell

The increase in touches of the ball enables an increase of player creativity on the ball. The use of small sided games there can be an increase in all round technical development, decision making, concentration, creativity, tactical understanding and enjoyment. The love of the game must never be lost.

The Development of the Brain

Mick Critchell, a former consultant for both Fulham FC and Southampton FC, argues that the long term development goes further than the simple rational conclusions that have been made above.

Critchell believes that the English game is often played through the logical and rational part of the brain (the left) and the right hand side of the brain (emotional and intuitive skills) is then underdeveloped because of a lack of creativity and freedom of player expression.

Bulgarian scientist Lozanov made the suggestion of a *'super learning method' in the 1970's, which candidly put, requires both hemispheres of the brain to be stimulated.'[12]*

The side of the brain that the English have developed well (the left) is too slow acting for a fast moving game like football.[13]

Players are best developed and prepared for the adult game when both sides of the brain are developed. It is only then that decision making, creativity and technique merge into one simple effortless activity.

This is the kind of action that Xavi of Barcelona demonstrates on every occasion he touches the ball.

"One thing our coaches don't do that foreign coaches do is teach [the children] to pass the ball, to a player under pressure [and] then coach [aspects such as the] one-two and how to protect the ball under pressure.

Foreign players do that much better than us [which is] one reason why they keep possession better. FA coaching courses need a right old shake up in my humble opinion if we are to move forward, [there are] some really good bits but some ancient bits too."

Rio Ferdinand[14]

Inadequate Academy Training

Despite the vast amount of research that highlights the importance of small sided games for developing players, research carried out by Liverpool John Moore's University found that 50% of training time at English football academies is spent on fitness training or unopposed practices and less than 20% spent on playing small sided games.[15]

12   Wein, H (2007). Developing Youth Football Players. Human Kinetics Europe Ltd. 6.
13   Critchell, M (2011). The Blizzard Magazine issue 3. Sunderland: A19. 99.
14   Ferdinand, R (2012). [Twitter] May 2012 [Accessed July 2012]
15   Critchell, M (2011). The Blizzard Magazine issue 3. Sunderland: A19. 99.

11   Critchell, M (2011). The Blizzard Magazine issue 3. Sunderland: A19. 99.

*"...not only are we developing poor technical players...
we are creating poor decision makers. We need players
who have the ability to play in the future - a vision to
know what to do before receiving the ball. This wont
change unless we get rid of the drills."*[16]

Mick Critchell

Professor Geir Jordet of the Norweigen School of
Sport Sciences analysed 55 English Premier League
midfielders' head movements during matches. Jordet
found that the higher frequency that these players
examined their surroundings, the more successful
their passing rate would be.

*"the visually most active third of the players completed
almost twice as many forward passes as the least
active players."*[17]

Professor Geir Jordet

Glenn Hoddle, is a man who now exclusively concerns
himself with youth development in England and
whose 60% win rate as England manager was
only bettered by Sir Alf Ramsey and Fabio Capello.
Hoddle believes that the misguided youth football
development in England is largely at blame for the lack
of technical ability:

*"We must get these kids having 1000 touches of the
ball a month rather than the 200 they get now."*

Glenn Hoddle, 2011

---

16   ibid
17   ibid

The English FA's Plan for Changes

By the beginning of the 2014-15 season, the English FA hopes that football in England will have fully implemented changes that impact the English game profoundly.

Players will not play 11 v 11 until the age of 12, the 5 v 5 format will be used from under 7 to under 8, with only age appropriate proportional scaled fields and goals.

Then from under 9 to under 10, a 7 v 7 game format will be implemented and the under 11/12's will play a 9 v 9 format with appropriately sized pitches and goals.

These changes will come into place in every league around the country along with new rules that are designed to promote good football being played, such as the 'retreat line.'

The 'Retreat Line'

This is a simple rule where the opposition must make their way back to the halfway line during goal kicks and it is only when the ball has been played out by the goalkeeper that normal play is resumed.

This particular rule is designed to encourage players to play out from the back without competitive pressures for the youngest age groups.

"We were not seeking to emulate one particular country but to look at the best things across Europe and try to develop a new model which is best for English football,...The smaller versions of the game will enable more touches, dribbles, one-on-ones, more involvement and more enjoyment. Where children are enjoying the game more, they are getting better, so that runs hand in hand with development."

Official English FA Statement, 2012[18]

The improvements will have far-reaching benefits on the English game and there will be a positive impact on both the English national team and number of English players playing at the top level of club football.

The English Premier League will no longer be seen as a finishing school for the world's elite, but an arena at which the best English players compete in number alongside the very best the rest of the world has to offer.

"It helped that I had so many quality players' around me. They all seemed so comfortable on the ball (which explained why so many converted from left wing to left back or from midfield to sweeper). They could all pass the ball and had sweet first touches.

In England it was so often the case of 'don't pass to him, he can't handle it."

Chris Waddle on his time at Marseilles

---

18   Conn, D. (2012). FA votes for smaller-sided matches for young footballers. Available: http://www.guardian.co.uk/football/2012/may/28/fa. Last accessed 28 May 2012

Futsal

Futsal is widely considered the national sport of Brazil and is fundamentally a competitive small sided game. It is widely credited for the development of many of its greatest players. It is said that Juninho did not set foot on a full sized pitch with a size 5 football until the age of 14 due to his preference for Futsal.

Being an invasion game, players go about organising their positions collectively in unison to increase the number of shots to goal (directly related to goals) and reduce those conceded by increasing the opportunity to tackle when out of possession.

Frencken and Lemmink (2009) studied this transition between the organisation of players with the ball and then without. The researchers concluded that valuable tactical information can be learnt through the frequency of which the players experience such transitions.

Frencken and Lemmink concluded that the differences in pressures of attacking and defending manipulate the relative positional play from players in a fixed formation, as the damage caused by a possible mistake increases players' (whether consciously or not) learnt ability to tactically narrow down the space around the teammate in possession.

Therefore, from this study we can conclude that futsal and other small sided games do not ignore tactical aspects of the game and are not set about in a free-for-all manner, but founded upon strategical cohesiveness between the teammates dependant on the increased likelihood of danger and where the ball is in possession. This cohesiveness is of great desire in larger sided formats.

Conclusion

This book places a great value of importance upon the significance of well planned and conditioned small sided games as a means of development and the English FA educates its' own coaches to follow the "technique to skill to game" procedure for training sessions for the earliest of age groups.

That is to say the basic functional technique should be isolated in some form for a simplistic drill that enables coaches to intervene and prompt progress through this preferred method of coaching (guided discovery, instructed etc).

The functional technique should then be placed into a game related context in a skill designed drill; it is important that the complexity of the drill is increased to implement the functional technique they have learnt into a game scenario.

Finally, the session should lead to an appropriately designed game that enables the developing player to demonstrate to himself that he can transfer the technique to a game situation effectively and it is here that a small sided game may be the appropriate format of which to enable such a transfer to occur.

You will find a variety of small sided games recorded from observed professional training sessions in the second part of this book and it should be understood that suitable exercises are considered for the element of play the coach is looking to educate players about.

The most important message to take away from this particular format is that it is not necessarily the drill or exercise planned, but the overall message and isolated element of play the coach concentrates his or her effort on.

Keeping training sessions unique and themed is evident throughout professional youth development and keeps the football messages clear and simple for developing players to comprehend.

2. LACK OF CENTRAL PHILOSOPHY
A Critical Analysis of the Long Ball Approach

If you have chosen to pick up and read this book, the likelihood is you are looking to fathom the secrets of how to produce an adapted version of tiki-taka football.

You therefore, may not want to hear about Stoke (under Pulis) or Bolton (under Allardyce) and their strong footballing philosophies. However, to a certain extent they are both excellent proof that there is no right and wrong way of playing football. It is important to understand the targets and aims of other football philosophies.

The long ball methodology is one based upon research and is both as artistic and scientific as tiki-taka. There is something about the way in which Greece won the European Cup in 2004 that was met with universal appreciation.

For you as a coach to begin to educate developing football players, you should understand why you are looking to play with a particular style of play.

You should not aim to artlessly replicate Barcelona's style of play (in terms of player roles) without considering the profile of each and every player you are presented with.

Instead of educating a player to play exactly how an existing celebrated player does, it is often better to focus on the strengths and weaknesses of the developing player and aid the development of each and every unique individual.

"The most important thing in football is to have a style of play, a set of principles that offer organisation to the team."
Jose Mourinho[19]

The 'long ball' philosophy was first conceived in the 1950's by an English theorist called Charles Reep, a man who studied football his whole life and in particular became obsessed with the method and processes of scoring goals. Reep concluded from his studies a number of different outcomes:

- The 3 pass optimisation rule: statistics showed that between three and five passes were evident before the majority of goals scored since the 1954 World Cup; *"over 80 per cent of goals result from moves of three passes or less."*[20]

- 9 shots per goal (the average number of shots taken per goal for each team).

- The average distance that goals were scored from is 12.3 yards from goal.

- The optimum position for an assist was found to have been between the corner flag and the six yard box.

- *"60 per cent of all goalscoring moves begin 35 yards from an opponent's goal."*[21]

Charles Hughes, who acted as head of coaching for the English FA during the 1990's was often criticised for his over-reliance on Reep's findings and the way in which the long ball game has developed at all levels in England.

The publication of the Winning Formula (1990) stood as the English FA's manual and contained several pages under the heading of *"Passing Techniques - Lofted Passes"* and only two that come under the heading of *"Improvisation and Inventive Play."*

The terms 'playing the percentage game,' 'get rid of it' and 'just get the ball in the box' are all inadvertent outcomes of Charles Hughes and Charles Reep's reports. A set of very specific way of playing has developed off the back of their research.

Be that as it may, the game has evolved in many ways since Reep published his findings. Wingers,

---

19   Anon., (2011). Mourinho's 10 commandments. Available: http://www.tonys-soccerschool.net/jose-mourinho-real-madridchelsea-10-tips.html. Last accessed January 2012.

20   Ronay, B. (2003). Grim Reep. Available: http://www.wsc.co.uk/the-archive/918-Playing-the-game/2502-grim-reep-. Last accessed January 2012.
21   Ibid.

Coaching The Tiki Taka Style Of Play

for example were heavily relied on as a source of creativity and provided the assists for many of the goals scored. This may still be true today, yet now the emergence of the central playmaker is one found in abundance across world football.

Modern day footballers have not only become elite athletes and therefore run far greater distances compared to the 1950's, the game itself has changed with the introduction of new laws that have had profound effects on the game.

That said, the long ball tactic is still evident in modern day football. The long ball tactic is one where the ball is played forward into a more advanced zone on the field as often as possible; to increase the number of shots taken per game and at the desired optimum distance from goal.

Furthermore, the effectiveness of crossing from the 'optimum position for an assist' as a methodology of assisting goals is one that has diminished since the 1950's. In modern day football it is considered that a winger has a good crossing success rate at between 25-30%. This means that 70-75% of the time possession is handed over to the defending side.

Opta defines a cross as:

"A pass from a wide position into a specific area in front of the goal."

During the 2011/12 English Premier League season, the average number of crosses per team was 837.2, which equates to just over 22 crosses per game.

Liverpool FC attempted more crosses than any of the other teams (1192 or 31.4 crosses per game), Manchester United attempted 1018 (26.8 per game) and Wolverhampton Wanderers attempted 999 (26.3 per game).

The teams who attempted the fewest were Blackburn (610 or 16 per game), Fulham (649 or 17.1 per game) and Swansea (721 or 19 per game).

Interestingly both Wolverhampton Wanderers and Blackburn were relegated from the English Premier League during this relevant season.

More important however, was the number of crosses per goal. Liverpool required 421 crosses from open play per goal, equating to a cross to goal rate of 0.25%.

In consequence, by allowing Liverpool to cross the ball in the game, the opposition were able to regain possession. Wigan were the team with the next most crosses needed per goal (294) as they had a cross to goal conversion rate of 0.34% and at the other end of the scale Manchester United needed 44.5 crosses per goal, Norwich 45.1 crosses per goal and Arsenal 48.4 crosses per goal. This translates as Manchester United scored one goal every two games from a crossing situation.

It should be noted that all three of the teams with the highest cross to goal ratio are far from being teams with long ball tactics. The average number of crosses needed per goal in the English Premier League for the 2011/12 season was 79 open play crosses per goal with a crossing success rate of 20.5%.

We try and condense these statistics into one general piece of meaningful data. By employing a tactic that forces the opponents to have possession in the wider areas of the field, you are likely to regain possession 79.5% of the time and likely to concede a goal 1.3% of the time.

These figures are far lower than the likelihood of conceding a goal through a more central attacking threat and this explains why teams often chose to play with a narrow, compact defensive approach, one that manipulates the opposition to play in the wider areas of the field and provides you with the opportunity to regain possession in behind the opposition's winger and attacking players.

When the long ball game is successful, a team can be devastating with their attacking processes.

Reep suggests that it was irrelevant as to whether the long passes found their intended target or not:

"While the intention should always be to find a teammate with each long forward pass,...the long pass not received brings valuable gains, and is by no means wasted."

Charles Reep

Charles Reep goes on to claim that his findings suggest that 5 long passes that do not find their target are as effective as 4 long passes that do find the intended target.

There are a number of modern day developments that pose problems for Reep's viewpoint. As modern day football has developed players have become far more effective with their possession retentive passing approaches.

Reep and Hughes' studies assume that both teams are frequently trying to score and therefore willing to lose possession in their bid to score goals.

Nevertheless, research carried out since the turn of the millennium has offered insight that suggests that Reep's research may well be out of date and impractical for modern day football.

Opta statistics that covered the 2008-2010 English Premier League seasons suggest that in only 30% of games did one team have 60% possession or more and as a result won 52% and only lost 25% of the games.

Furthermore, if a team won 70% of the possession or over, they would win 67% of the time and lost only 17% of games.

To summarise, a team that has 50-59.9% possession lost 31% of games, won 43% and drew the remaining 26% of games. There is a clear correlation between winning the possession battle and winning games.

Other managers have conducted their own statistical research with their own teams over the years and arrived at team-specific data:

"If you are better than your opponent with the ball you have a 79 per cent chance of winning the game."
Brendan Rodgers

In a more pragmatic battle of tactics, it is easy to see how the long ball team (if ineffective with their long passes) will continually return possession back to the possession based team and therefore go on to spend the majority of the game chasing shadows.

What becomes more interesting still, is when you see how Opta calculate their possession statistics.

One would assume that this statistic is calculated by using two stop-watch style timing devices that are then both drawn as a percentage out of 100%.

Opta, however, uses the number of passes rather than the number of minutes in possession and subsequently, we can adjudge that the team who

passes the ball more is more likely to win games. This is an outcome that Charles Reep and Charles Hughes did not arrive at.

Possession play does require more than just 'passing' as the only objective to conquer the opposition. Organisation is imperative to how players should win games, the organisation of defending and attacking.

The one time AC Milan manager, Arrigo Sacchi, set about proving that organisation was far more effective than passing freely to dominate possession.

"I convinced [Ruud] Gullit and [Marco] Van Basten by telling them that five organised players would beat 10 disorganised ones...And I proved it to them. I took five players: Giovanni Galli in goal, [Mauro] Tassotti, [Paolo] Maldini, [Alesandro] Costacurta and [Franco] Baresi. They had 10 players: Gullit, Van Basten, [Frank] Rijkaard, [Pietro Paolo] Virdis, [Alberigo] Evani, [Carlo] Ancelotti, [Angelo] Colombo, [Roberto] Donadoni, [Christian] Lantignotti and [Graziano] Mannari.

They had 15 minutes to score against my five players, the only rule was that if we won possession or they lost the ball, they had to start over from 10 metres inside their own half. I did this all the time and they never scored. Not once."
Arrigo Sacchi

So we can ratiocinate that a modern day football philosophy should be based on organisation first and foremost. A lack of cohesion with either philosophy (short passing or long ball) would be one defeated by any organised philosophy.

"It is more realistic to decide on a system; deciding, for instance, that you want to play the ball on the floor, not in the air, and then you need to create a philosophy at your club where everyone has the same one."
Rafael Benitez[22]

A sustainable philosophy is one where the approach is implemented throughout the whole club; a global approach. This way, a clear line of sight can be given to an under 13 academy player and the first team spots that he wishes to one day compete for.

---

22 Benitez, R. (2012). Rafael Benitez: England have the talent – but not the philosophy. Available: http://www.independent.co.uk/sport/football/news-and-comment/rafaelbenitez-england-have-the-talent--but-not-the-philosophy-7881158.html. Last accessed 26 June 2012

Coaching The Tiki Taka Style Of Play

An unsustainable philosophy is one that can not be continued, one that relies on the size, speed, strength or any other unique variable of the players in the first team; for example, the success of Bolton Wanderers from 1999-2007 under Sam Allardyce relied heavily on the basis that a Kevin Davies type player was ready to be called on when Davies was unavailable.

It is far more likely that Mark Davies (Bolton's technical midfielder) could be replaced to some degree in a system of short passing than Kevin Davies could be replaced in Bolton's long ball approach.

The point here is that one system is a whole approach that requires the cohesion of all eleven players and the other one (long ball) relies on the success of one or two stronger players.

"I'm a team player. Individually, I'm nothing. I play with the best and that makes me a better player. I depend on my team-mates. If they don't find space, I don't find them with the ball and I become a lesser footballer."
Lionel Messi[23]

At Barcelona, their own unique playing philosophy flows down the spine of each and every squad through an incredibly structured and hierarchical development model.

Once you have decided on a proposed way of playing and developed the basic principles of play unique to your playing squad, you should consider both the structure of the club and propose a central philosophy that is both achievable and backed up with theoretical and practice evidence.

---

23   *Hunter, G (2012). Barca: The Making of the Greatest Team in the World. Glasgow: BackPage Press Limited*

3. A GLOBAL FOOTBALL PHILOSOPHY
Barcelona

"The example of the Barcelona model was a great influence and inspiration to me. When I was at the Chelsea academy, that was how my players would play, with that high, aggressive press, combined with the ability to keep the ball."

Brendan Rodgers[24]

The philosophy at Barcelona is a global approach that runs throughout the entire makeup of the club. The club identity starts in 'PreBenjami' squad made up of players aged 7-8 years and it is here that the club begins 'tactical training', often through outnumbering teams in training in favour of the team in possession.

The players then continue to develop the technical and tactical elements of their game through a series of squads that make up different age groups:

- **PreBenjami** (ages 7-8)
- **Benjami** made up of 3 teams: Benjami A, B & C (9-10)
- **Alevi** A, B, C and D (11-12)
- **Infantil** A and B (13-14)
- **Cadet** A and B (14-15)
- **Juvenil** A and B (16-18)
- **Barcelona** A and B (16+/18+)

Within the club there are thirteen different teams that cover a variety of different ability levels and it is the flexibility of ability levels rather than age groups that provides much of the clubs training success.

Realistically, very few survive more than 3 years at the club. Barcelona handled 256 players between all the teams at the club during the 2011/12 season and released 82 players in the summer of 2011 as 80 new players were added.

These 80 new players were chosen from the 4,763 trialists. This natural competitiveness benefits the club in a number of different ways and spirals right up to the first team.

The club is in a position to expect the maximum effort from its players throughout the club because of the competitiveness.

However, this competitiveness is set about in a way that does not leave younger players feeling that they have no chance to succeed, as there is a clear line of sight from the youngest age groups through to the first team.

"You will retire me, but Iniesta will retire us both."

Pep Guardiola to a young Xavi

Of the 114 La Liga goals that Barcelona scored during the 2011-12 season, 78% of them were scored by La Masia graduates. Very few clubs worldwide can claim such a success story with their global club philosophy.

"The player who has passed through La Masia has something different to the rest, it's a plus that only comes from having competed in a Barcelona shirt from the time you were a child."

Pep Guardiola

---

24   *Vickery, T (2012) The Blizzard Magazine. Sunderland: The Blizzard Media Ltd.*

Ajax

It is by no means a coincidence that there are direct links between Barcelona's success and the famous Ajax academy and 'totaal voetball' of the 1970 and 1980's: Rinus Michels, Johan Cruyff, Johan Neeskens, Louis Van Gaal, Frank Rijkaard, Ronald Koeman, Frank and Ronald de Boer etc.

The Dutch philosophy, like La Masia, is one that pays careful treatment to the development of youth and consistently produces football players with an excellent level of functional and ideal technique.

Like La Masia, players at De Toekomst of AFC Ajax receive a footballing education that coincides with the first team's methodology from the youngest age groups at Jong Ajax.

"We try to develop players through a specific culture, a specific philosophy, and to show them in general terms how Ajax want to play football. It is an advantage if players have already played in the same system for many years. So yes, in that sense, it is very important for Ajax."

Danny Blind

The Dutch approach to youth development is an approach that has been honed over many years. They have based their development schemes on a set of principles:

- Youth development is a joined responsibility of the Association and the Clubs.

- The best players play with the best against the best.

- Talented players have about 6 training sessions and 1 or 2 competitive games per week.

- Well educated and football experienced coaches for talented players.[25]

A report from the KNVB Academy coach Albert Stuivenberg suggests that training is to be purposeful and match orientated from day one.

The Dutch development programme isolates particular characteristics that the training should cover.

The core training methods that are ball orientated should set out to improve passing, receiving, dribbling, shooting, heading and sliding.

Without the ball, the programmes sets out to improve attributes, such as running into free space, squeezing, pressing, marking and covering.

The development programme also identifies core supportive characteristics that are to be trained:

Insight of the game, the individual player, player choices, observation skills, promotion of both team tasks and the team function.

The team functions are the attacking, defensive and transition stages of the game. The team tasks are to prevent the opposition from scoring and the build up play of your own attack.

The KNVB Academy identifies an age related training programme that aims to simplify the more complex components of the end product, the team philosophy:

Under 6 - Learning to control the ball (training to train)

Under 7 - Goal orientated actions with the ball (training to train)

Under 10 - Learning to play goal orientated together (training to play)

Under 12 - Learning to play from a basic task (training to play).

Under 14 - Fine tuning of basic tasks as a team (training to play).

Under 16 - Playing as a team (training to play).

Under 18 - Learning to be competitive.[26]

---

25   Stuivenberg, A. (2008) The Dutch Vision On Youth Development. Amsterdam: KNVB Academy.

26   Ibid.

Coaching The Tiki Taka Style Of Play

What has become evident is that the training towards the first team philosophy is strategic and set up in a way so that no player is lost within the youth academy development process.

Every player starts his youth academy education with a clear line of sight on a futuristic first team opportunity.

"The basic methodological concepts must be instilled in both the elite and the base. At Porto I regularly met with the youth and reserve team directors to explain exactly how all the different teams should play. That way no player gets lost when making the step up. Everything is already trained into his mind"

Jose Mourinho

4. ESTABLISHING A CENTRAL PHILOSOPHY

Barcelona's 2012 position as the perfect role model is a result of over 40 years of hard work, since 1971 to be exact. Barcelona's identity would eternally stem from the day *Rinus Michels* landed after the outspoken manager transferred from an extremely successful Ajax team.

It was not for another 8 years that the entire club received a global makeover after **Johan Cruyff** recommended to Josep Núñez that the academy should be remodelled in 1979.

The first graduates started to arrive 9 years later:

Guillermo Amor, a midfielder who went on to play in 311 La Liga matches. Amor was shortly followed by goalkeeper Carles Busquets, the infamous Pep Guardiola and Albert Ferrer (857 La Liga appearances between them). All of whom made their debut under the management of Johan Cruyff, who was appointed first team manager in 1988 and brought with him an evolved total football philosophy, one that would later lead to **Louis van Gaal** and **Pep Guardiola** moulding into what tiki-taka is perceived as today.

Liverpool FC

When Pep Segura (a former Barcelona youth coach) was drafted in by Rafa Benitez at Liverpool FC in 2009 to facilitate a youth academy overhaul to bring a 'global approach' to the club, no one was expecting immediate pure home grown success.

Pep Segura brought in wholesale changes to the way in which the club operated and listed a number of criteria to achieve a successful global club approach:

- Everyone must do the same work.

- We must be inspired by street football.

- *"Street soccer is the most natural educational system that can be found."*
  Rinus Michels[27]

- Street football is gone and we have to work hard to make up for it.

- We must use rectangular surfaces to work on depth and breadth.

- We must always breathe offensive spirit.

- Explain to children the meaning of 4-2-3-1 to understand it [formation].

- Develop the game from the defensive line.

- Teaching the collective game based on our system.

- Emphasise creativity:
  The English player is disciplined and easily learns automation and order, but the Spanish player is more creative and we must move in this direction.

- The game related detail is difficult to apply to players and coaches because they are awaiting orders without thinking for themselves. When they do receive the detail, they work hard, but they suffer when they have to bring their own creativity.[28]

The horizontal and vertical collaboration across the entire club, from the ages of 8 to 21 has been stressed throughout; the remainder of the criteria is founded on attempts to improve technique, creativity, tactical and philosophical understanding.

In short, the information found in the first part of this book make up much of the rationale and the foundations behind moving forward to developing an adapted unique playing philosophy such as tiki-taka.

"I wanted to see the connection between the first team and...the child. I wanted to see from close how the club worked on developing the under-9s, how they put that ethos of technical continuity into practice."
Brendan Rodgers[29]

The Liverpool (re)model proposed a progressive training building block style approach to development similar to those of the Barcelona, Ajax and Dutch models.

- The youngest base their training around playing games, technical skills.

- As the players develop, the youth are to then progress: technical skills, tactical work starts, physical work starts.

- As players approach the age of 15-16, the training should specialise and concentrate heavily in areas such as technical skills, tactical work, physical work and psychological.

- As young adults (16-18), players should learn to win, they should begin to work towards the in-depth training capacities: technical skills, tactical work, physical work and psychological work.

"The program is a great tool to implement and not just having a good criteria for selection of players. It's the idea and style that make an organisation strong."
Pep Segura

27 Michels, R (2013). Team Building: The Road To Success. Reedswain Soccer.
28 Perarnau, M. (2011). El programa de la Liverpool Academy, por Pep Segura. Available: http://martiperarnau.blogspot.co.uk/2011/06/el-programa-de-la-liverpool-academypor.html. Last accessed June 2012.

29 Auclair, P (2012) The Blizzard Magazine issue 6. Sunderland: The Blizzard Media Ltd.

The program also sets out a strict regime, one that details the quantity of hours that the academy should provide for their youth at each relevant age:

- **Ages 8-12:** 35 weeks of competition and 3 sessions weekly.

- **Ages 13-15:** 35 weeks of competition and 4-5 sessions weekly.

- **Ages 16-18:** 40 weeks of competition and 7-8 sessions weekly.

- **Ages 19-21:** 42 weeks of competition and 7-8 sessions weekly.

With the assumption that each training session is 1 hour and 30 minutes long, we can calculate that from the age of 8 to 21, a graduate would have received between 4,000 and 5,000 hours of training at the academy.

This equates to 4000-5000 hours of a purposeful and progressive education that works towards a potential place in the first team squad.

"I try to educate players. You train dogs, I like to educate players both on and off the field."
Brendan Rodgers[30]

By breaking the club up as a project that has the goal of fulfilling roles in the first team, the youth development teams are just that, 'youth development.'

Therefore, the importance of results is taken away and a coach is measured by how well developed players are, not by how well the team has done in the cup or league competitions.

"Menezes argued that Brazil's clubs count on good structure in which to develop young players, but especially in contrast to Barcelona, were lacking any philosophy of formation.

There was no long term, collective vision, he said. The project is always an individual one - usually the quest for the youth team coach is to do well enough to gain promotion to the more senior ranks...In Brazil, even in youth football, we are not able to live without giving priority to results."

The global approach begins at the under 9's level with a view on the first team, an education into how to fit within the club's philosophy, an education of 'belonging.'

This education however, is a loose one that enables the player to grow into their own mould of themselves. They must picture how they will better the existing.

You do not educate players in such a way to say, 'you'll be taking Xavi's role, so become the next Xavi.'

Each player is to understand the philosophy and yet fit within the system with his own unique playing style.

"There's a first question: What do we want to replace Xavi, who has the script of number 4 (Xavi)? My idea is that we think that in ten years we will continue to play equally wonderful football, but not as we play now. We will have other things. "
Andoni Zubizarreta[31]

Subsequently, you do not educate players to mimic the existing first team member in your position, it's about evolution and that perennial drive forward into the unknown. New players come together to form a new and adapted version of the present.

"There may be one who understands my words that I will change the system and I will transgress the game model, 'now let's play something else'... Laudrup is not the same as Messi, both play the false nine role. Both are excellent companions and providers of power and force opponents to go out and create space behind. But if we wanted to clone Laudrup, Messi would not have come..."
Andoni Zubizarreta[32]

"The football of the past we have to respect, the football of today we must study, and the game of the future we should anticipate"
Bora Milutinović [33]

30   Darby, J. (2012). Brendan Rodgers unveiled at LFC press conference. Available: http://www.anfield-online.co.uk/lfc-news/2012/brendan-rodgers-unveiled-at-lfc-pressconference/. Last accessed June 2012

31   Perarnau, M. (2011). El programa de la Liverpool Academy, por Pep Segura. Available: http://martiperarnau.blogspot.co.uk/2011/06/el-programa-de-la-liverpool-academypor.html. Last accessed Ju
32   Ibid.
33   Wein, H (2007). Developing Youth Football Players. Human Kinetics Europe Ltd. 248.

5. A LOCAL TALENT IDENTIFICATION PROGRAMME

The successful academies of Ajax and Barcelona have produced some of the games greatest ever talents. You would be forgiven if you assumed that the best academies are a product of the world's best scouting networks, flying to all corners of the globe to draft in the best talent available.

Interestingly though, both academies have not only found much of their talent in their own countries, but within their own local regions through their **T.I.P.S** (Technique, Insight, Personality and Speed) approach to talent identification.

There is evidence to suggest that the success of a youth academy is not down to the scouting network, but founded upon competitiveness and a purposeful education and development process.

The German national team and domestic league is one that showcases one of the most successful progressive development procedures put into place in recent years. Of the 525 players currently playing in the German Bundesliga, 275 (52.4%) have been trained in one of the countries elite academies.[34]

Bayer Leverkusen 04 for example, drafts 90% of all it's academy members from nine local catchment areas and 20% of players in German professional football are still contracted to the clubs of which they received their academy education.[35]

What this shows is that through a progressive line of sight at the youth academies and an effective development procedure, it is possible to produce professional football players who are able to one day fit within a first team structure.

It is therefore not necessary to over spend on squad rotational players at any level of football, as they can be developed within in abundance.

Youth players are available at a local level, and it is about development, it is about the global philosophy.

It is not about purchasing the next best young group of Brazilians. Barcelona's La Masia is made up of 90% Spanish and of which 50% are Catalan.[36]

This suggests that while talent is both diverse and complex, it is in abundance all around you. There is no need to travel the world. It is a matter of educating the existing players in a progressive manner and promoting player development through all the stages in a way that enables the player to blossom, to fulfil his or her potential.

34   Bender, T (2011). 10 Years Of Academies. Frankfurt/Main: Bundesliga
35   Ibid.

36   Scottish Football Association (2009). Scottish Football Review. Glasgow: Independent Consultant Paper. 49.

6. PLAYER POTENTIAL AND DEVELOPMENT

They say it takes 10,000 hours of purposeful practice to produce an expert. That's 2 hours and 44 minutes every day for ten years of progressive training (Ericsson, et al., 1993; Ericsson and Charness, 1994, Bloom, 1985; Salmela et al., 1998; Coyle 2009; Syed 2011; Rasmus 2012).

"Improvement is no accident. It comes with hard work, practice & a love for the game."
Thierry Henry

Scientific research has suggested on a number of cases that there is no such thing as a person born with talent or the ability to become an expert in any chosen field. Instead, people become experts through purposeful practice, of somewhere around 10,000 hours.

"We deny that these differences [in skill level] are immutable; that is, due to innate talent...instead we argue that the differences between expert performers and normal adults reflect a life-long persistence of deliberate effort to improve performance."
Anders Ericsson[37]

"There is absolutely no evidence of a 'fast track' for high achievers."
John Slobaboda[38]

Child prodigies such as Tiger Woods, Mozart, Venus and Serena Williams, Lionel Messi and Sofia, Susan and Judit Polgar are all examples of people who simply crammed in their thousands of hours at a much earlier age. It is said that Mozart was to have clocked up 3,500 hours of practice by the age of 6.[39]

---

37   Syed, M (2011). Bounce: The Myth of Talent and the Power of Practice. London: Fourth Estate
38   ibid. 18.
39   Ibid.

'Geniuses Are Made Not Born': The Polgar Sisters Chess Experiment

Sofia, Susan and Judit Polgar are all sisters whose Father Laszlo Polgar (an educational psychologist) believed that **"geniuses are made, not born,"** so much so that Laszlo actually set out to train world class performers before they were even born.

Laszlo convinced Klara to take part in such a proposal, one where Laszlo set out to prove this theory. Chess was to be the chosen area of expertise due to its objectivity of confirming expertise. Susan was the first to undergo Laszlo's 10,000 hours of progressive educating in the game of Chess and at the age of just 15 Susan became the top ranked woman in the world, a title she kept for the next 23 years, winning numerous competitions along the way (including the title of Olympic Champion).

Sofia Polgar was the next to undergo Laszlo's educational experiment and believe it or not, at the age of 14 she won the "Magistrale di Roma" tournament, defeating several Grandmasters, including some of the greatest male players, and recorded the strongest performance in history by a 14 year old.

Finally, Judit completed the trio of successful sisters by becoming the youngest person ever to win the Grandmaster at the time, aged just 15 years and 4 months. Judit is now universally considered the greatest female player of all time.

After Susan became the first female grandmaster in history, Laszlo was approached by a Dutch billionaire named Joop van Oosterom and asked to adopt three boys from a developing nation to see if he could replicate the results.

Lazlo was hooked by the idea but Klara, his wife, declined the proposal. In her mind, they'd proven the theory and did not want to repeat the years of progressive dedicated educating required to replicate such results.

"Children have extraordinary potential, and it is up to society to unlock it."
Laszlo Polgar[40]

Many believe they see a child who is naturally gifted, one who has inherited the ability. In reality they are witnessing what is called "the iceberg illusion," the result of thousands of hours of purposeful training rolled up into the product that is presented before the onlooker.

"[Some] say it was a coincidence that a man who set about proving the practice theory of excellence using chess just happened to beget the three most talented female chess players in history. Maybe some people just do not want to believe in the power of practice."
Klara Polgar[41]

Other recorded findings that suggest that the powers of practice results in improvement lie within the Olympic records.

In 1891 the world record for the 100m was set by Luther Carey at a recorded time of 10.8 seconds and over time each perceived unbeatable and supernatural like record has been beaten, time and time again.

The world record in 2012 held by Usain Bolt stands at 9.58, a time many now consider unbeatable. The same is true across every recorded event at the Olympics, as progress prolongs our existence and each and every purposeful hour is progress.

To say that the improvements over time have been a result of Darwinian evolution is incorrect; evolution takes place over a much larger time span.

Laszlo Polgar believes that **"geniuses are made, not born"** and in proving that statement, the biggest variable amongst all the improvement is not one based around a natural gifted ability but one that comes down to the number of hours practiced and the methodology used to further development. The power of practice exists.

---

40 ibid. 85.

41 ibid. 99.

7. FC BARCELONA CASE STUDY
Approach to Purposeful Training Hours at La Masia

When a 20-year old has completed ten years at La Masia of Barcelona he would have accumulated 5,600 hours of organised and structured training (not including any hours before the age of ten or outside of the organised training).[42]

Typically a Barcelona player will have arrived at La Masia aged ten, having already accumulated somewhere between 3,000 and 5,000 hours.[43]

The **5,600 hours** are broken down as follows:

- 1000 hours of practicing conservation games, learning individual skills and correcting errors

- 1000 hours of rondos. The rondo is a training exercise that will be explained in the latter parts of this book and put simply harvests all the benefits of small sided games and futsal.

The players are constantly attempting to find and make space where there seemingly is not any and keep the ball in a selected size zone.

- 1750 hours of tactical and positional training. These are extremely purposeful and tie together the above in the form of a playing strategy and identity, known to us as tiki-taka.

- 1250 hours of competitive partidillos (practice matches). These are competitive in the sense of perfecting the strategies and philosophical ideologies but games are not played for points or a place in a competition, therefore the result is not important.

It is said that Iniesta and Xavi lost more matches than they won between the ages of 18 and 19 and won nothing at all from the ages of 12 and 14.[44]

- An average of 600 hours of official competition minutes per player throughout the ten year period.

The 5,600 hours are purposeful and start at hour one; the hours are all aimed at one singular concept of the first team playing identity.

So to conclude, a player who has arrived at age 20 and has completed his La Masia training is likely to have undergone between 8,600 and 10,600 hours of training.

Typically, the player would still be expected to endure a further 3 years before truly challenging for a first team place at Barcelona A at the age of 23.

The final stages of learning at Barcelona B are then the most complex, difficult and demanding of all the hours.

The players are expected over the course of 1.5-2.25 years to complete three distinguishable stages of development in the Barcelona B set up. These three stages offer a clear line of progression and development for both the players and coaches to analyse.

Barcelona B Stage 1 *(6-9 months)*

Players at this stage are expected to make mistakes and will be rotated with one another for a spot in the first team. It is vital that there are spots in the first team available for these rotational players. Players should play enough games over the course of the 6-9 months to prove their worth as a first team player.

42   Perarnau, M. (2011). Las fases del aprendizaje. Available: http://martiperarnau.com/articulos-de-futbol/formativo/las-fases-del-aprendizaje/. Last accessed June 2012

43   Somewhere between Felipe from Rocinha who will achieve 10,000 hours by the age of 13 and the average English footballer who won't achieve 10,000 hours until his late twenties. The Gold Mine effect 32%

44   Ankersen, R (2012). The Gold Mine Effect: Crack the Secrets of High Performance. London: Icon Books Ltd

Coaching The Tiki Taka Style Of Play

Barcelona B Stage 2 *(6-9 months)*

Stage two players are now regarded as first team players, but are often the players who are either substituted or rotated with stage one players.

These players are on the other hand, now to be considered as part of the permanent structure and are now expected to play a significant role in matches.

Barcelona B Stage 3 *(6-9 months)*

These players are regarded as key players and work closest with the first team squad. Stage three players are expected to lead the team by example and have progressed significantly since their stage one development level.

Mistakes are to have been corrected and minimised, a confidence is expected for these players to take the weight of expectation and pressure of good consistent performances.

Any player who does not fulfil the set stages would be a mark for concern in his progression, no player is allowed to stagnate.

Across the board however, players will need to improve the fundamental skills to meet the levels required to fulfil the concepts of the playing style.

Through the maturity of each stage, players will learn a number of different important character traits that will become useful for them in their journey to the first team.

There is a constant reminder that each player is expected to perform with a growth mindset.

8. PURPOSEFUL TRAINING

Now, whether or not you believe in Ericsson's theory; whether or not you believe the innate qualities in a person contribute to his or her talent, there are some themes found in Ericsson's scientific theory (evidence or otherwise) that this book employs as an underlying structure to it's educational progress of the students.

Each and every hour spent training should be set about in a way that suggests that no hour has gone unplanned.

This is something that the great Jose Mourinho underlines with great importance, the value of planning and purposefulness of every training session.

'Purposeful training' is a term to suggest that training is to be carried out in a very particular way for it to be included in the 10,000 hours of training.

It is worth noting that while others might, this book does not claim that after 9,999 hours, 59 minutes and 59 seconds of training you will then be classified as an expert or elite performer. There are many other aspects of development and training that collaborate to produce such an observation. Nevertheless, aspects such as the psychological development and the correct mindset contribute to the exact definition of purposeful training.

What is meant by 'Purposeful Training'?

(Sometimes referred to as 'deliberative practice')

Imagine yourself driving your car to work for the ten thousandth time and now try to recapture your thoughts and feelings the very first time you sat in the drivers seat to pull away.

The level of concentration, eagerness to learn and progress from the very first hour have probably all been forgotten, you now drive with the music on and often either talking with someone else sat in the car or day dreaming.

If your car driving experience is anything like the above, you're now in 'autopilot' mode as you have established a skill level appropriate for driving your car and are no longer interested in further learning.

You may well have driven over ten thousand hours, but the reality is you may well only have the ability of a driver who has the experience of two thousand hours. That is to say you stopped progressively learning how to drive way before your ten thousandth hour.

Similarly, when a football player feels that training has become all but too easy and that they have the talent to turn up and put in flawless performances without much effort, training then is far from 'purposeful' or progressive.

A player who believes that he has the talent to do just this will absolutely stall in his development. Time and time again we see child prodigies fall from their cloud and plummet into obscurity, not because of injuries but because of a failure to sustain a growth mentality.

Many candidly believe that potential is something destined and their talent is one given to them. They forget how hard they have worked to get to where they are, an ability level that has brought them a flurry of interest from the talent scouting media.

9. GROWTH MINDSET: CAROL DWECK'S EXPERIMENT
'Always Praise Effort and Not Talent'

Carol Dweck (1998) conducted an experiment that sheds light on the fall of child prodigies such as Cherno Samba (a former Millwall player destined for greatness in the English game and considered the greatest talent the country has ever seen at the age of 14).

Dweck took 400 children, all aged 11 and presented them with simple puzzles.

After the children completed the puzzles, they were then given their qualitative scores and a simple six word qualitative phrase. 50% of the children were praised for their intelligence (ability) and were told "you must be smart at this", the other 50% were instead praised for their effort, "you must have worked really hard."

The next stage in the experiment was to ask the children whether they would like to try a harder test or another puzzle equally as hard as the one they had just completed.

Astonishingly, two thirds of the students praised for their intelligence opted for the easier puzzle of the two, where as 90% of the children who were praised for effort opted to attempt the more difficult test.

The effort-praised group were not interested in success but exploring their own potential in a more fruitful challenge. On the other hand the ability praised group did not want to risk losing their 'smart' label.

The final stage of the experiment was for all children to then complete a final puzzle that was no harder than the first original puzzle.

Remarkably, the ability praised group results declined by 20% and the effort praised group increased by 30%.

The findings of this experiment are significant to the way in which we should view progress in development as the effort praised children were 61.5% better than those who were praised for their ability.

We can presume 2 things from this experiment:

1. Always praise effort and not talent.

Talent is often viewed as something that comes naturally and without any elaboration, whereas effort implies that one has worked hard to get to where they are.

Praising children's talent can harm their motivation, performance and progress. Effort praising prompts a growth mindset and enables progression.

2. 90% of the effort-praised group decided to take a harder test in between these two easier puzzles.

By testing oneself on the edge of their own ability, even momentarily, one can significantly improve their ability [read on to see why].

"I prefer inspired perspiration to momentary inspiration, talent to strength, the action of effort to the over-performance of sacrifice."
Marcelo Bielsa[45]

---

45   Loftheim, T (2012). Josimar Magazine; June. Oslo: Josimar

10. TRAINING AT 'THE EDGE OF YOUR ABILITY'

"A player learns and grows by trial and error. The important thing is to learn from mistakes"

Laurence Moorhouse and Leonard Gross[46]

In 1981, Pierce and Stratton conducted a study where 453 youth sport participants were asked to state their worries that may lead to them not playing the sport in the future.

62.5 % identified that making a mistake was their single biggest concern. 44.2 % stated that the anxiety of making a mistake prevented them from playing at their full potential.

The importance of the coaches role in ensuring mistakes are not blown out of proportion by either themselves or other players is very important.

In most cases the player who has made the mistake has already identified themselves that it occurred and therefore do not need reminding or highlighting again.

Offering a strategic insight to a player who continues to make the mistake and cannot find his own resolutions is another matter all together.[47]

It has become unclouded that the most effective way for one to learn is to learn through failing, to understand why they are failing and then correct the actions. For that reason, by training at a level just beyond the comfortable reach of your playing ability, you are in a zone that is described as the edge of your ability.

The German proverb *"you will become clever through your mistakes"* is one that this handbook works from as it's base line.

"Striving for what is just out of reach and not quite making it; it is about grappling with tasks beyond current limitations and falling short again and again."

Matthew Syed[48]

The paradoxical perception of failing to succeed is a concept found throughout success in all forms of sport.

"I've missed more than 9000 shots in my career. I've lost almost 300 games. 26 times, I've been trusted to take the game winning shot and missed. I've failed over and over and over again in my life. And that is why I succeed."

Michael Jordan

Progress is in effect, built upon the foundations of necessary failure and Colm O'Connell is in agreement when he states that *"a winner is a loser who has evaluated himself."*[49]

In the following paragraph there are two columns and ten listed collaborative words. Your instructions are to find a pen and paper, a quiet spot to concentrate and simply read over both columns and identify each word. Then, close the book and write down as many of the words as you can remember.

COLUMN A	COLUMN B
(1) painting/brush	a-chitectu-e/house
(2) dog/collar -	e-taurant/waiter
(3) knife/plate	li-r-ry/books
(4) window/door	paper/pla-tic
(5) light/dark	Lon-on/Par-s
(6) sugar/tea	bic-cle/wheels
(7) bin/rubbish mobile	ph--e/p--ne bo-k
(8) sofa/pillow	we-dnesday/thur-day
(9) perfume/odour	pink/w-ite
(10) Tokyo/New York	boo-/magazine

46   Moorhouse, L; Gross, L. (1977) Maximum Performance. New York: Mayflower Granada Publishing
47   Wein, H (2007). Developing Youth Football Players. Human Kinetics Europe Ltd. 8.
48   Syed, M (2011). Bounce: The Myth of Talent and the Power of Practice. London: Fourth Estate. 111
49   Ankersen, R (2012). The Gold Mine Effect: Crack the Secrets of High Performance. London: Icon Books Ltd

Coaching The Tiki Taka Style Of Play

If you are like most people, it would not have been close, you will have remembered around 3 times more of the words in Column B. The 300% increase is down to the milliseconds of struggle you encountered when identifying the word.

The experiment above is based on the work of Robert Bjork, who acknowledged that through struggle, learning can accelerate. Bjork identifies perseverance and struggle as key aspects of learning successfully.

"You think effortless performance is desirable, but it's really a terrible way to learn."

Robert Bjork

The lessons learnt from above are that your selected training methods should also aim to be at the edge of the players' abilities, a selected and targeted method of struggle to force the players to slow down and correct mistakes.

By slowing down one is able to act more attentively to errors in a way that creates a higher degree of precision. Then, through adjusting the speeds at which players learn, the players acknowledge the skill's inner architecture and build a working perception of the necessary blueprints.

The players then fully comprehend the shape, rhythm and technique of the skills; a holistic understanding of how to perform the relevant skills successfully. When failure arrives, the player then has a strategy of how to fix the failure to execute his task.

It is imperative to perform at a speed that allows you to understand exactly what you are doing wrong in order to put the mistakes right.

"If you don't know what you are doing wrong, you can never know what you are doing right."

Chen Xinhua[50]

Under these circumstances, training should always be test ability.

FUTSAL

One of the fundamental reasons Futsal functions so successfully as a driver of development is down to the testing structure to the game. There is a reduction of space and time that forces players to learn how to succeed in such extreme scenarios not found on a full sized pitch as often.

"No time plus no space equals better skills. Futsal is our national laboratory of improvisation."

Dr Miranda[51]
(Professor of football at the University of Sao Paolo)

Futsal is a prime example of how a well designed training method can improve particular aspects of a players game in relation to the understanding of space and time on a football field, as you have to create your own time and space that scarcely seems to exist.

It is through the increased opportunity to fail that the players enhance their abilities in such scenarios.

In conclusion, it is easy to understand just how training at the edge of one's ability can enhance the opportunity to progress.

Therefore, a mindset should be installed that enables players to understand the success in failure, that failure is the most important aspect in development.

"Try again. Fail again. Fail better."

Samuel Beckett

---

50 Syed, M (2011). Bounce: The Myth of Talent and the Power of Practice. London: Fourth Estate.

51 Cited in Coyle, D (2010). The Talent Code: Greatness isn't born. It's grown. London: Arrow.

Coaching The Tiki Taka Style Of Play

11. COGNITIVE TRAINING

Implementing a successful football playing identity is a transition that entails an extremely complex set of ideologies to be put across in the simplest form possible.

The building blocks to 'good decision making' on a football field can be learned through the processes of 'chunking' information and recognising patterns. It must be experienced and lived and cannot truly be taught as a spectator.

"Good decision making is about compressing the informational load by decoding the meaning of patterns derived from experience. This cannot be taught in a classroom; it is not something you are born with; it must be lived and learned. To put it another way, it emerges through practice."

Matthew Syed[52]

Put plainly, decision making is something that can be learnt through experiencing a particular situation and learning how to achieve the correct outcomes.

Andre Villas-Boas is a scientific based football coach and believes in the fundamentals of rehearsed improvisation; that is to recognise patterns in a chaotic and emotional sport decoded through the tactics and strategy employed. This means identifying important elements and placing them into a meaningful framework.

The method of chunking can be trained in an unclouded and well thought out manner. First, one needs to see and understand the finished product of the skill they are attempting to accomplish.

Then the finished product should be divided into it's smallest possible chunks, much like learning the lyrics to a song, you learn the chorus and verses separately before putting them all back together.

Lastly, the training method requires a variance in the time to slowing the action right down and then speeding the action back up. This gives the player control and teaches him an understanding of the skill's inner architecture.

In response to that, when learning how to keep possession, the coach should break possession down to it's simplest components (playing out from the back, off the ball movement, passing combinations, understanding the geometry of the spaces on the field etc) and then bring them all back together.

The coach should be able to suggest particular training methods that are appropriate to the given playing ability before him. More importantly, the coach should be able to identify when a team can move on and progress through the levels of training difficulty:

"The second they get to a new spot, even if they're still groping a little bit, I push them to the next level."

Linda Septien[53]

The coach is present to point out errors or failures using his or her theoretical knowledge and to then offer a strategy to improve. This aids progressive development and purposeful training hours.

Remember, if there is a choice between telling students what to do or letting them discover the answer themselves, always opt for self discovery.

"You've got to make the kid an independent thinker and problem solver."

Robert Lansdorp[54]

When training for rehearsed improvisation you have to remember that no two scenarios are ever the same on a football field and therefore, to successfully train players to make good decisions in moments of improvisation that still fit within the framework of your playing identity, you should opt for a training method of chunking.

52   Syed, M (2011). Bounce: The Myth of Talent and the Power of Practice. London: Fourth Estate. 60.

53   Coyle, D (2010). The Talent Code: Greatness isn't born. It's grown. London: Arrow. 119.
54   ibid. 195.

Coaching The Tiki Taka Style Of Play

Remember in spite of that, you are attempting to teach the principles of situations and not show them the correct thing to do time and time again.

The players need to form a deep rooted understanding of what to do in each scenario and space and not learn a specific pre-learnt pass for each scenario. Independent thinking and problem solving are key aspects of a players tactical make up and you should directly aim to focus on training these aspects of cognitive development.

The learning on the other hand, must be taken out in an experiential way.

"According to John Whitmore in Coaching of Performance, a pupil remembers 19 percent of what the teacher taught him some three months ago through instruction or telling, whereas he can recall 32 percent of what was demonstrated and explained.

Yet in cases where pupils were given the opportunity to generate the information on their own, but with the help of a teacher, fully 65 percent of the information was memorised."

Horst Wein[55]

---

55   Wein, H (2007). Developing Youth Football Players. Human Kinetics Europe Ltd.

12. THE POWERS OF TRAINING THE MENTAL ASPECTS OF A PLAYER

It will come of no surprise to you that effective creativity, decision making and tactical understanding are some of the most difficult aspects to isolate and train in football.

Many youth coaches have therefore made the conscious decision that a player's mental attributes, such as mental toughness and experiential maturity are ones that develop naturally and therefore should not be directly covered when drawing up a training scheme.

Nonetheless, these mental attributes offer some of the most important aspects of developing football player's capability of playing football at the highest level.

"The psychology of the game...it's the single biggest thing that I concentrate on once you take away the technical and tactical side of football."
Brendan Rodgers[56]

56   Liverpool FC Magazine, Issue 01 (2012). Liverpool: Liverpool Football Club.

The Power of Imagination: Effective Visualisation

In 2004 Dr. Judd Blaslotto, a researcher at the University of Chicago, conducted an experiment that highlights the fundamental advantages of effective visualisation.

Blaslotto split a basketball team into three equal sized groups: Group A, Group B and Group C. All three groups were to record how many free throws they could score with a limited amount of free throws.

After this, the three groups were given three different tasks over a period of a month.

Group A were asked to not practice free throws for a month at all, Group B were asked to practice free throws for an hour a day and Group C were asked to only visualise perfecting free throws for the same period of time.

After a month all three groups were recalled and asked to repeat the recording of how many free throws they could score with the same limited amount of free throws.

As expected, Group A (having not practiced) did not improve at all, Group B scored 24% more free throws after practicing an hour a day for a month.

Remarkably, Group C improved by 23% without having physically practiced at all. Visualisation had therefore been almost as effective as physical practice.

The act of thinking over exactly how to perfect a free throw and immersing yourself in this zone led to a significant improvement. It is important to note that the person(s) visualising the act must do so in the first person, they must visualise themselves and not be a spectator.

In this particular experiment the basketball player would have visualised the feeling of the ball, the movement in the body and power behind throwing the free throw, the sound of the ball bouncing in preparation, leaving the fingers and then hitting the net or board and visually the participant would have seen the ball spinning through the air from the fingers and the ball swish through the net.

The vision requires that all of the small details be considered and each of the senses be satisfied; touch, smell, sight, sound and even taste.

Mental imagery has been suggested by a number of different studies[57] to enhance the abilities in an athlete in a number of different ways:

- Reduce the risk of injury
- Increase motivation
- Maximise enjoyment
- Increase energy levels
- Boost your immune system
- Increase focus
- Improve performance

Michael Phelps famously set a world record during the 2008 Beijing Olympics in the 200 metre butterfly event and afterwards he was asked by a reporter what it had felt like to win. Phelps responded *"It felt like I imagined it would."*

What many forget to remember is that during that particular race, Phelps' goggles had completely filled up with water and he set the world record effectively swam blind in the third turn and final lap of the race.

57   (1)Isaac, A. R. (1992). Mental Practice- Does it Work in the Field? The Sport Psychologist, 6, 192-198

(2) Martin, K.A., Hall, C. R. (1995). Using Mental Imagery to Enhance Intrinsic Motivation Journal of Sport and Exercise Psychology,17(1), 54-69.

(3) Orlick, T., Zitzelsberger, L., LI-Wei, Z., & Qi-wei, M. (1992). The Effect of Mental-Imagery Training on Performance Enhancement With 7-10-Year-Old Children. The Sports Psychologist, 6, 230-241

(4) Pavio, A. (1985). Cognitive and Motivational Functions of Imagery in Human Performance. Journal of Applied Sports Science, 10, 22-28.

(5) Porter, K., Foster, J. Visual Athletics. Dubuque, Iowa: Wm. C. Publishers, 1990.

(6) Roure, R., et al. (1998). Autonomic Nervous System Responses Correlate with Mental Rehearsal in Volleyball Training. Journal ofApplied Physiology, 78(2), 99-108

(7) Theodorakis et al, 1997

Coaching The Tiki Taka Style Of Play

He could not see the line along the pool's surface beneath him or even the black T-mark that indicates that a wall was approaching and a turn was required. Even so, Phelps was prepared.

"Watch the video tape. Watch it before you go to sleep and when you wake up" [58] Bob Bowman (Phelps' swimming coach) would say to Michael Phelps as a young teenager. The video tape was not real, it was a mental visualisation of every stroke and action before, during and after 'the perfect race'. Phelps would imagine himself stepping up to the block as his name would be called out, swinging his arms three times (as he still does today) all the way through to the moment he would rip his swimming cap off from his head again and again, until he knew every moment by heart.

Bowman would later instruct Phelps to 'get the video tape ready' before big moments in competition and Phelps would carry out each and every second of his visualisation to the smallest of details.

In many ways, Phelps' preparation for any swimming race does not begin the moment his alarm clock wakes him in the early hours, but the preparation for every race began many years before, during the mental visualisation of his perfect race.

Over the many years, Bowman would challenge Phelps' visualisation with a situation that may occur, such as the moisture of his goggles causing his vision to become blurry.

These visualisations and the many hours spent training in the dark (an intentional ploy from Bowman to encourage Phelps to truly think about each and every action) had prepared Phelps for his 2008 Beijing Olympics triumph despite losing his sight in an Olympic final.

Some coaches will argue that sporting success is generally made up of (estimated) 90% mental and only 10% physical performance.[59] Visualisation can be seen as a useful tool for overcoming performance anxiety, mental trauma (past injuries for example) and negative thought patterns.

However, coaching visualisation to see the benefits is an extremely difficult thing to do, as the benefits are only seen when the student is able to find his or her own unique and extremely personal successful methodology of mental training.

The only realistic solution is to show just how other successful athletes prepare mentally and allow them to select what might work for them.

"Part of my preparation is I go and ask the kit man what colour we're wearing, if it's a red top, white shorts, white socks or black socks. Then I lie in bed the night before the game and visualise myself scoring goals or doing well.

You're trying to put yourself in that moment and trying to prepare yourself, to have a 'memory' before the game...when I was younger I used to visualise myself scoring wonder goals, stuff like that. From 30 yards out, dribbling through teams. You need to visualise yourself doing all that, and when you're playing professionally, you realise it's important for your preparation."

Wayne Rooney[60]

"I imagine the ball coming towards my bottom right hand corner, and see myself catch, parry or punch it away. Then I go through every variation of that short and save. Game days are a classic. I wake up in the morning, get breakfast or whatever, jump in the shower and then just stand there for 10 minutes going through it. Then jump in the car, I stop at the traffic lights, catch a few crosses and go on. When my teammates are up the other end of the pitch, I'm busy visualising what might take place."

David James[61]

58   Duhigg, C (2012), *The Power of Habit: Why We Do What We Do in Life and Business*, London: Random House Books.
59   Weinberg, R. and Gould, D. (2006) *Foundations of Sport and Exercise Psychology*. London: Human Kinetics

60   Jackson, J. (2012). *Wayne Rooney reveals visualisation forms important part of preparation*. Available: http://www.theguardian.com/football/2012/may/17/waynerooney-visualisation-preparation. Last accessed June 2012.
61   Anon., (2004) *David James*. Guardian Newspaper 22nd May 2004

Eliminating Doubt

Some of the most problematic negative thought patterns that lead to sporting error stem from doubt.

"The power of doubt lies in its self-fulfilling nature. When we entertain a lack of faith that we can sink a short putt, for example, we usually tighten, increasing the likelihood of missing the putt. When we fail, our self-doubt is confirmed...Next time the doubt is stronger and its inhibiting influence on our true capabilities more pronounced."
Timothy Gallwey[62]

The viscous cycle of doubt is one that can sometimes be to blame for the downfall of an athletic career. Performance can be affected significantly.

The most effective way to combat doubt is to tackle the situation by preparing for training and playing using an appropriate methodology. Timothy Gallwey (in his book *'The Inner Game of Golf'*) provides us with an insight into one way of overcoming immediate doubt before an important action (such as penalty or free kick taking).

'By vividly associating with this easy act there is no room left in the mind to associate the upcoming putt with failure...each time I succeeded in totally immersing myself in this concept, there was not a trace of doubt in my mind about sinking the putt."
Timothy Gallwey[63]

In this situation, Gallwey speaks about visualising a simple action such as picking the ball up out of the hole, in order to overcome the more complex action of putting the ball in a high pressure scenario.

Matthew Syed, the former three time Commonwealth Table Tennis Championship winner is one of a large percentage of professional athletes who undergo an extremely strategic and structured pre-match mental preparation process.

Syed sets out his strict procedure in his book 'Bounce' and goes into great detail of how exactly he prepares:

- In a quiet private spot, Matthew close his eyes and a uses a series of breathing exercises to quiet down the body and mind.

- Followed by a visualisation process that begins with third person imagery, he imagines himself watching a great game of table tennis as a spectator, remembering what he loves about the game and immersing himself in the position of a an enthusiast watching over wonderful shots and touches.

- The visualisation perspective then shifts as he becomes the player. Syed replays a retrospective memory of all his most successful touches and shots.

This is a first hand replay of his greatest moments, remembering what it felt like to make the best shots of his career.

- The visualisation then switches again, now he is playing the game against the opponent he is to face.

Syed imagines all the tactical ploys he has prepared working perfectly, a harmonious successful performance. He imagines the shots, touches and movement around the table and imagines the feelings and sounds to accompany the visual aspects.

- Lastly, Syed completes his prematch preparation by repeating the phrase 'YOU can win' over and over, as he importantly speaks to himself in the second person. Only when the adrenaline kicks in and his mind and body are at ease, only when confidence is oozing, only then does Syed open his eyes.

It is easy to see how such a strict perfected system can work in drastically altering your mindset before a game.

---

62   Gallwey, T (1986). *Inner Game of Golf.* London: Pan.
63   *Ibid.*

Coaching The Tiki Taka Style Of Play

Matthew Syed knows that this preparation will also go a long way into improving his technique during the opening moments of the match, since 'under-pressure technique' and your mental state are directly related.

Confidence solidifies and the right state of mind has developed.

Arsène Wenger

Arsène Wenger knows that confidence, the elimination of doubt and optimism are all key components in preparing yourself before a game.

Wenger relies on the philosophy that you must set your mind on the possibilities of success, rather than the probabilities of failure or error.

It goes without saying that the mental characteristics of a player are clearly key components in performance and successfully completing purposeful practice.

Possessing the abilities to irrationally believe that you are capable of winning and preparing yourself mentally for a competitive match or purposeful training session are fundamental requirements in elite performance in football.

'To perform to your maximum you have to teach yourself to believe with an intensity that goes way beyond logical justification.

No top performer has lacked this capacity for irrational optimism; no sportsman has played to his potential without the ability to remove doubt from his mind.'

Arsène Wenger[64]

---

64   *Syed, M (2011). Bounce: The Myth of Talent and the Power of Practice. London: Fourth Estate.*

Mental Toughness

The term 'mental toughness' is typically used *"to describe players who seem to possess an unchangeable confidence, an unrivalled determination to succeed and an unparalleled control of their emotions and environment."*[65]

Mental toughness is in a sense, the umbrella term given to many of the mental issues mentioned to this point and there can be no argument about the importance of the mental attributes of players and the links with their performance.

"One of the most consistent relationships ever identified in science is the association between time spent practising and improvements in performance."
Farrow, Baker & MacMahon[66]

"[in any case, the] difference between winning and losing can come down to the head, and not the body."
John Kremer, Aidan P. Moran[67]

Scully and Hume (1995) carried out a study on elite athletes and found that mental toughness was perceived to be the most important determinant of success in sport and many other studies have arrived at the same conclusion.

This book has posited the idea that while mental toughness is key to match performance on the pressure based competitive match days, the development of a successful mental approach starts well before the match day. The purposeful training requires a detailed and successful mental approach too, as mental toughness is such an important component of any sport.

"When it comes down to it, there are two qualities that are necessary for victory in any sport: ability and mental toughness."
Michael Sheard[68]

The variety of situations well covered by mental toughness branches over the ability to cope with pressure, stress and adversity,[69] overcoming setbacks[70] and possessing the ability to persist or a refusal to quit,[71] sustaining the ability to withstand heavy criticism (undeserved or otherwise) and avoid becoming upset (to disadvantage) when losing or performing poorly.[72]

Much undisputed research has been carried out which concludes that successful elite sports performers have a seemingly superior psychological skill-set to others[73] and it should come as an unquestionable facet of football development that throughout the development of players and a football identity, it should never be forgotten that each development procedure should be unique to the individuals in the playing squad.

What may work for one team may not work for another set of similar aged players, purely down to a difference in culture or other experiential football and life paths.

Angela Lee Duckworth, an assistant professor of Psychology and the University of Pennsylvania, has noticed that throughout her studies on success (in teaching, sales professionals and students) the most successful are generally those who have combined

---

65   Doherty, M. (2012) Mental Toughness in Adolescent Athletes and its Use as an Indicator of Competitive Performance. Oxford Brookes University
66   Farrow, D., Baker, J., and MacMahon, C., (2007) Developing Sports Expertise. London: Routledge. 29.
67   John Kremer, J., Mora, A., (2012) Pure Sport: Practical Sport Psychology. London: Routledge. 13.

68   Sheard, M., (2010) Mental Toughness: The Mindset Behind Sporting Achievement, Second Edition London: Routledge. 4.
69   Bull et al, (2005); Clough, Earle & Sewell, (2002), Gould et al, (1987); Jones, Hanton & Connaughton, (2002)
70   Gould et al, (1987); Jones, Hanton & Connaughton, (2002)
71   Cashmore, (2002;) Gould et al, (1987); Jones, Hanton & Connaughton, (2002)
72   Clough, P.J., Earle, K. & Sewell, D.F. (2002) Mental toughness: The concept and its measurement. In I. Cockerill (Ed) Solutions in Sport Psychology, London: Thompson. 32-47.
73   Crust & Azadi, (2010); Golby & Sheard (2004);Gould, Dieffenbach & Moffett, (2002)

a passion for a clear and well defined target with an unshakable determination to achieve their goals, regardless of any 'interference' in the way.

She calls this **'quality grit,'** but it is obvious for all to see the parallels with mental toughness and it is present from a very early age and one that matures in your mid-twenties.

"In England we've judged players by the time they are 17 or 18."

David Webb[74]
(Southampton FC professional football scout)

Yet those who have been released are neither fully developed physically or mentally. With players generally reaching peak physical fitness in their late twenties and early thirties (dependant on position) and the brain not being fully developed until the age of 25, it seems absurd that there is an overriding importance put on physical attributes, opposed to the player's mental fitness.

Players will continue to develop physically beyond the age of 17 and 18 and it is arguably far too young to make a judgement on whether the academy player is one suited to professional football.

It is far more realistic to use Jamaican sprinting coach Stephen Francis' model of judgement and understand that a lack of experience, psychical and mental development are all different types of interference (Performance = maximum performance level - interference).

So much emphasise is put on a football players physical make up, you should wonder just how much is really put on the mental toughness of a player, far beyond just their confidence. They need a growth mindset and everything else that is in the cocktail in the approach to development and purposeful training.

"I think that coaches either forget, or don't even realise, that football is a hugely cognitive sport."

Kevin McGreskin[75], *Uefa-A license coach*

---

74   Sinnott, J., (2011). The Blizzard Magazine issue 3. Sunderland: A19. 98

75   Ibid.

13. PURPOSEFUL TRAINING, A SUMMARY AND CONCLUSION

"The chinese bamboo takes 10 years to grow six inches. It then grows 10 feet in six months. Ask yourself: Did the plant grow 10 feet in six months or 10 feet and six inches in 10 years and six months?"[76]

The development of the 10,000 purposeful hours of training is a vastly complex statement and one that starts at hour one, without those first few significant and important hours players will find it difficult to progress at the rate expected.

Many will disagree and will not be willing to budge from their belief that one's ability is a mixture of both biological and the environmental factors (remember that neither has been proven beyond all doubt).

What cannot be argued is the importance of the mental elements of a player and how one should go about purposeful hours of training.

Purposeful training should include:

- Transforming the mindset (to a growth mindset).

- Praising effort and never ability or talent.

- Setting itself on the edge of one's ability prompting failure.

- Coinciding with the concept of chunking and pattern recognition (whole-part-whole) where appropriate:
  - Whole scenario
  - Broken down
  - Slowed right down
  - Sped back up
  - Put back together

- Placing a high level of importance not on the current mental and physical attributes, but the understanding and addressing of the mental training preparation and comprehension.

Throughout this part of the book, much of the rationale behind why particular coaching methods are successful or not have been explored.

The conclusive outcome should be one of a mixed approach to coaching and that from time to time, one particular approach may be better suited than another (guided discovery, whole-part-whole, to instruct and command etc.

It is important to remember that you should not instinctively follow the messages of this book or those learnt from the studies of professional clubs.

To attempt to mimic the current model of the tiki-taka philosophy that the likes of Spain or Barcelona present us with would not be wise.

Firstly, by the time you have mastered it you will be decades behind the new breed of the tiki-taka playing identity.

Secondly, by moulding players to play as the next Xavi or Messi (if such a thing is even possible) is absolutely the wrong message.

Michael Laudrup

Michael Laudrup was widely considered as the greatest role model for such a player who plays as a 'false 9' or withdrawn forward.

"Pele was the best in the 60's, Cruyff in the 70's, Maradona in the 80's and Laudrup in the 90's."
Franz Beckenbauer[77]

"I have played against Maradona, Platini and Baggio. But the player I saw do the most indescribable things was Michael Laudrup."
Roberto Galia

76   Cited in Durand-Bush, N., & Salmela, J. H. (2001). The development of talent in sport. In R. N. Singer, H. A. Hausenblas, & C. Janelle (Eds.), Handbook of Sport Psychology (2nd ed., pp. 269-289). New York: John Wiley

77   Boisen, A., Boisen, C., Nordskildem H., (2008) Laudrup - Et fodbolddynasti. Copenhagen: Lindhardt og Ringhof.

"Who is the best player in history? Laudrup."
Andres Iniesta[78]

"...he was so classy and a real thinker. A master of the blind pass and impossible through-balls and I will never forget his 'spoon' pass in a game against Osasuna. He lifted the ball right over the defence and Romario touched it in first time."
Albert Ferrer[79]

With Michael Laudrup universally considered as one of the game's greats, you would have been forgiven for thinking that La Masia should have aimed to replicate Laudrup's greatness. However, if this had been the case, Leo Messi would not be who he is today.

The Evolution of Tiki Taka

The same is to be said of entire tactical approaches that are celebrated in each decade. After all, tiki-taka has evolved from total football, which itself is argued to have stemmed from influences such as the creativity of Hungary and by River Plate's La Maquina which were both thought to have revolutionised the sport in the 1950s.[80]

Tiki-taka itself has undergone a series of alterations in the way it functions, as each manager and player that has come in to the first team has stamped his own mark on the playing identity of Barcelona.

"He [Pep Guardiola] has created a different philosophy for Barcelona. I think the [Johan] Cruyff era laid the foundation for the width they used in their game and using the full size of the pitch. If you look at their midfield players over the last 20 years they have all been small. What has changed is the pressing and the areas in which they press the ball. That is what Guardiola has brought to the team."
Sir Alex Ferguson[81]

---

78   Diaz, J. (2010). Iniesta: El mejor jugador de la historia ha sido Laudrup. Available: http://www.elconfidencial.com/deportes/andresiniesta-mejor-jugador-historia-laudrupespaña-mundial-20100701-67135.html. Last accessed August 2012

79   Ferrer, A. (2009). Perfect XI. Available: http://fourfourtwo.com/interviews/perfectxi/209/article.aspx. Last accessed July 2012.

80   Ornstein, D. (2008). Dutch substance over style. Available: http://news.bbc.co.uk/sport1/hi/football/euro_2008/netherlands/7415457.stm. Last accessed July 2012.

81   Singh, I. (2011). Quote of the Day: Sir Alex Ferguson. Available: http://www.totalbarca.com/2011/news/quote-of-the-day-siralexferguson/#more-76890. Last accessed July 2012

Nonetheless, there is a framework and philosophy learnt by each of the playing members of the Barcelona squads. There is a loose framework that allows creativity and freedom to flourish, a framework that enables the freedom of creativity by design. You need to immerse yourself in the principles of the philosophy and build your own framework to fit within.

Having said that, there is much to be learnt from studying the historic and current state of tiki-taka football. We evolve through understanding the current.

"The best coaches are the greatest of thieves."
Fabio Capello[82]

This Book's Aims

The emphasis of this book is to emphasise sustainability as an objective and to use the successful philosophy of tiki-taka football as a model, measure and mentor.

There is no suggestion of direct mimicry of 2012's Barcelona or Spain, as your total understanding of tikitaka football should not be based on a set of truisms about the present.

For one to mimic 2012's Barcelona, one would have skipped over decades of vital progress that has been made, years and years of developing the club's central philosophy based upon sound information about maximising the physical, mental, technical and tactical aspects of a players education. All players play as one and not as eleven individuals in 1 v 1 battles.

If you do not understand the principles or how to get where you want, you will be left with bits and pieces that present the semblance of a whole rather than what you are truly striving towards. The reason you are reading this book is because the end product and the mastery of it inspires you to love football. How it could potentially be learnt intrigues you and asks you revisit how you view football, an uplifting alteration in the perception of football itself.

Within the pages of this book it is all here, but just remember it is a global approach, a whole approach, one where the goalkeeper's duties are intertwined

---

82   Pereira, L.M., Pinho, J.M (2011). André Villas-Boas: Special Too. Stockport: Dewi Lewis Media Ltd

with that of the striker at the other end, one where the first kick of the ball in your under 9's training session is one step on the path of development with a linear line of sight to what is in truth the most complex path you will take. This is a model where the under 9's interim coach is as important as the first team manager. It is an approach that needs to be experienced to truly understand.

Passionately invest in the principles of this philosophy and I promise you progress will be made, but be humble in your successful playing-identity and remember that there is not any one right way of playing.

"My way of working is different. It doesn't make it right. It doesn't make it wrong either."
Brendan Rodgers[83]

Through the next 3 parts of this book, it is imperative that you continue to consider 'how' you will look to execute an idea and 'how' you should educate players to understand the way of thinking you wish to adopt on a football field.

83   Auclair, P (2012) The Blizzard Magazine issue 6. Sunderland: The Blizzard Media Ltd. 75

PART 2

50 PRACTICES TO COACH THE TIKI TAKA STYLE OF PLAY

TRAINING METHODS

The second of the 4 parts of this book presents you with 50 recorded training methods that the author has observed and analysed over a period of two years at a number of professional football clubs:

FC Barcelona, Liverpool FC, Swansea City FC, Wigan Athletic FC, Villarreal CF and from a number of other clubs and professional coaches across an array of developmental stages.

The preferred method of training session delivery generally tends to follow the procedure:

Technique to skill to game (each defined by the author below).

Technique

A training drill that isolates the desired functional technique required to fulfil the fundamental activities that occur during a match situation.

A 'technique' drill is often unopposed and at first, broken down into the most simplistic version of the activity. While drills may be repetitive on a week to week basis, it is apparent that at all clubs, coaches progressed the complexity and/or difficulty of the drill as the drill took place.

Skill

A training drill that takes the learnt and practiced technique into a game situation (often opposed). It is important that this stage of progress aims to bridge the development gap between the basic concept of technique and that of the game.

This drill is often similar to a small sided game and looks to maximise the opportunity to demonstrate the ability to execute the given technique.

Game

This training method can range from a full sized game right down to a small sided game consisting of a 4 v 4 scenario. It is important that the selected technique

that has been learnt and practiced should be worked on and remain within the coaches main interest.

The Training Session

Each and every training session observed follows the basic understanding that sessions are planned around a particular theme (pressing, playing out from the back, defending out-numbered, dribbling, running with the ball etc). The particular theme should be chosen so that the technique learnt and practiced benefits the group you are to coach.

On the advice of a number of professional coaches, training sessions should be planned around a period of one and a half hours (the duration of a game) and begin with dynamic stretching as opposed to the dated static stretching often used at the grass roots level.

Dynamic stretching refers to the stretching of muscles through continuous movement (from light to game related movement). A number of researchers[1] have reasoned that dynamic stretching allows the muscles to react best to explosive movements through being in a warm, fast and reasonably elastic condition (increased muscle tone).

Dynamic stretching includes heel-toeing forwards and backwards, skipping forwards/backwards, cross-leg steps, knee-raise jumps and other game related movements.

Training sessions should however, look to relax muscles when completed. Subsequently static stretches are an appropriate method to achieve the desired post-match condition and recovery. These stretches look to lengthen the muscle and help to find the ideal muscle condition for match recovery.

As important as the appropriate stretching type, is the consistent intake of fluid as there is an increased risk of injury that occurs during training sessions where

---

1   Poel, G. van der (1995). Dossier Stretching, deel 1, 2 & 3. Richting Sportgericht 50 (1): 2-5, 50 (2): 101-105 en 50 (3): 165-169.

players are tired and players are unable to perform at the levels required of them to concentrate and play at an intensity level expected for effective development:

"Research shows that if you lose a litre of fluid (in a game you lose 1-3 litres of fluid), your level of stamina averages a 10% decline."

Raymond Verheijen

This book offers the reader with a variety of small sided games, a means of tactical development and focuses very little on physical related training drills and supports the view that any minutes spent concentrating on (marginal) improvements to speed, strength and power are expensed at valuable time that could be spent on developing players as 'readers of the game.'

While a 100m sprint may find these marginal improvements highly beneficial, football is a game that allows us to effectively alter the starting point of each player in the race to the ball. In consequence, positional focus is far superior to a players ability to be quick, strong or powerful.

It is imperative that training exercises are kept as match realistic as possible. **Jose Mourinho** is said to train his team for ninety minutes per day and not a second longer. This time is used to replicate the length of a football game.

Paolo Di Canio expects his players to run as far as they do in matches as they do in training and vice versa and lastly, it is said that **Rafa Benitez** conducts his training sessions with shorts bursts of intensity of exactly six minutes and twelve seconds to replicate the match realistic intensities before taking a twenty to thirty second break.

The training philosophy of this book looks to follow those methods previously mentioned.

In an ideal scenario, the length of training and timings of intensity should be specific to the age group and team itself. It would be possible for you as a coach to research and analyse your team's performance or relevant data to conduct a team specific training regime.

PRACTICE FORMAT

Each practice includes clear diagrams with supporting training notes such as:

- Name of Practice
- Objective of Practice
- Description of Practice
- Progressions/Variations (if Applicable)
- Coaching Points of Practice

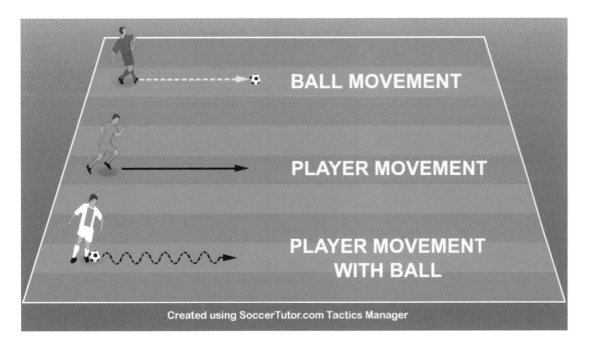

Created using SoccerTutor.com Tactics Manager

TERMINOLOGY

Kaasters: Dutch for 'rebound' and are often neutral players who are positioned at the sides of the designated space and are instructed to play quick one or two touch passes back into play as appropriate.

Coaching The Tiki Taka Style Of Play

1. FC BARCELONA: **The Rondo**

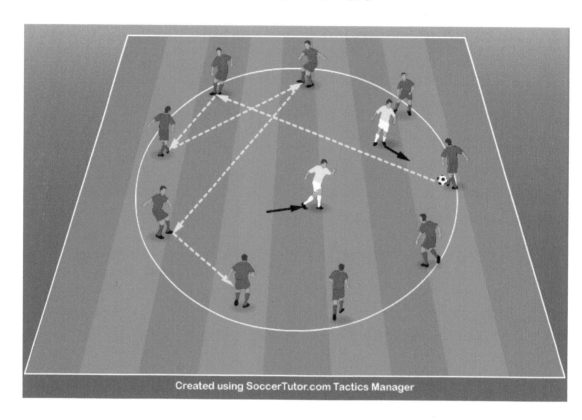

Created using SoccerTutor.com Tactics Manager

Objective

For the players to warm up through a high intensity possession based skill practice with players developing technical aspects used in high pressure game related scenarios.

The Story

The Rondo is an exercise that former Barcelona youth team coach and first team manager Laureano Ruiz has claimed to have first invented. Ruiz's book **'The True Method'** reveals he designed El Rondo from analytical work he carried out on the great Hungarian team of the 1950's.

"I started with parties 'two on two' plus a wildcard in the middle that went with the one that had the ball, to find triangulations, then I expanded and was born on rondo." **Laureano Ruiz**[2]

The exercise has since formed the foundations to Barcelona's modern day philosophy. Carles Rexach, the former youth coach at Barcelona who educated the likes of Xavi, is said to have emphasised the speed at which a player must pass the ball with "a mig toc" (half a touch).

---

2   Pallàs, J.J., Poquí, J.. (2011). Laureano Ruiz: "El Barça tiene recorrido si conserva el estilo". Available: http://www.mundodeportivo. com/20111024/mundo-barsa/laureano-ruizmundo-barsa-seccions-barca-la-masia-fc-barcelona_54234633618.html#ixzz2S99uNqBZ. Last accessed July 2012.

Description

Players are to position themselves in a circle around 2, 3 or even 4 central players who aim to intercept passes or pressure (not tackle) the players positioned on the outside. The players should attempt to retain both possession and the basic circular shape during play and demonstrate their ability to play intelligent short passes through their speed of thought and prepared body positioning.

Rondo sizes vary from 4 v 2, the popular 5 v 2 right the way up to those that aim to replicate game situations.

It is important that the following terminologies are understood:

First, second and third line of pass, half a touch (a rebound pass) and teasing the ball player.

The **first line of pass** is simply the pass that does not bypass any of the players in the middle and is often a pass to one of the nearest 2 supporting players.

A **second line pass** often bypasses the 2 players in the middle but not through the middle. It is the pass that cuts 'around' players in the middle and is often the players furthest away on the supporting adjacent side of the space.

A **third line pass,** the most desirable pass, is the one that splits through the middle of the 2 players in the middle. It is important to think of a third line pass as the type of pass that runs from a central defender into the feet of a striker dropping off of his marker on the halfway line. These terminologies are to be explained to the players and are later key for the progression of the rondo.

The **rebound pass** (Rexach's "a mig toc") is a useful tool in the rondo. The ball needs to be played in to a player hard and the receiving player then just needs to redirect the pass (reducing the time required to kick the ball) and as a result speeds up the rondo. This type of pass can become particularly useful when transferred to the full scale game.

'Teasing the ball player' is simply the understanding of the 2 players in the centre of the rondo. The 2 defenders need to be close enough to cut off first line passes, be positioned with their bodies to cut off any second line passes and appear to offer a third line pass between them. However, the differences in angle mean that each of the 2 players in the middle could cut out the third line pass - they are in effect, teasing the ball player to try and play the third line pass. This idea of teasing the opposition, or 'making play predictable' is essential for pressing effectively in a full scaled game.

In the typical rondo it is important that BOTH players change when the ball is given away. Therefore, the player who gave the ball away AND the player who passed him the ball before should immediately switch with the 2 in the centre. It is vital that this change over is done at the highest speed possible to replicate the concept of 'transition'.

If bibs are being used by the 2 central players get them to carry them (not wear them) and on the changeover, no player should wait, they should throw the bib onto the floor instead or at the players chest and let the bib become the presser's problem. The speed of change over is essential and no players should be walking or pausing during the change overs. Coaches should have a constant flow of spare balls should a ball run out of play so the exercise is continuous. Only pause the exercise when giving a coaching point.

Progressions / Variations

1. Reduce the players to only being able to make one first line pass before having to look for another, i.e. no player can make 2 first line passes in a row (as an individual principle).

2. The coach should look to constrain the players to 2 touch and then 1 touch to increase the speed of thinking and the exercise itself.

3. The size of the space, number of players and position of the players can be varied to replicate essential elements of the game. Positional rondos then become invaluable in that you set the rondo up with the central defenders and wide players taking up the spaces around the square and eventually have 2 teams of midfielders in the centre (see practice 10 for an example of such a progression).

Coaching Points

1. Coaches should emphasise the importance of this exercise and allow ownership to be handed down to the players themselves as a regular team practice.

2. Players should protect the ball by receiving the ball with the furthest point of their body from the defender.

3. Encourage second and third line passes whenever possible.

4. The 2 pressing players should look to tease and 'trick' those in possession through a collective approach to block second line passes and should be able to pounce on first and third line passes.

5. Encourage the use of "half touches."

6. At no point should the practice pause or stop. Emphasise the importance of the transitions.

Coaching The Tiki Taka Style Of Play

2. FC BARCELONA: The Double Rondo

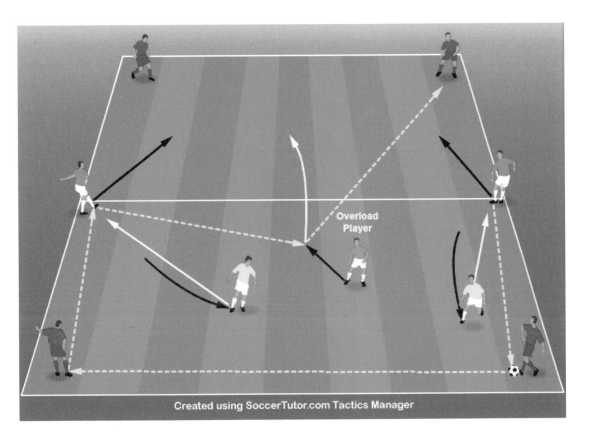

Overload Player

Created using SoccerTutor.com Tactics Manager

Objective

For the players to warm up through a high intensity possession based skill practice with players developing technical aspects used in high pressure game related scenarios.

Description

This is a progression from the previous drill.

Progress can be furthered by altering the basis of the space itself. 'The Double Rondo' requires players to position themselves in two rectangles (6 players) and then a further overload player in the centre against 2 pressuring players in the middle.

After the ball is switched, the 2 pressuring players join the outer rectangle and the 2 central outer players (red) become the pressuring players within the opposite space. This is a more complex skill related exercise that explores themes that occur within a match (transitions and playmaking etc.).

Variation

Coaches can vary the number of passes required before the switch occurs.

59

Coaching The Tiki Taka Style Of Play

3. FC BARCELONA: The Adjacent Passing Square Exercise

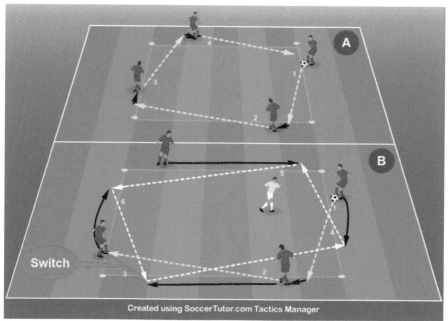

Created using SoccerTutor.com Tactics Manager

Objective

This is a technique to skill practice involving 5 to 6 players.

Players are to follow the particular pattern of passing required and work in coordination with each other.

Description

4 Players play a passing sequence and are positioned on the outside, limited to each side of the square (10 yards) and should always be positioned in the nearest corner to the side that the ball is on.

The 2 supporting players should move to the side of the player who has the ball and the player opposite should also be inline with the ball - this is the form desired.

The start of this exercise should be done with no player (Part A - unopposed) in the middle so that they can become familiar with the patterned movement. This is a high intensity exercise and players are expected to demonstrate high levels of awareness and concentration as well as the ability to retain the functional technique of passing.

No passes across from one end to the other are allowed as you can only pass to the supporting players either side of you. Players can change the direction of the passing by laying the ball back to the player who has just passed to them (as shown in Part B - marked 'Switch').

Progressions

1. Introduce a player in the middle to make the drill opposed (Part B). The opposed player is added to invite pressure to the player on the ball (at all times).
2. Change the size of the area to increase the intensity of movement and passing.

Coaching Points

1. Players should look to take 2 touches to enable sufficient time for movement.
2. The ball should be received across the body at all times to open up the options available.

Coaching The Tiki Taka Style Of Play

4. FC BARCELONA: The Laureano Ruiz Simplified Triangulation Exercise

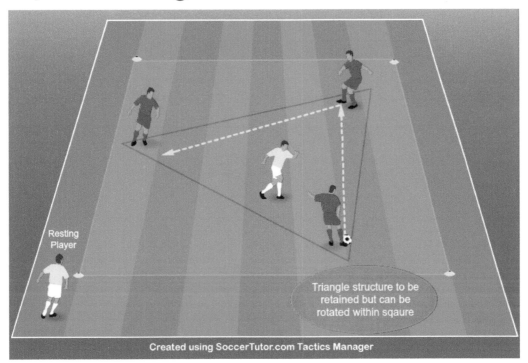

Resting Player

Triangle structure to be retained but can be rotated within sqaure

Created using SoccerTutor.com Tactics Manager

Objective

This is skill exercise that aims to work on retaining possession in a given space (marked out square) in a 3 v 1 situation with a focus on high intensity.

The game requires a resting man to maintain the levels of intensity desired.

Description

The triangular form should be maintained within the marked out space (10 yards x 10 yards) and the players should aim to move the ball around with 1 or 2 touches where possible (but never restricted to).

Each cycle should last no longer than 60 seconds before the middle man is rested and replaced to maintain the high intensity of pressure and passing.

For the duration of ball circulation, the triangle structure should be kept and can rotate freely within the area.

Progressions

1. Progress can be made by altering the marked out space, but the space should be appropriate for the players to move around in the triangular structure.

2. Coaches can alter the number of players and introduce a neutral player to add mental complexity to the exercise.

Coaching Point

Coaches should emphasise the importance of receiving the ball across your body to open up the options where appropriate.

Coaching The Tiki Taka Style Of Play

5. AFC AJAX: 4 v 4 (+2) End to End Possession Game

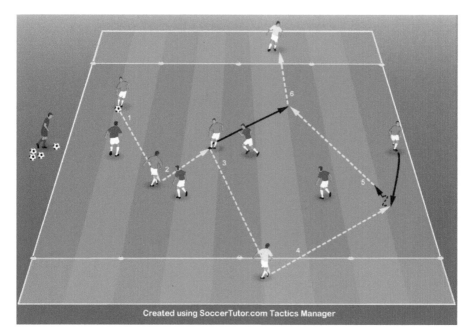

Created using SoccerTutor.com Tactics Manager

Objective

The objective is to dominate possession using your teammates and the 2 neutral kaasters (rebound players) who are limited to the length of the line they are situated on.

This exercise progresses well into a tool for educating players in the 'triggers' of when to press as rules are introduced.

Description

This exercise requires a minimum of 8 players but is best suited to 10 players so that the principle of 'making the pitch as big as possible' and using the whole space can be emphasised. We have 4 v 4 in the middle with 2 neutral players at the end who play with the team in possession.

The kaasters should look to play quickly and play the ball back to the same team that passed them the ball.

Variations of this game allow a number of different objectives to be carried out.

Variation

Allow the kaasters to act as interfering (pressing) players should one of the teams fail to successfully demonstrate an isolated theme (shielding the ball, a poor first touch, rushing the play or failing to create space for each other). After interference, the kaaster should rotate with an internal player.

Coaching Points

1. During the process of kaasters becoming interfering players, it may be necessary for the coach to call out when a 'trigger' occurs.

2. This exercise provides the coach with many options and aspects of the exercise such as the number of attackers, defenders or touches a kaaster can make are variable to help the coach achieve his own goals.

3. As with all these passing drills, you can introduce triggers such as - "if it is a heavy pass, that means the support is behind you" and vice versa.

6. AFC AJAX: 4 v 4 (+1) Corner To Corner Possession Exercise

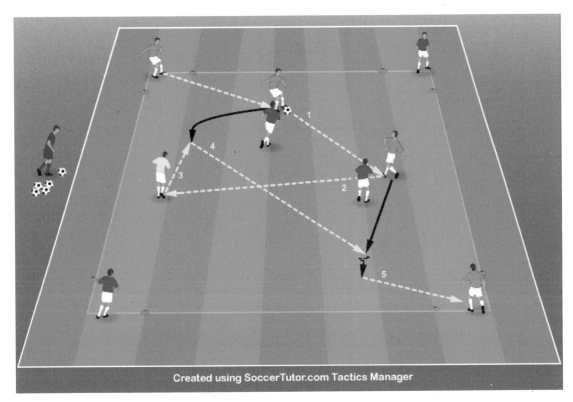

Created using SoccerTutor.com Tactics Manager

Objective
We work on passing, moving possession play and pressing.

Description
Each team consists of 2 central players, 2 kaasters positioned in each corner diagonally opposite and we have a central neutral playmaker. The aim is to play the ball from corner to corner, but with a minimum of 3 passes in the central zone.

The coach can vary the specific outcomes (number of passes before playing the ball in to a kaaster). The coach should concentrate on both the possession team and the 2 defender's ability when outnumbered.

The central neutral player can be limited to 1 or 2 touch, or simply instructed to play quickly where possible (and should be a player who demonstrates the ability to be a playmaker with his off ball movement and high levels of passing consistency).

Coaching Points
1. The coach can vary the number of passes required per team, the maximum number of touches per neutral or kaaster player and number of players per team.
2. As the kaasters are instructed to act as rebound players with only 1 touch allowed, the coach is expected to emphasise the importance of the players' positioning to provide the kaasters with options.

Coaching The Tiki Taka Style Of Play

7. FC BARCELONA: Shielding the Ball and Waiting for Support with 3 v 1 Play

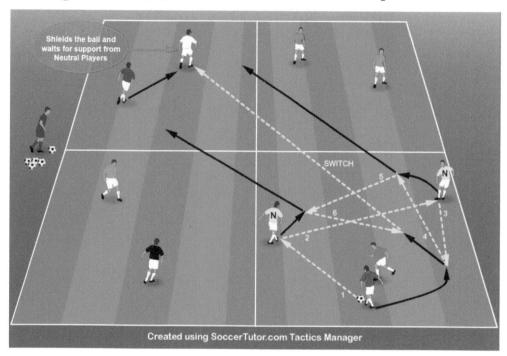

Created using SoccerTutor.com Tactics Manager

Objective

This exercise aims to allow players to practice their ability to shield the ball and wait for support.

Description

In each square there should be 2 players, each on opposing sides. There are 2 neutral players (yellow) who create a 3 v 1 scenario in a square and should look to play 6 passes before playing the ball into a player in any of the other 3 squares.

The player receiving the ball should look to shield the ball from the opposing player and await support from the 2 neutral supporting players to arrive inside the pertinent square. If the ball is won by the opponent, the ball should be played by this player into a new square and the process begins again.

Variations / Progressions

This exercise can be altered heavily. You can begin with a free passing exercise with 3 or 4 groups where one player passes the ball in, another lays the ball off and the third travels with the ball into another square.

You can then progress this exercise into a skill-based exercise by introducing 3 v 1 scenarios in each box whilst watching for appropriate support (not in the corners but on the sides!). This example given represents a technique to skill exercise for passing, shielding and movement.

Coaching Point

The coach should look to help the player who is shielding the ball from his opponent with good instructions on their starting position, first touch, body positioning etc.

8. AFC AJAX: Directional 6 v 6 '3 Goals Game'

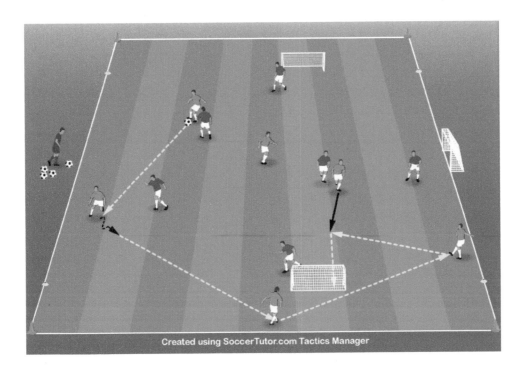

Created using SoccerTutor.com Tactics Manager

Objective

We provide players with the problem of how to defend in a three dimensional way and regain possession of the ball with an equal number of players per team.

Description

We play a 6 v 6 game with 3 goals positioned as shown in the diagram.

You are allowed to cover the goals but you are then left with a 6 v 3 scenario in the central space. The winning team is either the team that has scored the most goals, or if failing that, the team that has had most possession (an incentive not to cover goals).

Variation

You can vary the game by allowing players to use the space behind the goals (like in Hockey, as shown in the diagram) - this may encourage players to create appropriate tactics.

Coaching Points

1. Strategies to find balance between covering goals and regaining possession of the ball should be created by the players themselves.

2. The coach should look to help the defensive team find an appropriate form to win the ball and protect the three goals.

3. If the team with the ball are struggling to retain possession (and force the defenders to adopt a defensive form) you can add a neutral player in favour of the possession team.

9. FC BARCELONA: 5 v 4 Breaking Out of the Middle Third

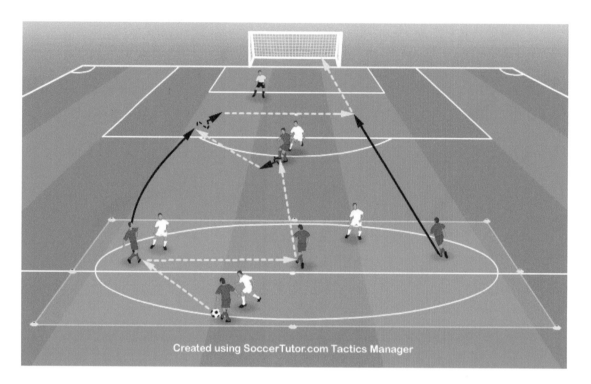

Created using SoccerTutor.com Tactics Manager

Objective

To link ball circulation and attacking play together.

Description

This practice looks to isolate a particular area of the field (variable) and requires 4 players to play a select number of passes before looking to break from the designated space. We have a 3 v 3 situation in the zone on the halfway line as shown with each team having an extra player outside, plus a goalkeeper.

The exercise asks the team in possession to play a minimum of 5 passes before playing a ball into an attacker and outnumbering the opposition's defence. The first touch for the striker is at first a free touch, and then on the second, the defender can look to win possession. A maximum of 2 attackers may join in the attack and at first, no defenders may leave the area.

Variation

The exercise can be altered to represent different moments or scenarios in a game. The number of passes required, number of attackers or defenders that can exit the box and the restrictions on the defender are all variable to progress the session to suit your own needs.

Coaching Point

Coaches should focus on the flow of movement and angles of runs while off the ball as a starting point (as these are the most common areas of possible improvement).

10. LIVERPOOL FC: Position Specific 8 v 8 (+1) Possession Exercise

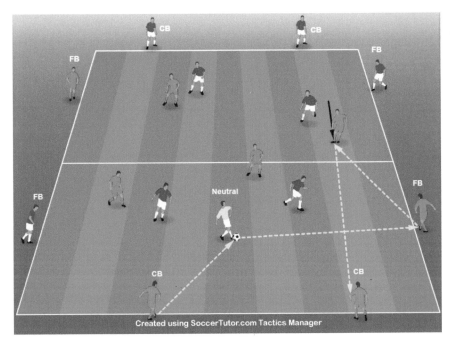

Created using SoccerTutor.com Tactics Manager

Objective

This exercise aims to develop building up play while replicating familiar positions taken up on the football field by specific positions within Brendan Rodger's 4-3-2-1 formation.

Description

The team in possession pass the ball from one central defender, across the 'halfway line' and back to the central defender as a method of controlling possession (mimicking non-directional or non-goal orientated play).

It is imperative that the relevant players position themselves in the desired position on the outside of the 25 x 50 yard space. The neutral player should be considered the playmaker of the team and have an excellent ability to play with and without the ball (he cannot be man marked).

The players on the outside are limited to controlling the ball and then quickly playing the ball back into the space and should not dwell on the ball. Inner players can only shadow or block players in the outside areas and cannot tackle the player unless he enters the central space (by mis-controlling the ball).

Variations

1. The practice can be altered to reflect progress by differentiating the maximum number of touches a particular position or group of players can take (and restrict outside players to only being able to pass the ball internally).
2. Request that a minimum number of passes be played before returning the ball to a central defender.

Coaching Point

The exercise is designed to familiarise players with the field of play in their selected position and is an exercise that demands problem solving abilities to be practiced.

Coaching The Tiki Taka Style Of Play

11. VILLARREAL CF: **The Gridded 4 Goal Game**

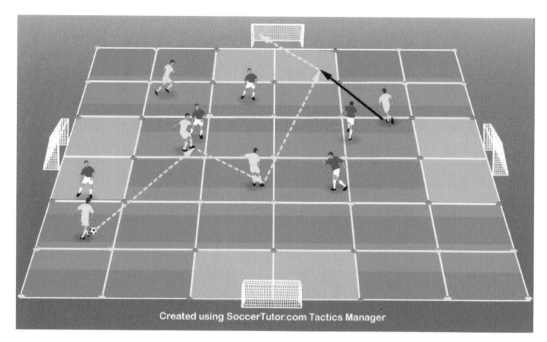

Created using SoccerTutor.com Tactics Manager

Objective

This exercise aims to improve the players' problem solving abilities by placing a number of strategic demands on the team in possession.

Description

We play a 5 v 5 game with the grids marked out as shown and the teams can score in any one of the 4 goals, but must not pass within the same horizontal or vertical line of play that they are positioned in.

Goals can only be scored from within the yellow zones (2 grids nearest the goals), where defending players can be restricted from if the game is not progressing.

Ensure that colours are used effectively to enable players to distinguish between squares, using flat cones to keep the flow of game.

Variations

1. If a team is struggling to find goal scoring opportunities, you can add in a neutral playmaker who isn't bound by directional passing limitations.
2. The number of zones, players and minimum/maximum number of passes are all variables that can be altered to meet own requirements.

Coaching Points

1. Players should come up with their own strategies to find space in this space-limited game.
2. Zones should be marked out by flat markers to enable passing within the game's space (for 5 v 5, this could be 30 x 30 yards but depends on the level of the players).

12. VILLARREAL CF: Match Realistic Overloads in a 3 Zone Small Sided Game

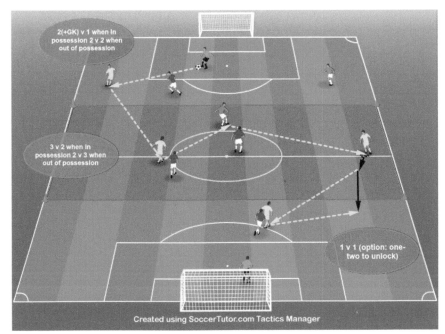

2(+GK) v 1 when in possession 2 v 2 when out of possession

3 v 2 when in possession 2 v 3 when out of possession

1 v 1 (option: one-two to unlock)

Created using SoccerTutor.com Tactics Manager

Objective

To promote the idea that overloads can be created by 'the system'.

Description

We consider the Barcelona 3-4-3 (or better still, the 3-5-2 when Messi drops deep) or even the Wigan 3-5-2 which you will become familiar with by the end of this book.

We play 4 v 4 + 2 neutral players and 2 goalkeepers.

2 defenders and the goalkeeper build up against 1 striker (3 v 1) in the first third, 3 central midfielders against 2 (3 v 2) in the middle and then a 1 v 1 situation in the final third.

Teams are to play within their thirds at first. The team in possession are expected to play through the thirds, whilst the other team can play on the counter attack and skip the central third should they choose to do so.

The 2 neutral players (red) will play for whichever team is in possession, meaning that team are placed in a risk/ reward scenario with their passing into the final third. If a midfielder can play a one-two with the striker, he/ becomes unlocked and is allowed to enter the final third (creating a 2 v 1 situation in the final third).

Progression

You can progress this by removing the zonal constrictions but shape must be kept. Players are advised not to watch the passes and to scan the field every 3-4 seconds to know the direction of their first touch.

Coaching Points

1. The weight of the pass is to act as a trigger as to where support is.
2. The player on the ball should be supported to the side, directly behind (defender) and ahead of him at all Times if possible which creates overloads through the player intelligence and movement.

13. LIVERPOOL FC: Playing through the Lines in a 4 Zone Passing Exercise

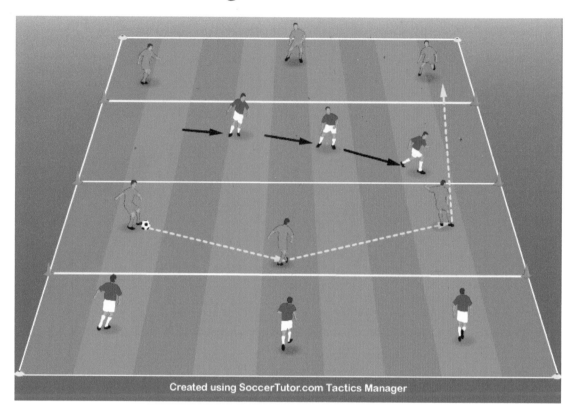

Created using SoccerTutor.com Tactics Manager

Objective

This exercise works on passing through the lines and primarily looks to aid the midfield trio to work in unison to block passes through to the opposition's attack.

Description

This exercise requires 12 players (two teams of 6) to position themselves as shown in the diagram, with 3 players in each zone, alternating teams. The players are required to make at least 2 passes within their own zone before looking to pass the ball through to the desired zone (to allow the blocking players time to find their shape).

Players must stay within their zones and players cannot tackle (they only shadow within their own zone).

Coaching Points

1. Ground passes are to be encouraged and the coach should look to assist the team without the ball and encourage them to think about their shape and approach to regaining possession.

2. If the exercise proves that possession is too easy, it is advisable to remove a possession player and add him into the midfield block.

3. The coach can apply rules such as a minimum or maximum number of touches per player or passes per team within the zones.

14. FC BARCELONA: Playing through the Thirds with 1 v 1 Duels

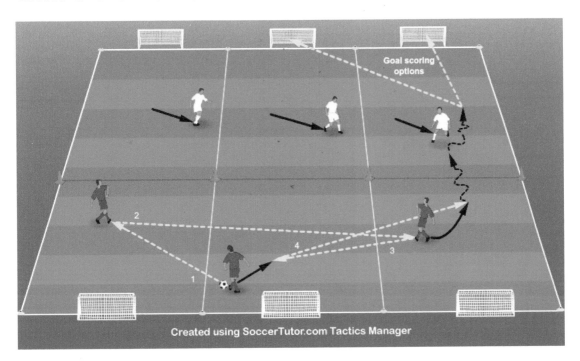

Created using SoccerTutor.com Tactics Manager

Objective

This exercise looks to educate both the blocking players and the possession players.

In this exercise, the objective is to pass the ball between your own team a set number of times (to force opposition out of shape) and then when appropriate dribble past the player (1 v 1) and score into the mini goal (representative of a player or space on the field).

Description

The ball should be passed between the 3 players (to force opposition out of shape) and then when appropriate, one player dribbles into a channel and past a white player (1 v 1) and shoots into the mini goal (representative of a player or space on the field).

Tackling is allowed when the player enters the opposition half (past the red cones). When the ball is intercepted, possession is given to the defending side and the team roles switch. The build up should be patient and should identify the right time to attack and move into the channel.

Coaching Points

1. Educate players to recognise when the relevant situation arises (when the opponent is out of position).

2. The team in possession need to be patient with the ball.

3. Players should always receive the ball across them with an open body shape, play quickly with a minimum number of touches and the middle man should act as the playmaker.

15. AFC AJAX: 10 v 4 Playing through the Middle Third (Zone)

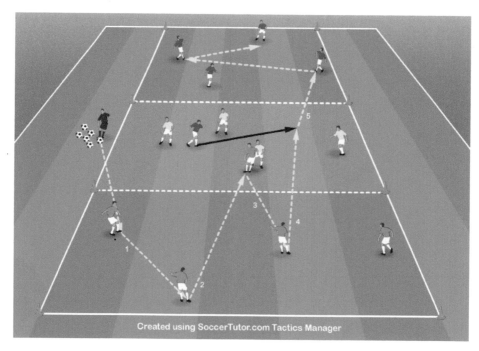

Created using SoccerTutor.com Tactics Manager

Objective
We work on possession play and passing through the midfield line.

Description

The team in possession must get the ball over to the opposite third and use the middle third at least once before switching the ball. We use 2 teams of 5 with 4 middle players.

Each team of 5 has 1 player in the middle.

This exercise has a number of variations. At first it may be beneficial to start simply by asking the team in possession (all red and blue players act as team of 10) to play at least one ball into the central zone every 2 switches (this will encourage the middle players to mark spaces rather than the players).

You can progress this exercise by placing further restrictions, the red middle player can only pass to other red players and blues likewise (but you then must restrict the middle opposition players to mark space only).

No players can leave their zone and a point is only given when the ball is played through the middle and out to the other side (you may work on a 2 point/1 point system to favour playing through the middle third).

When the ball is won 3 times, the teams switch roles.

Coaching Points

1. Coaches should focus on players *'making the pitch as big as possible'* when in possession and the opposite when without possession.

2. The coaches are expected to identify the players' capability to perform this exercise with the appropriate amount of restrictions.

3. You should look to advance to one touch play in the middle third (as they have little space) and you can then start to place time restrictions on the teams (number of switches per minute).

Coaching The Tiki Taka Style Of Play

16. AFC AJAX: 7 v 7 Three Zone Small Sided Game

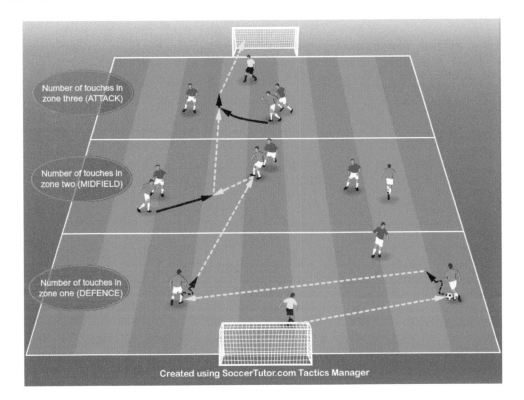

Number of touches in zone three (ATTACK)

Number of touches in zone two (MIDFIELD)

Number of touches in zone one (DEFENCE)

Created using SoccerTutor.com Tactics Manager

Objective

We play a typical 7 v 7 game, but with restrictions placed on players within each third.

Description

At first, it may be suggestible to restrict players to their own zones to get comfortable with playing in particular spaces. You can then allow certain players to break into particular zones and then eventually restrict players to a number of touches in each zone rather than positional restrictions.

The number of touches allowed in each zone should reflect the ideology of play you wish to implement; 3 touches in zone one, 1 touch in zone two and 2 touches in zone three may encourage teams to play from the back and look to work on their off the ball movement to open up passing options when they receive the ball in the central third.

You should refrain from demanding players only take one touch in the final third as shooting is a complex aspect of play and may require the ball to be under control before shooting. You will find that with this example given, as the midfield will look to use the defence more often than they would without conditions placed upon them. In a touch conditioned game, you can free up the positional conditions.

Coaching Points

1. You should look to find a balance that suits your own objectives and encourage players to play quickly when they are entering the final third.

2. Keeping possession and maximising opportunities are the foundations of this exercise.

73

17. AFC AJAX: Passing in Behind the Defensive Line in a 4 v 4 (+2) SSG with 2 End Zones

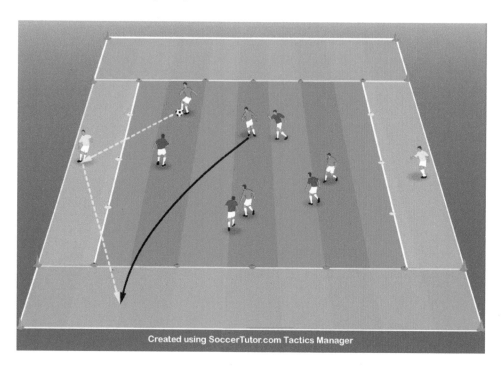

Created using SoccerTutor.com Tactics Manager

Objective

We work on the timing of the run in behind and the weight of the pass into the end zone in this 5 zone small sided game.

Description

We have 2 teams of 4 who have the aim to retain possession as a defensive strategy but look to make the appropriate attacking runs and off the ball movements to break into the end zone, timed as the ball is played in there. Teams are encouraged to use the 2 neutral players positioned in the side zones, who are not allowed to leave their zones and cannot be tackled.

In the example shown, a red player passes the ball out to the neutral side player and his teammate makes a run in behind the opposition to receive the weighted pass in the end zone. The end zone line should be treated as an offside line so players need to time their runs well.

The end zone should be large enough to allow for the players' ability to trap/control the ball (6 yards for example) and the entire area size should reflect the ability level and the number of players participating.

Coaching Points

1. It is important to allow the exercise's natural mechanisms to 'teach' the players how to arrive with their own tactical conclusions.

2. The one thing we should stress is that a straight run may be suitable for a diagonal pass and a diagonal run is best suited to a straight pass.

3. You can advance this game by placing restrictions on the neutral player (such as no assists or a limited number of touches).

74

Coaching The Tiki Taka Style Of Play

18. FC BARCELONA: Using Width in Your Own Half SSG

Created using SoccerTutor.com Tactics Manager

Objective

This is a typical 7 v 7 small sided game and we encourage the players to use the full width with unopposed side zones.

Description

In the example given, the defenders build up play (reds in possession) and can take up positions in the side zones and cannot be marked or tackled in these 'safe zones'.

This exercise aims to encourage teams to play the ball wide when in possession of the ball in deeper zones.

Players cannot enter the opposition's safety zones and are expected to play centrally in attack.

Players who receive the ball in the safety zones are expected to play the ball quickly (typically 2 or 3 touches) but should not be rushed if the option of a pass is not available. This game essentially expects the possession team to use their defensive players and goalkeeper as a 'pressure relief' and as a way of retaining possession.

Coaching Point

As the game advances you should ask the team the question *'If you are aiming to make the pitch as big as possible when in possession, what do you think you should be trying to do when you are defending?'*
(Answer: To keep the pitch as small as possible for the opposition).

Therefore, by carefully marking the wider spaces before the ball is played out (but with the balance of protecting the central areas) teams can both defend and attack effectively as they would in an 11 v 11 game.

19. FC BARCELONA: Playing Out from the Back 3 Zone SSG

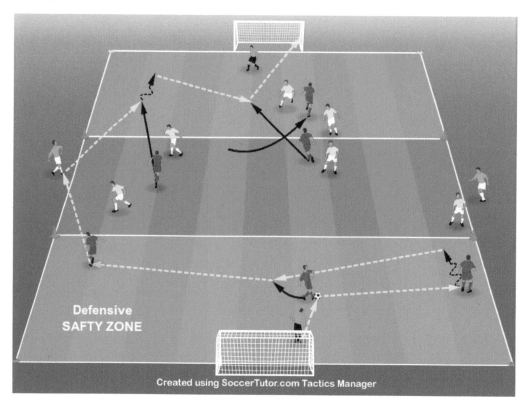

Defensive
SAFTY ZONE

Created using SoccerTutor.com Tactics Manager

Objective

We play a typical game that encourages teams to use particular spaces on the field as a way of 'pressure relief' or to build up the play from the back and from wider areas.

Description

We play a 7 v 7 game with 2 extra neutral players on the sides, with the area split into thirds.

This exercise introduces a safety zone in the defensive third for central defenders and the goalkeeper to play with the ball without pressure. The opposition therefore fall back into an organised block.

It is imperative that although it may seem easier to use the wider safety zone players (neutral) and the defensive safety zone, that the teams constantly try to create goal scoring opportunities.

Coaching Points

1. This game will encourage the team in possession to play out from the back, but the coach's focus should be on the opposition's defensive organisation (as the game's conditions help the team with the ball).

2. To encourage the conditions to teach the players, you may introduce the condition that the safety zone can only be used once the ball has initially crossed the halfway line.

3. The neutral wide players are expected to be used to stretch the play and should pass the ball quickly (possibly restricted to 2 or 3 touches).

Coaching The Tiki Taka Style Of Play

20. FC BARCELONA: 8 v 9 Phase of Play - Playing against the Deep Block

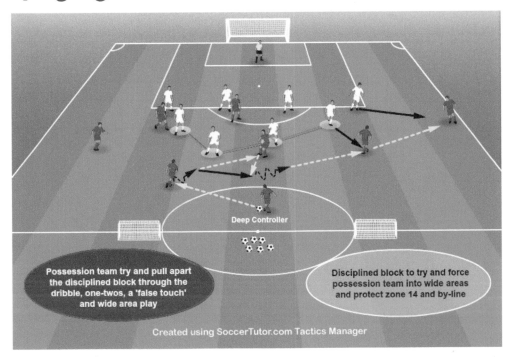

Deep Controller

Possession team try and pull apart the disciplined block through the dribble, one-twos, a 'false touch' and wide area play

Disciplined block to try and force possession team into wide areas and protect zone 14 and by-line

Created using SoccerTutor.com Tactics Manager

Objective

We work on a phase of play with one team (8 outfield players + 1 goalkeeper) looking to counter attack and the other team (8 players) trying to break down a well disciplined deep defensive block.

Description

This phase of play takes place using half a full sized pitch and requires a minimum of 8 attackers (2 full backs, 3 central midfielders and 3 forwards - as in the 4-3-3) and 9 defenders (2 lines of 4 and the goalkeeper).

There has to be 2 goals positioned on the halfway line to represent the 2 strikers that the counter attacking team will look to pass the ball to which encourages the defensive side to attack as well as defend (match realistic).

There are a number of methods a team should look to use to break through a deep lying block, one of which is the 'false touch,' a touch that appears to be mis-controlled which entices the defenders out of their disciplined organisation to try and tackle them.

This exercise is extremely match realistic and will test the possession teams creativity against the defending team's discipline (think Barcelona vs. Chelsea in 2012).

Coaching Points

1. The coach should stress that key areas should be protected (central and by-line) by the defending side and that the possession team should encourage the use of a deep lying playmaker who controls possession and sits to protect any counter attacks.

2. Width should be treated as a non-assist zone, except from the by-line (when isolated 1 v 1) by the possession team to encourage the desired philosophy.

21. SWANSEA CITY FC: Position Specific Pattern Play

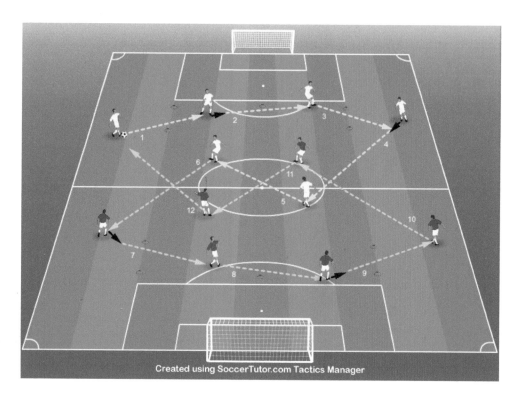

Created using SoccerTutor.com Tactics Manager

Objective

To encourage players to be comfortable in their positional system and encourage ball circulation in deeper spaces on the pitch.

This exercise is an extension of practices 25 and 26 from Barcelona in this book.

Description

This is an unopposed exercise that requires players to memorise the patterns of the opposition's defence. We use a full sized pitch and each team has 6 players positioned as shown in the diagram.

Teams should look to play the ball to every person on their team in a particular pattern and then pass the ball to the opposition. The other team then replicate the same passing pattern they have just seen (see diagram).

Coaching Points

1. For what seems like a simple exercise, it is vital that the coach looks at body positioning and the players' first touch.

2. The players need to check spaces around them before they receive the ball, to find space (pretending there are opponents around them).

3. Players should look to stay the desired distance apart and move as a unit within their given zones (marked out by cones).

4. On a full sized pitch, players should look to remain 20 yards apart at all times during the exercise.

22. SWANSEA CITY FC: 8 v 6 Phase of Play - Playing Out from the Back

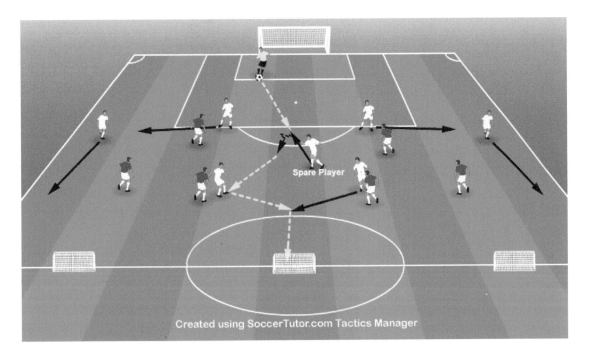

Spare Player

Created using SoccerTutor.com Tactics Manager

Objective

To encourage the building up of play from the goalkeeper with pressure from the opposition.

Description

We have a goalkeeper, 4 defenders and 3 midfielders (if you play 4-3-3) against 2 attackers and 4 midfielders (to represent the midfield and attack in a 4-4-2). This phase of play always starts with the goalkeeper and the team in possession have a numerical advantage in the defensive third. They must use this when building up the pitch from the back (7 v 6 for outfield players).

The team in possession should look to use the spare man to play the ball out to one of the 3 goals (which represent the 3 forwards and can only be scored in when within 5 yards). The front 3 (goals) can be marked but the goals should be big enough so when doing so, players can still score with the right angles.

Progression

To further this exercise, you could add a further 2 defenders who would represent full backs or change the formation of the defending side all together.

Coaching Points

1. The defending team should look to find a balance between high pressing and zonal marking the 3 goals as a tactical ploy.
2. The team in possession should be patient and look to play with a controlled manner and dominate possession.

Coaching The Tiki Taka Style Of Play

23. ATHLETIC BILBAO: Finding Space within the Block (Pattern Play)

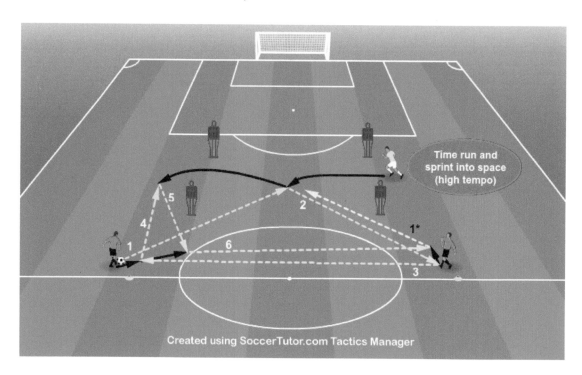

Time run and sprint into space (high tempo)

Created using SoccerTutor.com Tactics Manager

Objective

To introduce basic pattern play into the central midfielder's movement amongst a middle third zone.

Description

We work with 3 players, with 2 defenders (red) and 1 midfielder (yellow). This exercise requires a particular pattern to be learnt (example shown in the diagram's numbered sequence) and for each and every pass to be executed at a match realistic tempo.

The timing of the midfield player has to be immaculate and should consist of short sprint bursts rather than continuous movement. All players should look to play with 2 touches at every station.

Once the first cycle is completed, the second cycle should completely mirror the first on the opposite side (in the diagram the first pattern starts from the left, so the mirrored sequence starts from the right) in a continuous sequence.

Coaching Points

1. The coach needs to enforce the pattern of play and emphasise the importance of short sprints into space that are both well timed with the pass and appropriately positioned within the markers (which represent opponents).

2. The runs into space should be curved and the pass into the midfield space should aim to be disguised when possible.

Coaching The Tiki Taka Style Of Play

24. ATHLETIC BILBAO: Finding Space within a Compact Block (Pattern Play)

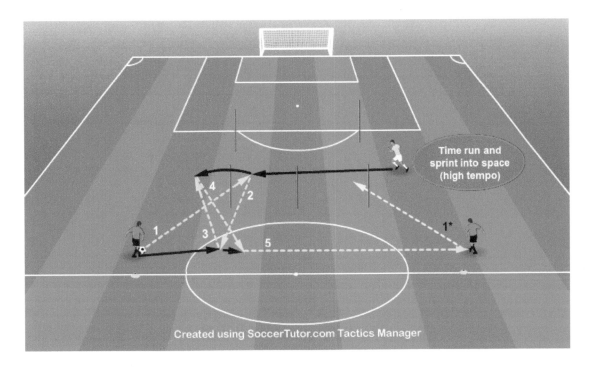

Time run and sprint into space (high tempo)

Created using SoccerTutor.com Tactics Manager

Objective

To introduce a more complex pattern play in a highly congested midfield zone.

Description

This exercise is similar to the previous practice (23), but requires players to become more accurate with their passes and timing of their runs. Once again this exercise looks to mimic a real game situation with a midfielder running in amongst the opposition and the 2 ball playing defenders being patient in their build up approach.

All players should look to use 2 touches and are expected to time their runs well and play their passes with the appropriate weight. All movement off the ball should look to be disguised and through a series of short sprints rather than continuous movement.

The pattern should consist of 5 passes and once they are completed the sequence is mirrored and the continuous exercise replays from the opposite side.

Coaching Points

1. Enforce the pattern of play and emphasise the importance of short sprints into space that are well timed with the pass and appropriately positioned within the markers (opponents).

2. The runs into space should be curved and the pass into the midfield space should aim to be disguised when possible.

25. FC BARCELONA: Team Positioning When Playing Out from the Back (Pattern Play)

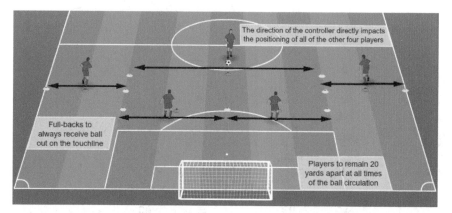

The direction of the controller directly impacts the positioning of all of the other four players

Full-backs to always receive ball out on the touchline

Players to remain 20 yards apart at all times of the ball circulation

Objective

To encourage comfort in a passing network between the back 4 and the deep lying midfielder who tries to control possession.

Created using SoccerTutor.com Tactics Manager

Description

This pattern play exercise requires players to understand the relationship between their own position and the location of the 'play.'

Players should look to be positioned within their 'station' in accordance to where the ball is. In the first diagram, players are positioned in the neutral central position, but if the ball were to be shifted over to the left back (receiving the ball on the touchline), all the other players shift over to the far left of their own zone.

Players should always be on the move within this 'system of play.' The exercise breaks out of this cycle when the coach calls players to break forward (through a full back or controller) and then the coach calls for play to 'start again', where players are now expected to fall back into position as if it were a match (moving forward, backwards and from side to side as a unit).

Coaching Points

1. The ball should always be received across the body where possible (to open up the field of opportunities) and players should look to play confident and appropriately weighted passes (using 2 or 3 touches).
2. The coach is expected to keep good standards and the play should be maintained at a high intensity.

26. FC BARCELONA: Team Positioning When Playing Out from the Back From a Throw-in (Pattern Play)

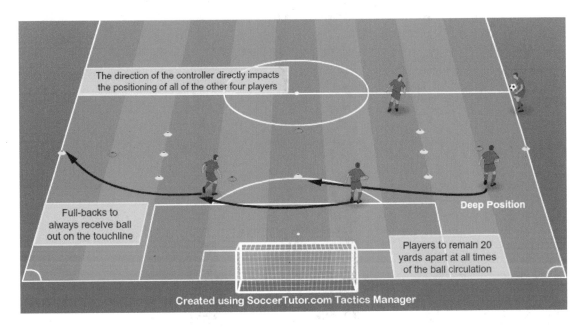

The direction of the controller directly impacts the positioning of all of the other four players

Full-backs to always receive ball out on the touchline

Deep Position

Players to remain 20 yards apart at all times of the ball circulation

Created using SoccerTutor.com Tactics Manager

Objective

We work on positioning and pattern of passing using a regular game-like starting point.

Description

This pattern play exercise isolates the throw-in as a regular match specific starting point. Players should take up the positions as shown in the diagram and look to shift across as normal (see exercise 25).

The ball should be played across the width of the pitch 3 times (full backs should use both the controller and the nearest central defender) before the throw in is repeated, but from the opposite flank.

The ball should be thrown in to either the central defender who has positioned himself in a deep right back position or to the controller who should then play the shortest pass available to him. The central defender in the full back position should look to receive the ball on his second touch on the edge of the zone closest to the centre of the field (to allow the thrower to take up a wider position in play).

Coaching Points

1. The ball should always be received across the body where possible and players should look to play confident and appropriately weighted passes (using 2 or 3 touches).

2. The coach is expected to keep good standards and the play is to be maintained at a high intensity.

27. LIVERPOOL FC: Shooting Practice with Quick Passing

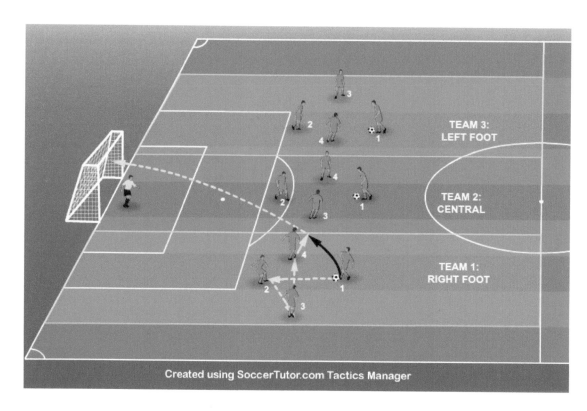

Created using SoccerTutor.com Tactics Manager

Objective

We work with the players to shoot from outside the box after a series of quick one touch passes.

Description

This exercise requires competitiveness and should therefore be done in teams of 4. The first player should pass the ball forward and only receive the ball to shoot after the correct series of one touch passes have been made.

The player who is set to shoot is allowed to take up to 3 touches, but should look to take a controlled shot with the minimum number of touches. The team with the highest number of goals between them wins the exercise and each team should take it in turns to shoot at the goal (with the goalkeeper).

We have 3 zones, one where players shoot with their right foot, one with their left foot and a central zone where both feet can be used. Players should rotate their positions within their teams in a clockwise direction.

Coaching Points

1. This is the coaches opportunity to encourage players to use their weaker foot and to really concentrate on all aspects of their shooting (body position, arm position, head angles, type of shot etc).
2. This exercise should remain fun and as match realistic as possible.

84

28. FC BARCELONA: Feeding the Ball into the Front 3 (3 v 3 (+GK) Attacking Practice)

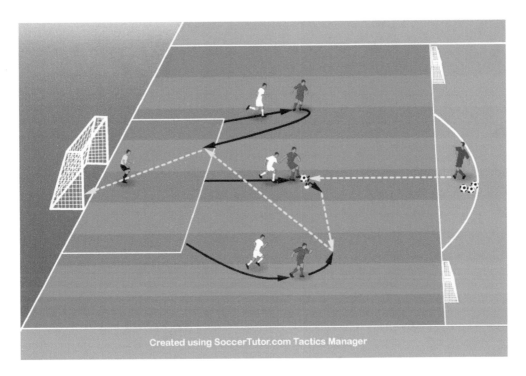

Created using SoccerTutor.com Tactics Manager

Objective

We work with the players to think about how they can turn against opponents who mark them tightly in a high pressure environment.

Description

We work with 3 defenders, 3 forwards and 1 goalkeeper.

The forwards should take up a starting position on the edge of the 6 yard box, with the defenders right behind them. The coach or a spare player should feed the ball into the striker's feet or chest. The 3 forwards then work as a team to try and score in the full sized goal against a goalkeeper.

This exercise should be executed at a high intensity. Therefore we introduce an incentive for the defenders who have to try and win the ball, counter attack and score in one of the two wide positioned mini goals. They should not build up slowly from the back.

Once a goal is scored or the ball goes out of play, the exercise starts again with the coach/spare player and all players go back to their starting positions.

Coaching Points

1. The striker should be able to shield the ball and be patient in finding the appropriate situation to turn with the ball.

2. The coach should alter the angle, height and speed of the pass in.

3. While the first striker may be shielding the ball, the coach should analyse the movement of his 2 teammates to help create space and goal scoring opportunities.

85

29. WIGAN ATHLETIC FC: Finding the Centre Forward in the Box 3 v 3 (+GK) Practice

Created using SoccerTutor.com Tactics Manager

Objective

We work on a 3 v 3 situation and want the forwards to work out how they can find space 'in behind' the opposition in tight spaces.

Description

This is a similar practice to the previous one. The drill starts with the coach passing a ball along the ground to one of the kaasters who then plays the ball to one of the forwards. The 3 forwards should look to work in combination with the kaasters who are limited to 2 touches and are positioned outside of the area, as shown. The forwards look to find space behind a tight marking defender and the kaasters look to play the ball in behind/over the top of the defence.

The offside rule applies in this exercise (and is advisable to use the coach's position). As the game progresses, the coach should look to limit the kaasters to 1 touch to encourage quick thinking and pre-meditated movements, especially encouraging the 'third man' movement.

Should a defender win the ball, they can become the attackers (optional). The coach can change the positioning of the 3 kaasters and place conditions on the game (i.e. no one-two's for assisting a goal etc.).

Coaching Points

1. The coach should focus on the movement of the 'third man', i.e. the player who passes to the player who then passes to the player who will attempt the assist.

2. In Dutch football there is a great deal of emphasis put on thinking two steps ahead and this exercise looks to accomplish this way of thinking.

3. The coach should help players disguise their runs and create an understanding amongst the squad about 'faking' the direction of runs (or double faking) to create space and lose a marker.

Coaching The Tiki Taka Style Of Play

30. FEYENOORD FC: Raymond Verheijen's Sprinting & Finishing Under Pressure

10 second rest before next short sprint & Inside player rotates

Created using SoccerTutor.com Tactics Manager

Objective

This exercise looks to focus on short bursts of sprinting with an end product that are match realistic. The objective for the players is to beat the opponent to the ball and score under pressure.

Description

The coach stands in between the 2 players and passes the ball forward, as shown. The players can sprint as soon as the ball is struck and compete to win the ball and then score in the goal past the goalkeeper.

This exercise demands high intensity and short sprints from a very particular type of pass into play from the coach. This pass in may be short, long, high or along the ground but should remain fair for both players to compete for. The first person to arrive at the ball is to be the attacking player and the other the defender.

Coaching Points

1. While seemingly straight forward, this type of drill is by far the most effective practice of short sprints and providing a match realistic end product.

2. The ball should be controlled, shielded or shot (in a controlled manner) despite the initial high pace approach.

3. There should never be queue's in any of your exercise longer than the 'recovery time' is needed to be and therefore you should look to have a turn over of 10 seconds per pair.

Coaching The Tiki Taka Style Of Play

31. AFC AJAX: 3 Man 1 v 1 Duel 'Moves to Beat' Dribbling Exercise

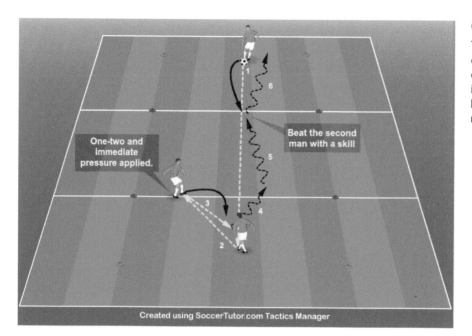

One-two and immediate pressure applied.

Beat the second man with a skill

Created using SoccerTutor.com Tactics Manager

Objective

To encourage creativity in 1 v 1 duels and bringing in new skills to be learnt in match realistic conditions.

Description

The 3 players in this exercise start in separate zones as shown. The ball is played from the deepest defender to the attacker, who then plays a quick one-two with the nearby second defender. On receiving the ball, the attacker should be under immediate pressure from the second defender and aim to beat this player with a single touch if possible.

The deep defender should then approach and the attacker has an opportunity to demonstrate a move to beat (pre-determined by the coach) and dribble into the end zone.

The 3 players then rotate and the exercise begins again. The defender should simply jockey backwards with the attacker at first with little pressure applied and as the session progresses, a more realistic attempt to tackle should be encouraged.

Coaching Points

1. This exercise has been designed to allow continuous use of a newly learnt skill to beat a man in a 1 v 1 scenario and therefore, the coach is in a position to introduce a move to beat and analyse as appropriate.
2. The move to beat should be aggressive, at pace and keep the ball moving. Players are to be reminded of the purpose of each skill and assess their own ability to deceive the opponent.

Moves to beat include: The Roulette (Zidane), The Elastic (Ronaldinho), The Chop (C.Ronaldo), The Step Over (Brazilian Ronaldo), La Croquette (Iniesta) or a change of pace and control of the ball (Messi) etc. Brazilian Soccer Skills and Coerver are two methods of coaching that can be inspirational for this particular type of coaching.

Coaching The Tiki Taka Style Of Play

32. FC BARCELONA: The 3 Station Interchanges Exercise (Losing Your Man)

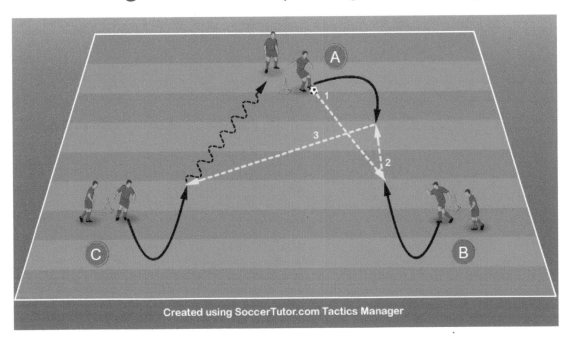

Created using SoccerTutor.com Tactics Manager

Objective

The 'feint' movement is to be introduced and practiced.

Description

We work with 6 players with 2 at each station (A, B and C). Player A passes to B, who passes the ball back and Player A passes to C who completes the sequence by dribbling back to the starting point (A). The players positioned at stations B and C should make a quick dummy movement away from the ball to 'lose their man' and then travel back towards the ball to then make the pass.

This is a continuous drill, whereby the feint or fake movement should look convincing and the player should be able to complete the next task with consistency (whether that be a pass or a dribble). Players should move to the next cone after completing their task at each station (A➔B, B➔C and C➔A).

Coaching Points

1. The coach should concentrate on the feint and making sure that the movement is both convincing and one that does not negatively impact the success of the next task (pass or dribble).

2. This exercise should remain at a high tempo and the queue behind each station should remain minimal.

3. Players should look to complete their tasks with 1 or 2 touches (if receiving the ball across the body).

Coaching The Tiki Taka Style Of Play

33. VILLARREAL CF: 4 v 4 Pressing Patterns

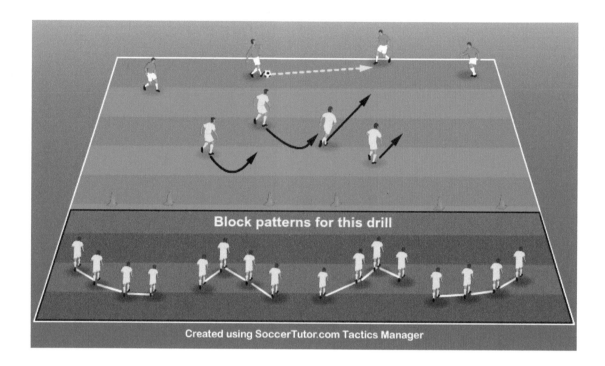

Block patterns for this drill

Created using SoccerTutor.com Tactics Manager

Objective

This simple but effective exercise looks to educate players about the importance of a well organised block (e.g midfield line in a 4-4-2).

Description

We play with 4 attackers and 4 defending players who defend 3 mini goals. You should let the players play without any instruction to begin with, only telling them they are to prevent the ball going in to any of the 3 goals behind them. You can add an extra possession player to outnumber the defenders.

After watching players develop their own tactics, you should ask them to stop and figure out the necessary angle to successfully block the attackers. To aid the process, you must ask the players in possession to play in an area that is between 8-10 yards away from the goals and ask the defenders to play within the area between the attackers and the goals (see diagram). Players should be marking spaces rather than players.

Coaching Points

1. The shapes shown above should be demonstrated to players to help their understanding of how an organised block is more effective than the chaotic individualistic methods.

2. This practice may benefit from performing the block at walking pace at first and then eventually building up to match speed.

3. Body positions should always be in a way that benefits the defensive method and attempts to make the opposition play as predictably as possible.

Coaching The Tiki Taka Style Of Play

34. VILLARREAL CF: 3 v 3 High Intensity Transition Game

Created using SoccerTutor.com Tactics Manager

Objective

This 3 v 3 exercise is a high intensity practice that really pushes players to their limits, by demanding players go from attack to defence with as much speed and intensity as children often go from defence to attack.

Description

We play a normal game of 3 v 3 as shown and when the ball is intercepted or given away, the team that lost possession is required to send the player that is furthest forward to the opposition by-line and back to the halfway line before he is allowed to take part in defending (they are left with a 2 v 1 outfield scenario until the player is able to get back.

This game rewards good defending and therefore when the ball is intercepted or overturned, the defence is rewarded and can play out from the back with little pressure (as the opponent furthest forward is required to sprint to the byline and back to his own half way line before he can participate again).

In the supporting diagram, the goalkeeper has given the ball away and the furthest forward attacker is having to race back to his halfway line to defend after coming from the by-line.

Coaching Points

1. This game requires an age appropriate space to be marked out for a 2 v 2 outfield scenario and plenty of balls around the edges to feed back in should the ball go out of play.

2. You should use 3 teams and have 1 team resting (gathering up loose balls) as the exercise is of high intensity.

3. Stress to the players the importance of getting back into position after an attack and create an urgency that many do not have.

35. FC BARCELONA: Switching Play through a Central Zone Transition Game

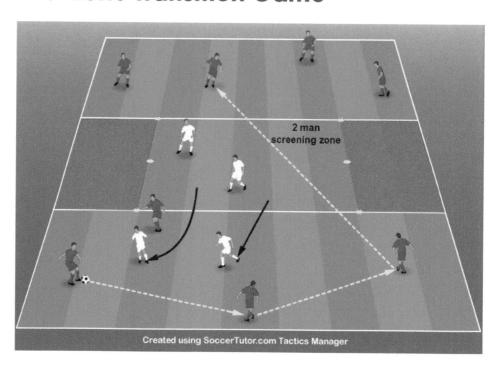

Objective

We work on possession play within preconditioned rules (number of passes etc) and in doing so practice switching the play through a central area.

Description

We have an 8 v 4 situation in this 3 zone possession game. The area (flexible in size) is split into 3 zones: 2 for the team in possession and 1 central zone for a team of defenders.

The defenders must work in pairs and look to press the attackers while they have to pass the ball between themselves a particular number of times, before looking to switch the ball through the central area to the other side (and the 2 blocking players within this space).

If the central players intercept the ball, they then switch roles with the 4 players at the end where the ball was lost. This should encourage all players to think about how they should defend.

Coaching Points

1. To maintain high levels of pressing, the coach should keep the number of passes required low.
2. This exercise may be difficult at first and you may need to restrict the players in the middle so that they do not block passes going through.
3. If players are struggling to keep possession, it may be beneficial to limit the number of defenders who are pressing to just one.
4. The area has been 'centralised' to represent a match-realistic scenario where defenders are defending deep in narrow and compact zones at the edge of the penalty area.

Coaching The Tiki Taka Style Of Play

36. FC BARCELONA: 5 v 2 / 5 v 8 Quick Transition Game with Central Square

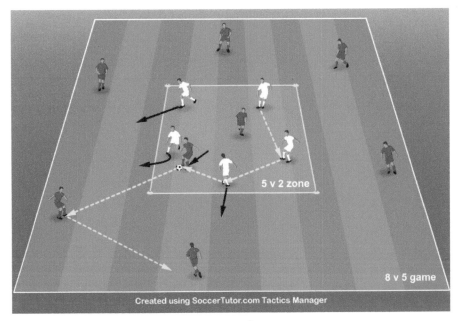

Objective

We work on keeping possession within a Numerical advantage and introduce the idea of quick transitions between having possession and attempting to win the ball back.

Description

This game is set up to encompass two different zoned games. The smaller space should be large enough for a 5 v 2 ball retention game where the 5 players are to keep the ball away from the 2 'chasers'. Should the 5 players lose the ball to the 2, the ball should be played out by one of the 2 defenders to any of their 6 teammates positioned in the larger space.

The game then becomes an 8 v 5 situation where the whole space is to be used. When the ball is won by the 5, the smaller 5 v 2 game in the smaller central zone is repeated.

1 point is scored per 5 passes (or fewer if both teams struggle). The transitions of the ball should be left unopposed (i.e. the moment the ball is played back into the smaller zone or out into the larger space).

Progression

You can progress this game to allow players to enter the central area when a 'trigger' occurs. Triggers include a poor touch, a poor pass etc. These triggers are to be learnt by the players in small doses and more can be read on 'triggers' within chapters about pressing in this book.

Coaching Points

1. Coaches should encourage players to think about using the whole space and in turn, the collective positioning of the team.
2. You should look to introduce ideas such as the use of a playmaker (unmarked) when in the larger space.

Coaching The Tiki Taka Style Of Play

37. AFC AJAX: 7 v 7 Transition Game with Blocking Zone

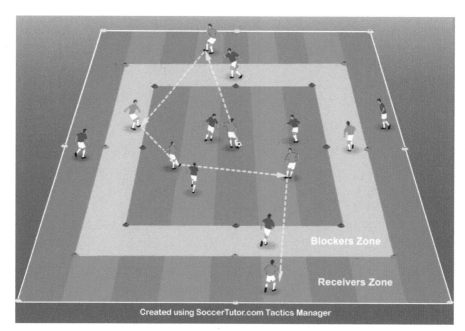

Blockers Zone

Receivers Zone

Created using SoccerTutor.com Tactics Manager

Objective

We practice with a 7 v 7 possession based exercise that requires teams to play amongst high pressure and 'blocker' players.

Description

This game requires 3 zones to be marked out (see diagram) that allow for 3 different uses. In the central square there is a 3 v 3 situation and these players are not allowed to leave the square. 1 point is scored every time players are able to pass the ball out to one of their 2 receivers and then receive it back into the central square.

Receivers position themselves in the outer zone and should look to find space despite being marked by a player in the blocker zone. Players are not allowed to leave their zones. Each zone should be at last 5 yards deep to allow depth of play and movement away from a marker.

Receivers are allowed to take a maximum of 3 touches and are instructed to play the ball into the central space as quickly as possible. The blockers for the team in possession act as 'kaasters' and are restricted to 1 touch.

Variations

1. Receivers could use their team's blockers as a way of passing the ball back into the space if they are comfortable with playing a pass with their first touch (reward for first touch play) for example.
2. You can impose conditions such as a maximum and/or minimum number of passes within the central square.
3. You may add in a neutral central player if the game is stalling along with other conditions.

Coaching Points

1. Coaches should look to encourage disguised movement and for players to maximise the use of their space.
2. Players are expected to think about the angles of their passes and movement carefully in this game.

94

38. FC BARCELONA: Pressing Organisation Position Specific Pattern Play

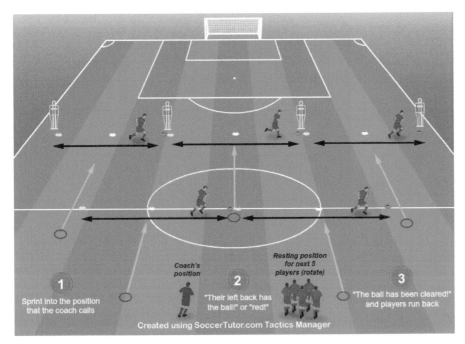

Objective

This practice is an unopposed pattern play exercise that involves the front 3 and central midfield duo in a 4-3-3.

The objective is to introduce players to the organised movement that takes place in a well organised team press when out of possession.

Description

The 5 players should take up the positions by the blue rings in the diagram within their own half and should sprint into the position that the coach calls for (movement shown by blue arrows).

This is a game situation 'press' that requires players to stay a particular distance apart during the initial movement (until the ball is won). The coach will call out "right", "left" or "central" and players must sprint into the relevant position. Coaches may call out colours (red, yellow or white - cones in the diagram) if directional calls are difficult to follow.

After around 5 or 6 changes of direction (5 or 6 calls from the coach), the coach will call out that the ball has been "cleared" and players should sprint back into their starting positions. Players should then be allowed to rest as another five players take up the positions and perform the same exercise.

Coaching Points

1. This exercise must be kept at the highest intensity possible.

2. You should look to keep the exercise as match realistic as possible and therefore should look to demonstrate to players what they are doing with a tactics board or with the use of opposition mannequins.

3. To aid the learning process, you should begin with a walking pace and repeat this exercise until players have demonstrated match level pressing (this exercise is also perfect for preseason fitness purposes).

39. LIVERPOOL FC: The Defensive Block Scoring Zone Game

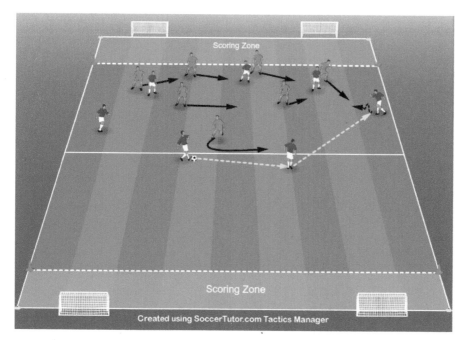

Objective

This exercise requires players to use the pressing techniques as a way of 'slowing down' the opposition's attacking play.

Description

This is a 7 v 7 game with the focus on the shape of a back 4 and midfield trio in their attempt to attack and defend. The team in possession have 2 goals to score in and must get in behind the defence as they are only allowed to shoot within the 'shooting zone' which is 5 yards deep.

Players should look to play freely until the coach begins to introduce match conditions. The aim for the team in possession is to score and the defending team try to limit their attack and win the ball to launch a counter attack of their own and score from within the 'shooting zone' at the opposite end.

Both teams need to be aware of their attacking and defending responsibilities, demonstrating good awareness and positioning throughout.

Coaching Points

1. This exercise asks players to think about how they are going to go from attacking to defending in quick transitions as there are 2 goals to defend.

2. Teams need to adopt a defensive block and formation that the opposition finds hard to break through (replicating the deeper defensive block in game situations).

3. The team in possession should look to employ different strategies to break down the opposition block (use of a playmaker and the false touch etc - see part 4 of this book).

4. You should ask the defending side to be disciplined and only aggressively press when appropriate to do so.

Coaching The Tiki Taka Style Of Play

40. AFC AJAX: Defensive Shape Transition Game

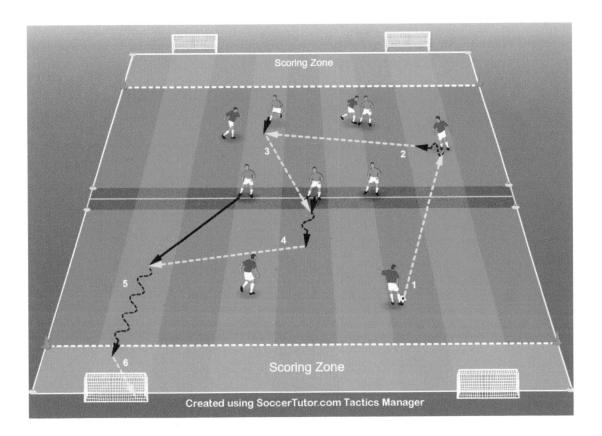

Objective

We work on encouraging the attackers to fall back into position after losing the ball (to the halfway line).

Description

This is a 5 v 5 game. The attacking 3 are instructed to fall back to the halfway line zone (a 3 yard space on the half way line). The 3 attackers cannot exit this zone until the ball is won (except for when further conditions are introduced - see progression). This exercise does not allow the central defenders to go into the opposition half and creates a 3 v 2 scenario in the attacking half if they manage to pass the ball in there.

Progression

When players become comfortable with the conditions of the game, you may begin to introduce pressing rules and triggers such as the 6 second rule (an aggressive press for the first 6 seconds after losing the ball) before asking the 3 attackers to fall back into the central zone.

Coaching Points

1. While in the central zone, the attackers should look to block passes through them without leaving the zone.
2. This game requires constant communication between the players and a disciplined attitude to defending.

Coaching The Tiki Taka Style Of Play

41. FC BARCELONA: 7 v 7 'Triggers' Pressing Game

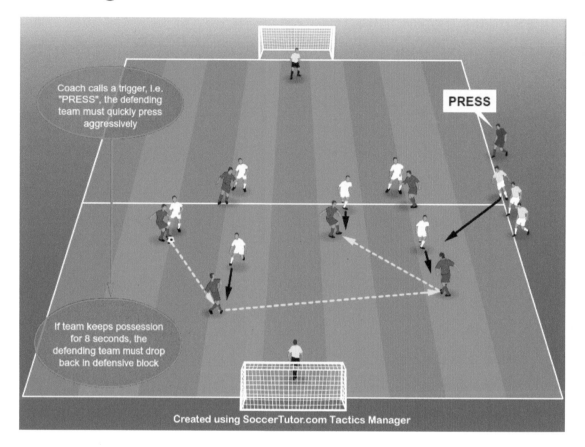

Coach calls a trigger, I.e. "PRESS", the defending team must quickly press aggressively

PRESS

If team keeps possession for 8 seconds, the defending team must drop back in defensive block

Created using SoccerTutor.com Tactics Manager

Objective

This small sided game looks to introduce the 'triggers' of pressing to a team of players.

Description

There should be a 6 v 6 outfield game (goalkeepers added if possible, if not include a 5 yard scoring line). The small sided game should continue as normal until a 'trigger' occurs that allows for the defending side to press aggressively and attempt to win the ball back.

Should a team keep the ball for 8 seconds while the aggressive press takes place, the defence should then drop back and look to defend in a defensive block again. The coach can begin to progress the game by introducing up to 3 additional players who would rest on the sidelines until a trigger occurs and then they should join the defensive team and help overload the defence. These pressers should be rotated to keep a high intensity.

Coaching Point

The coach may need to slowly introduce the triggers to the players and at first may need to instruct players until they are capable of understanding the triggers (see part 4 of this book).

42. FC BARCELONA: 7 v 7 '6 Second Rule' Pressing Game

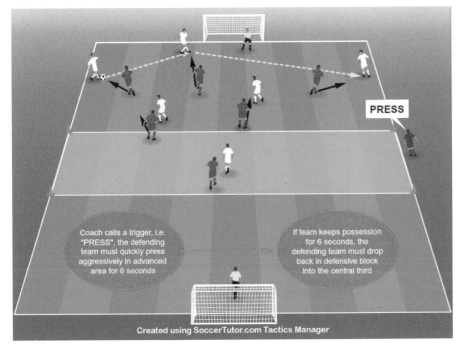

PRESS

Coach calls a trigger, i.e. "PRESS", the defending team must quickly press aggressively in advanced area for 6 seconds

If team keeps possession for 6 seconds, the defending team must drop back in defensive block into the central third

Created using SoccerTutor.com Tactics Manager

Objective

We play a 7 v 7 small sided game that allows the players to form an understanding of the 'pressing rules and triggers' through conditions introduced by the coach.

Description

We play a 7 v 7 game with a central zone marked out as shown.

Players must listen for the coach's call of 'press' and are expected to press in advanced areas aggressively for 6 seconds.

If the team in possession manage to keep the ball during this period, the defensive team are instructed to drop back into to a disciplined defensive block (into the central third).

If the team in possession builds up play successfully and enters the central zone with the ball, the defending team should drop in and out of their phases (defensive block or aggressive team press) for what they think is right.

Coaching Points

1. The coach is expected to use this format as a way of introducing pressing methods that allow defenders to come out of their disciplined block.

2. The coach is also expected to intervene as a way of introducing different types of blocks to the defending team (see part 4 of this book).

3. The coach should focus on promoting a disciplined defensive block as a way of defending and it is often recommended that this small sided game is started without conditions at first, so defenders can realise the importance of team organisation.

99

43. FC BARCELONA: Pressing Attacking Zone Game

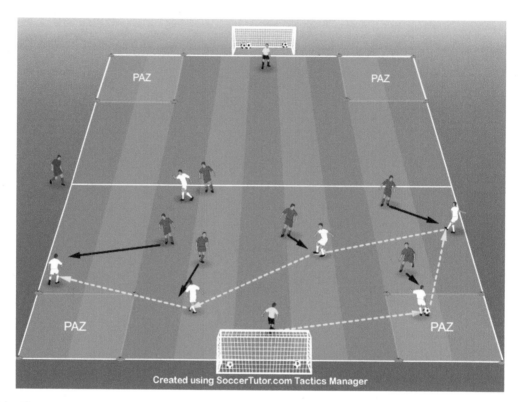

Objective

To encourage control of the game without possession of the ball by an organised team of players.

Description

We play a 7 v 7 small sided game with 4 corner zones, as shown in the diagram.

If a defending team can force the team in possession into the PAZ (pressing attacking zone) they gain possession either from a throw in or sideline kick-in. The team in possession must start with the first pass from the goalkeeper out into the PAZ before the defensive team can press (the only time the possession team should have possession of the ball in the PAZ).

Progression

To make the game harder for the team in possession, a rule should be introduced that they are not allowed to pass the ball back to their goalkeeper (as the game is designed to benefit the aggressive offensive press).

Coaching Points

1. The coach should focus on the shape of the defensive team and their recognition of the triggers as to when to aggressively press forward.

2. The coach may introduce passing conditions for the team in possession (i.e. a minimum of 5 passes before the ball can cross the halfway line) to encourage the defensive side to control their opponents possession.

Coaching The Tiki Taka Style Of Play

44. AFC AJAX: 3 v 3 / 6 v 3 Quick Phases Transition Game

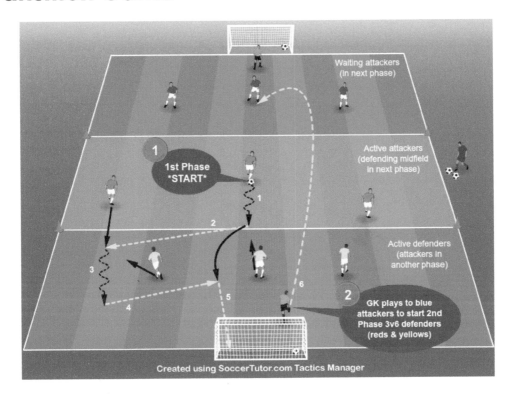

Objective

This is a 3 phase exercise that encourages players to turn from attackers to defenders very quickly and they have to adjust their mindset to match the speed of transition.

Description

We have 9 players and 2 goalkeepers for this practice with 3 players starting in each zone (as shown).

The game begins (first phase) with the middle third players (red) being instructed to dribble with the ball and attempt to score a goal by beating the defensive trio (yellow). When the ball is lost or the team have scored, the ball is played down the field to the inactive players at the other end.

These 3 players (blue) now have to attack against the 6 defending players (second phase).

Players can only become active defenders when the ball enters their given zone. When the ball is lost or the team have scored, the game is restarted but in the opposite direction (reds attacking blues 3 v 3 - third phase).

Coaching Points

1. The coach should encourage discipline and shape from the defending players. It is better for the team to 'make it difficult' for the attackers than to tackle the attackers quickly.

2. Conditions may need to be introduced to encourage the defending side to think about their shape.

3. Defenders should look to control the possession of the attackers by showing them outside into wider spaces (away from goal).

Coaching The Tiki Taka Style Of Play

45. SWANSEA CITY FC: Attacking in the Final Third (2 v 2s)

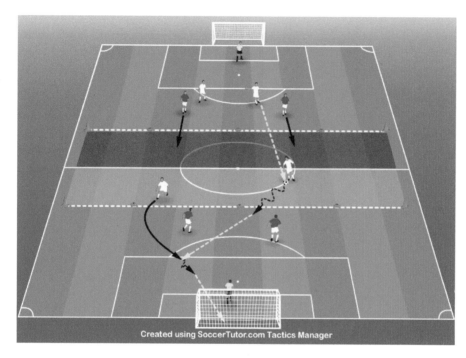

Created using SoccerTutor.com Tactics Manager

Objective

We simulate a game situation where forwards are fed the ball to beat the defenders in front of them (on the counter attack).

Description

We use a full sized pitch (relevant to the age of the players) with 8 outfield players and a zone should be set up either side of the halfway line to allow the attackers to pick up the ball unopposed.

The game starts with the goalkeeper who passes to one of his defenders. They then pass the ball to one of their attackers in the central unopposed zone, who receive the ball, turn and run at the 2 defenders in the final third and try to score.

If the ball is lost or a goal is scored, the ball should be played unopposed to the opposition attackers who should be waiting in their zone near the halfway line to repeat the same to try and score in the opposite goal.

The aim is for the attackers to get their shot away within the box (or from just outside should the defenders sit off too deep). This exercise should be done at full-pace to create a realistic game situation.

Coaching Points

1. The coach should give instructions such as *'movement without the ball to create space for your team mate'* and bring in learnt skills to a match related scenario.

2. The coach can vary the number of attackers and/or defenders to help create situations that the team experiences during games.

3. The inactive time without the ball should be considered 'resting' time but players are still expected to take up good starting positions for the next phase of play.

46. FC BARCELONA: 2 v 1 / 2 v 3 Quick Transition Game

The two attackers should sprint back to receive the ball and then turn to beat the lone defender and score

If the lone defender wins or intercepts the ball the 2 defenders on the goal-line will join to create a 3 v 2

Created using SoccerTutor.com Tactics Manager

Objective

This exercise tests a player with quick transition play.

We have 2 attackers trying to score against 1 defender and then defend against 2 attackers immediately after.

Description

The game begins with the defending goalkeeper kicking the ball over the halfway line where the 2 attackers should sprint back to receive the ball and then turn to face the defender. The 2 attackers should attempt to beat the defender but within the conditions of the game set by the coach (offside etc). The 2 attackers must get beyond the defender to shoot.

If the defender intercepts or wins the ball, the 2 supporting 'resting' players should sprint on to join the defender and create 3 attackers. The defender is rewarded and should an interception change the direction of the ball, the 2 attackers should allow him to take the ball unopposed.

The 2 attackers then become defenders. We now have a 3 v 2 situation where the 3 attackers look to beat the 2 defenders by the same conditions.

Coaching Points

1. The coach should place an emphasis on the speed of play and decision making of those on the ball.
2. The coach can vary the numbers of those playing in this game (3 v 2 becoming a 3 v 5 etc).

47. FC BARCELONA: Playing through the False 9 in a SSG

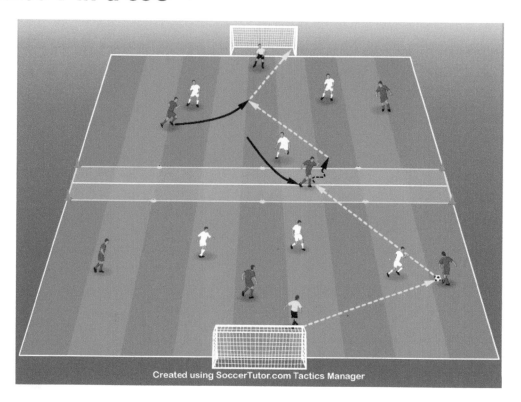

Created using SoccerTutor.com Tactics Manager

Objective

This small sided game encourages an attacker to drop back into an unmarked space to pick up the ball and turn to attack (opposed by a defender).

Description

We play a 7 v 7 small sided game with a central zone (3 yards) marked out where defenders are not allowed to enter. We have a 3 v 3 situation in each of the end zones.

The central zone allows the attacker to drop back into it to receive the ball and turn. The attacker is not allowed to be tackled until he exits the central zone and he is free to dribble or pass the ball out.

The ball must be passed through this zone before entering the final third of play.

The player dropping back into the central zone is limited to 2 touches and should therefore think carefully about the direction of his first touch. The attacker cannot spend more than 2 seconds in this zone without the ball being played to him, so the timing of the run is key. Only 1 attacker can enter the zone at one time.

Progression

The coach can progress this game to allow only the first touch to be free for the player in this zone before the defender can enter the zone and look to press.

Coaching The Tiki Taka Style Of Play

48. FC BARCELONA: 3 Team Vision & Awareness Practice

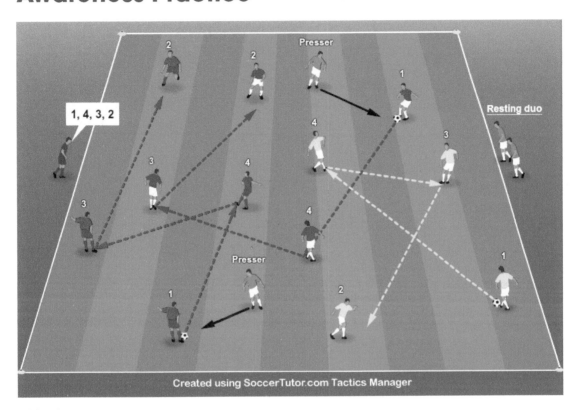

Created using SoccerTutor.com Tactics Manager

Objective

This practice works on awareness and problem solving within a chaotic and crowded space.

Description

We play with 3 teams of 4 in the playing area with 2 defenders. The players within the teams are numbered 1-4 (kept secret from the opponents) and the coach calls out the numbers in a given sequence, and then the players must then pass in this sequence (i.e. "1, 4, 3, 2").

The first team to complete this sequence without losing the ball wins a point.

There must be 2 resting players who rotate with the 2 defenders (pressers). Pressers are not allowed to mark a specific player and are encouraged to try and tackle players from all 3 groups (not focusing on only one team).

These pressing players should aggressively press at a high tempo before rotating with the 2 resting players.

Coaching Points

1. This game encourages players to use their peripheral vision in moments of 'chaos' and look to play out of trouble under high pressure (i.e. when they would win the ball back in the middle third in a match scenario).

2. Players should keep their head up and continually scan their surroundings (looking over their shoulders).

3. Players should look to use the whole area and play in amongst the other 2 teams.

4. You should encourage players to think about the 'third man' rather than just the current pass they are looking to complete.

49. FC BARCELONA: 3 v 1 / 2 v 2
Awareness Game

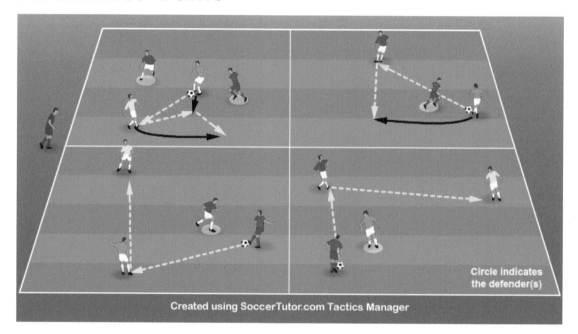

Circle indicates the defender(s)

Created using SoccerTutor.com Tactics Manager

Objective

We have an exercise that looks to create 'chaos' and provide problem solving scenario's for players who are in possession of the ball.

Description

We divide the space up into 4 equal squares and there are 3 players positioned in each square. In each square the 3 players should decide which 2 are on the same team and which player on their own.

A further 3 players (yellow in the diagram) are given the role as problem solvers and have the role to play in different squares and should react, according to the situation in the square. Should they pass the ball to one of the 2 who are in the same team, they help create a 3 v 1 scenario and keep the ball away from the solo player.

Should they pass the ball to the player on his own, they help create a 2 v 2 scenario and look to keep the ball away from the other 2 (circled players in diagrams are defenders).

The problem solver does not know however, which player is alone and which 2 are in the same team and therefore will need to react as quickly as possible to join his teammate(s). Defenders should commit immediately.

Completing 5 passes for the problem solver's team is 1 point. When the coach calls, the ball should be played in a clockwise direction. After 4 rotations, players should switch roles and there should be 3 new problem solvers.

Progressions

1. You may progress the game to constrict the problem solvers to 2 touches.
2. The coach may remove a line of cones to create 1 larger space and 2 smaller.

106

50. FC BARCELONA: 4 Corner Zone Dynamic Transition Game

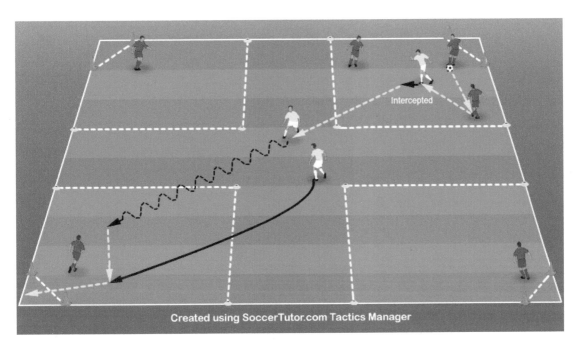

Created using SoccerTutor.com Tactics Manager

Objective

We work to recreate the same match pressures of the quick transition from defence to attack.

Description

The coach should set up 4 corner zones with each zone having a small goal (red cones). There is 1 player positioned in each of the other 4 corner zones. In the central space, there are 5 players; 2 floating possession players and 3 opposition players (who wear yellow).

The game begins with the 2 floating possession players joining one of the corners who then must keep the ball. A 3 v 1 situation is created as 1 defender (yellow) looks to intercept the ball in the chosen corner (sprinting in from the central cross area).

Should the defender win the ball, he should play the ball out quickly to the 2 waiting attackers (yellow teammates) in the central space, who then take the ball and look to attack any one of the 3 corners. They combine and try to score in a mini cone goal.

The player guarding the corner goal should look to commit to pressure the oncoming attackers (not just guard the goal) as they enter the corner. They should rotate after each attack so everyone experiences all roles.

A point is scored for each goal or for when 4 passes are completed in the 3 v 1 scenarios.

Progression

A more complex version of this game can be introduced where you play 2 games from corner to corner. This would create moments of 'chaos' where teams should look to make space for themselves amongst other teams.

PART 3

INFLUENTIAL FIGURES: THE EVOLUTION OF TIKI TAKA

1. THE TIKI TAKA FOOTBALL PHILOSOPHY

"Football is not about players, or at least not just about players; it is about shape and about space, about the intelligent deployment of players, and their movement within that deployment."

Jonathan Wilson[1]

Part three of this book turns the focus away from the development theory and training methodology, towards the tactical theory related to the tiki-taka football philosophy.

The tiki-taka philosophy at first requires for the intelligent and technically sound player to have mastered the basic requirements of a player that is comfortable with the ball at his feet.

Thereafter, coaches need to educate the team in an age appropriate language through team meetings and training sessions in the art of collective play and the fundamentals of football widely recognised as tikitaka football.

This book has made an attempt to break down the themes that make up the tiki-taka philosophy into the simplest components in an attempt to analyse just how the philosophy's strategies and system functions.

The 9 Pillars of Tiki-Taka

1. The spatial positional system and concept of 'formation.'
2. The transition differentials of a fluid and zone dependant formation; from the build-up play, attacking zones and defensive zones.
3. The defensive organisations.
4. The art of collective pressing (transition).
5. Ball circulation.
6. The attacking attitudes and off the ball movement.
7. Form follows process (relationships between the 4 basic states).
8. The individual basic tasks.

9. Tactical response and variations of the system.

Each of the relevant key strategies have evolved over the course of history, a concept of great ideas being passed down through the generations in a very linear, stagist and sequential view of history right up to what constitutes as tiki-taka today.

An understanding can be made through the historical study of tiki-taka to understand what components are variables and which are non-variables.

It is not good enough to ever mimic the current model of tiki-taka and that should not be your aim; to progress is to evolve.

---

1   Wilson, J (2009). *Inverting the Pyramid: The History of Football Tactics: A History of Football Tactics.* London: Orion

Coaching The Tiki Taka Style Of Play

2. THE EVOLUTION OF TIKI TAKA FOOTBALL
The 12 Men Who Changed Football the Most

This chapter briefly attempts to pick away at significant events in the history of football to identify how tiki-taka has evolved to its current state.

There have been a number of epoch-making events that took place to enable changes in the evolution of tiki taka.

Each change, no matter how slight, has played its part in the history of the playing philosophy and this chapter briefly highlights those who have made the biggest differences.

While Jonathan Wilson highlighted a McColl-McWilliam-Buckingham-Michels-Cruyff-Guardiola storyline in the foreword, I would like to propose an alternative route to contemporary possession based philosophies that jumps across continents starting from a little town in the West Central Lowlands of Scotland.

When Prime Minister Benjamin Disraeli remarked that the people should *"Keep your eye on Paisley"* in the 19th century it certainly was not directed at the events of football but it quite easily could have been.

Paisley was a town of radical political and industrial movements at the time. So that is where we will begin, nearly 100 miles north of the English border.

3. ARCHIE MCLEAN
From Paisley To Sao Paolo

The absolute origins of tiki-taka are not often thought to have stemmed from a Scotsman's journey to Brazil, but the suggestion that Archie McLean introduced the short high tempo passing game to South America is clearly a significant one given that the game most similar to tiki-taka first developed in the Americas.[2]

The English who travelled the world spreading the game of football took with them the more direct game together with the reliance of an awe-inspiring dribble. The Scots on the other hand, relied more heavily on fluid ball circulation, from player to player.

The differences of the 2 approaches really was thought to have been that distinct and clear cut and as early as 1872 (30th November) when the two giants of 19th century football met, an exhibition was put on for the fans to watch a short passing team (Scotland) play against a team with a long ball reliance and dribbling expertise (England).

"We also need to look at these great pioneers like McLean, who took the Scottish game across the world."

Richard McBrearty[3]
(Curator of the Scottish football museum)

Archie McLean, a textile engineer from Paisley, arrived in Sao Paolo in 1912 and almost immediately set up his own football club, 'The Scottish Wanderers,' a club who intrigued those in the Brazilian Paulista League by playing with a style not seen before.

The Scottish Wanderers played a fast attacking short passing game, employed with the stringent rule that there was no place for the long ball or selfish dribbles in their playing identity.

Before too long, this playing style became representative of the entire state and the Sao Paulistas would go on to challenge the neighbour state of Rio

de Janeiro playing in this very particular way that encouraged the ball to ebb and flow around the field in short and free interchanges.

This was a style of football that locals began to call the **'Tabelinha,'** a style dominated by one-two's and a fast paced short passing game (which was almost religious bias).

"Archie influenced the way Brazilians thought about the game and played the game."

Aiden Hamilton[4]
(Football historian)

Archie McLean, who is often compared to Garrincha, became affectionately known as O Veadinho (the little deer), was himself a clever thinking technical winger relying on flair, speed and his teammates movement around him.

The short passing game was one that benefitted him as he preferred the ball to his feet as often as possible, with the opportunity to dribble and play one-two combinations and break free from defenders.

---

2   *History can be interpreted in a number of different ways; this is simply the author's interpretation of the relevant history*
3   *Anon. (2006). The Scot who gave Brazil the most beautiful game of all. Available: http://www.scotsman.com/lifestyle/outdoors/features/the-scot-who-gave-brazil-themost-beautiful-game-of-all-1-1119924. Last accessed July 2012.*

4   *Ibid.*

4. URUGUAY 1930
John Harvey And Alberto Horacio Suppici

It is not too difficult to imagine how such a style would grow quickly in this region of South America, across the closest borders to Uruguay and Argentina.

But another Scotsman, John Harley, arrived in Uruguay in 1909 and like McLean he took with him a short passing style of play that would go on to influence a whole nation to give up their long passing game.

Harley would actually go on to represent the Uruguay national team 17 times and manage both the national team and one of the biggest clubs in Uruguay, Peñarol.

Harley's impact on Uruguayan football was recognised to be significant in the book *"100 Años de Gloria: La Verdadera history del Futbol Uruguayo" (100 Years of Glory: The True History of Uruguayan Football)* written by Atilio Garrido[5] as a key headline read *"Harley cambia la forma de jugar"* (Harvey changes the way we play) and goes on to detail how Harvey taught the nation how the ball should be passed out from the back with a fluidity that we still see today in the modern possession based philosophies.

When Uruguay dominated the world of football under Alberto Suppici in the 1930's they did so by being aggressive in defence, but also by championing technique with the ball and relying on a quick short passing game.

"We played for 20 years to learn to become players, to become what players had to be: absolute masters of the ball."

Ondino Viera[6]

"Their style of play - full of short passes and movement, invention and wizardry - was immediately seen as being much more attractive than the more muscular style of the day."

Tim Vickery[7]

Uruguay coupled this style of football with a W-W formation, a 2-3-2-3 (or 2-3-5) to take advantage of the interlocking triangles that were presented to them in this arrangement, encouraging the short pass and emphasising the importance in keeping the ball on the ground.

It was by no means a result of chance that the final of the first World Cup was played by two of the most technical short passing sides who understood space on the field, Uruguay and Argentina.

5   Garrido, A., (2000) 100 Años de Gloria: La Verdadera history del Futbol Uruguayo; [Uruguay] : El País : Tenfield.
6   Uruguayan domestic football manager during the 1930's; Viera, O. (unknown). Interview with Ondido Viera, Uruguayan Football Player. Available: http://www.pbs.org/wgbh/peoplescentury/episodes/sportingfever/vieratranscript.h tml. Last accessed August 2012.

7   Vickery, T. (2002). Football's debt to Uruguay. Available: http://news.bbc.co.uk/sport3/worldcup2002/hi/team_pages/uruguay/newsid_190700 0/1907148.stm. Last accessed August 2012.

Coaching The Tiki Taka Style Of Play

5. MATTHIAS SINDELAR
The World's First Great 'False 9'

Our journey to modern day tiki-taka now jumps across continents back to Europe, as a completely independent (consider the lack of worldwide communication in the 1930's, but note the significance on future developments) on pitch movement was taking place.

Matthias Sindelar was an Austrian forward, the player widely recognised as the world's first ever 'false 9' or at least the first notable player to play the role of a withdrawn central striker. He was the first great innovator of the false 9 role in Austria's Wunderteam of the early 1930's.

Whilst dropping back into a deeper role was common through short passing football cultures at the time, it was uncommon that a central striker was to make such a movement.

It was against England in 1932 that Sindelar's passing ability and intelligence in such a role first caused problems on an international scale. England won this particular game but found Sindelar to be extremely problematic for them as he drifted off into midfield and the man marking defenders followed him out of position, just as Nandor Hidegkuti would do playing the same role and scoring a hat trick some 20 years later as Hungary beat England 6-3.

England were shown to be both tactically and technically inferior to Hungary's Magical Magyars. Hungary's 35 shots to England's 5 highlights that Hungary's success was more than just their style, as Hidegkuti's final goal and volley, followed an awe inspiring 10 pass move.

"They were the greatest national side I played against, a wonderful team to watch with tactics we'd never seen before."

Sir Tom Finney
(Who played for England against Hungary that day)

One of Hungary's focal tactical successes, that of the withdrawn central striker, has a lot to thank Austria for and more precisely. Hidegkuti. He would no doubt have moulded his own game on that of Matthias Sindelar, a player who Egon Ulbrich (a life long friend) claims was tragically murdered along with his girlfriend by the Nazi Germany regime for refusing to play for Germany.[8]

Sindelar will no doubt be remembered for his significant tactical influence by being the world's first ever great 'false 9.'

---

8   Duffy, J. (2003). Football, fascism and England's Nazi salute. Available: http://news.bbc.co.uk/1/hi/magazine/3128202.stm. Last accessed August 2012.

6. LA MAQUINA AND EVOLUTION'S PATH
Renato Cesarini & José María Minella

Before we explore the tactical advances of the great Hungary team of the 1950's we must jump back across continents, not too far away from where we started, in Argentina. We land in La Maquina of River Plate in the 1940's to be exact, a team managed under the guidance of both Cesarini (1939-44) and then Minella (1945-59).

River Plate boasted some of the world's greatest attacking players in the 1940's and continued the success of the false 9 role as Adolfo Pedernera drew the opposition man marking defenders out of position, creating spaces for the remainder of their world class strikers, such as Angel Labruna, Juan Carlos Munoz, José Manuel Moreno and Felix Lostau to exploit and create havoc for the opposition.

Nevertheless, probably the most significant tactical aspect of River Plate's playing identity was not just that of the false 9 role, but the dynamism of the 5 forwards. Moreno, Pedernera, Munoz, Labruna and Lostau were all blessed with a great tactical understanding as well as technical abilities, which enabled River Plate to constantly rotate the attacking positions. This caused the fans and opponents to believe the front 5 had superhuman stamina in their quest to continually roam around the field without tiring, winning both games and admirers along the way.

"I play against La Maquina with the full intention of beating them, but as a fan of football, I would prefer to sit on the stands and watch them play."

Ernesto Lazzatti[9]
(The star of rivals Boca Juniors 1934-47)

---

9   Comme. (2011). A History of World Football in 100 Games - Part 23. Available: http://ademirtozizinho.blogspot.co.uk/2011/11/history-of-world-football-in-100-games.html. Last accessed August 2012.

7. THE MAGNIFICENT MAGYARS
Gusztáv Sebes

As River Plate continued to win the plaudits, another great side was just about to be born, that of the Magnificent Magyars, Hungary (1949-56). Hungary's Golden Team was founded on the genius of 6 key players: Ferenc Puskás, Sándor Kocsis, Nándor Hidegkuti, Zoltán Czibof, József Bozsik and Gyula Grosics.

Hungary were managed by the great Gusztáv Sebes, whose success can be ascribed to the way in which he revolutionised the tactical norm through 4 key innovations pulled together under one team and everything changed.

Similarities to La Maquina can be drawn from the following changes, but it was the gravity of the impact that leaves this Hungary team as one that cannot be ignored when considering who shaped tiki-taka along the way.

1. Sebes implemented fitness regimes for his players and began regular international training sessions, just like we see at club level today.

2. At the time the norm was to adopt the WM formation where the centre forward led the line, with an attacking line of three forwards and two wingers. Sebes also regularly dropped the wingers back into a deeper role and created an extremely flexible 2-3-3-2 formation, drawing the opposition's defenders out of position as they followed the deep lying striker out of defence. While this role was not first introduced here, the combination with this and other tactical features was highlighted here.

3. Sebes encouraged versatility in his players in a positional sense, a continuation of La Maquina's success. The Hungarian tactic of players constantly changing roles and positions contributed greatly to the success of the team.

4. When the team attacked all players were involved in this movement, from the defenders to the goal scoring forward. Generally speaking, teams and formations at the time relied on the two distinctive roles set out as defending players and attacking players, with no middle ground (hence the WM and WW formations).

"When we attacked, everyone attacked, and in defence it was the same. We were the prototype for Total Football."
Ferenc Puskas

Sebes' role in shaping The Magnificent Magyars cannot be downplayed. Under the forward thinking tactician and coach Hungary scored the most goals (27), still boast the highest average of goals per game (5.4) in a single World Cup finals stage and went 31 games unbeaten between 1950-1956, only to lose once against Germany in the 1954 final.

The 1952 Olympic Champions are of course equally as famous for their 6-3 and 7-1 victories over England and this was in large part put down to Sebes' methods of coaching Hungary to sustain superior levels of fitness and technique as well as decisive tactical innovations. There was also the inspiring individual spirit, self expression and creativity in a nation under authoritarianism.

Sebes was instrumental in piecing together the domestic club Honved with the bulk of the national side: Ferenc Puskás, Sándor Kocsis, László Budai, Gyula Lóránt, Zoltán Czibof, József Bozsik and Gyula Grosics were all either at the club or conscripted under the newly 1949 nationalised army club.

Players of Honved were all given military ranks and required to fulfil the full time fitness regime and dietary instructions by the club's coaching staff to ensure that players would be in the best possible physical shape to maintain the high tempo expected of them on the football field.

Sebes prepared for the infamous 1953 victory against England using specified training methods that would benefit The Mighty Magyars, by training with heavier footballs than those that were used in England and on a football field that was measured up to be the exact dimensions to those of Wembley.

Of all coaches in history that led change the most, Sebes' attention to detail was decades ahead of his counter-parts in gaining advantages through technical, physical and tactical innovations on an unprecedented level of change.

For this, football owes much to the great Hungary side of the 1950's, a side that inspired not just other nations over the next decade or so, but the game itself.

8. MASLOV'S PRESSING APPROACH

Along with Archie McLean and Matthias Sindelar, it is probable that Viktor Maslov is one of the lesser known men in this chapter to make a significant contribution to the evolution of tiki-taka based football. However, Maslov is every bit as important as anyone else in this linear timeline because he made a significant contribution on a number of different levels.

From 1964-1970, Maslov was in his prime in terms of his impact as the manager of FC Dynamo Kyiv of Ukraine.

As Vicente Feola's Brazil won the 1958 World Cup playing a distinctive 4-2-4 formation with two wide wingers, much of the world followed suit.

Maslov on the other hand, had other ideas. He brought the two offensive wingers back into the midfield and he scrapped the notion of attacking dribbling wingers all together. Maslov invented the 4-4-2 and in doing so outnumbered the two man midfield opposition. Maslov's impact though, goes far beyond a change of formation.

"The 4-4-2 was first invented by Maslov."
Jonathan Wilson[10]

Viktor Maslov saw his 4-4-2 as a system of roles that fitted together to form the collective roles of the whole:

- A midfield with no wingers, but wide midfielders who fulfilled the roles of working the space directly in front of the full backs.

- No player was to hold on to the ball longer than necessary and a pass was always favoured over a dribble.

- Full backs were to join in with the ball circulation.

- The midfield was anchored by a defensive midfielder who screened the back four.

- The most creative player was to be used as an advanced playmaker whilst in possession.

- The midfield hunted for the ball when out of possession as a tight unit or pack.

- Man making was to be abolished in favour of zonal marking and positional covering.

This notion of playing as a system of players had been loosely touched on in previous successful teams, but Never so stringently.

"No matter how talented the individual, if they did not function as part of the collective, they had no place within it."
Jonathan Wilson[11]

Maslov's machine-like system was set out to unreservedly diminish space for the opponents on the ball and win the ball back high up the pitch. A professional level of physical fitness and awareness was/is required to achieve such a devastating attacking approach to winning the ball back.

"[Maslov] introduced 'pressing' at Dynamo Kyiv, which may be seen as the birth of modern football. His sides would hound the opposition in possession, but their system was good enough that players covered those pressuring the man with the ball, closing up gaps that might otherwise have been exploited."
Jonathan Wilson[12]

Maslov almost religiously abolished man marking from his system of play, as instead he believed that through strategic zonal marking and players covering for one another, the ability to tightly press effectively was strengthened.

---

10   Wilson, J (2009). Inverting the Pyramid: The History of Football Tactics: A History of Football Tactics. London: Orion

11   Ibid.
12   Wilson, J. (2008). The end of forward thinking. Available: http://www.theguardian.com/football/2008/jun/08/euro2008. Last accessed July 2012.

Coaching The Tiki Taka Style Of Play

"Man marking humiliates, insults and even morally oppresses the players who resort to it."

Viktor Maslov[13]

Thanks to Maslov, the game learnt more than just a change of formation, but the advantages of playing with players who fit into a system of roles rather than a system that fits the available players was highlighted.

More than that still, the arts of pressing and zonal marking were introduced to the world on a worldwide scene for the first time and football would go on to change indefinitely, as other managers understood the notion of defending in such an attacking style.

---

13   Wilson, J (2009). *Inverting the Pyramid: The History of Football Tactics: A History of Football Tactics.* London: Orion

9. RINUS MICHELS
The Architect of Total Football

Rinus Michels is widely acknowledged as the father of total football or **total voetbal**, a style of football that is often thought to have been the first of its kind as it achieved worldwide recognition and praise.

Nevertheless, as you may have come to notice throughout this chapter, this statement is a highly contested one and ignores the methods employed by Hungary, La Maquina and Maslov.

Perhaps you could argue that never before had football been packaged together under one playing identity so well, or that the ability of players of players to switch positions so freely.

So although Michels' concepts were not born without precedent, the impact of the total football movement absolutely cannot be ignored when considering their importance to the tikitaka evolutionary history.

Rinus Michels managed a technically and tactically brilliant Ajax side between 1965 and 1971.

The foundations for the Ajax players to play in such a technical way had been laid years before by Englishman Jack

Reynolds.

What made **totaal voetbal** so unique was the way in which the philosophy intensified Maslov's thinking dominating space and outnumbering the opposition whether in possession or not, commanding total control and total football.

"Total football was, among other things, a conceptual revolution based on the idea that the size of any football field was flexible and could be altered by a team playing on it...

Seeing every run and movement as a way to increase and exploit the available space. When they lost the ball, the same thinking and techniques were used to destroy the space of their opponents."

David Winner[14]

"It was about making space, coming into space, and organising space-like architecture on the football pitch...We discussed space the whole time. Johan Cruyff always talked about where people should run and where they should stand, and when they should not move."

Barry Hulshoff[15]

"Every player has to understand the whole geometry of the whole pitch."

Gerard van der Lem[16]

The concept of talking about the football pitch as a series of spaces is one that had been touched on before in history, but never before so aggressively addressed as an issue.

When Michels' teams were in possession, the players would **'make the pitch as big as possible'** by spreading out over the whole space of the field of play. The wingers would push out onto the sidelines, the forwards advance forward to stretch and pull the defensive line, the midfield would then receive the ball with acres of space to play and circulate the ball at full potential.

Equally as interesting is how the team then closed down the space and reduced the possible space on the field for the opposition to play, 'making the pitch

as small as possible' for the opponents; the unit of the team would shift from left to right, thinking about geometry and the angles of play available for the opponents and through high pressing and a compact unit (defensive pushed right up), the opposition is left with a congested field of which to play on.

While the opposition is on the back foot, Michels' team (not in possession) would then attack aggressively through the art of collective pressing, hunting mercilessly. Each and every player on the field plays their part, from the goalkeeper and sweeper to the goal scorer, every player has their sense of importance in creating triangles of play and squeezing the opposition:

"Michels was the architect of this football. And I helped him the most."

Velibor Vasovic[17]
(Ajax sweeper 1966-71)

What has become clear is that totaal voetbal was the first to marry together the possession based theoretical concepts with Maslov's aggressive pressing approach.

Nothing about totaal-voetbal was born as an unprecedented idea, but the packaging of such an approach was so complete: it was total.

"I would describe what the journalists call 'total football', as 'pressing football'.

To me, this expression seems to put the emphasis on the type of football I was trying to create with Ajax and with the Dutch national team in the 1974 World Cup. What I wanted to create was a game in which all ten outfield players pressed forward all the time – even when we didn't have the ball!"

Rinus Michels[18]

"Pressure football, the 'hunt', was: regaining possession as soon as possible after the ball was lost on the opponents half during an attack.

The 'trapping' of the opponents in their own defensive half of the field is only then possible when all the lines are pushed up and play close together. This automatically means that you give away a lot of space on your own half and you are vulnerable for counter-

14   Winner, D (2001). Brilliant Orange: The Neurotic Genius of Dutch Football . London: Bloomsbury Publishing PLC; New edition edition.
15   Ibid.
16   Ibid.
17   Ibid.
18   Ibid.

attacks...

To not let the opponent get into their rhythm of play through being well organised as a team is the basics for your own build-up and attack."

Rinus Michels[19]

"You need to control the opponent if you want to play an attacking style football."

Rinus Michels[20]

We have seen before how switching positions and how a withdrawn player in a positional sense, can aid the attack in finding space to create goal scoring opportunities while in possession.

Michels' strategy of position switching offered more than that though, his teams had the ability to stay fresh and continue to press so mercilessly without any breaks in the waves of pressing.

"Fitness has to be one hundred per cent, but how can you play for 90 minutes and remain strong? If I, as left-back, run 70 metres up the wing, it's not good if I immediately have to run back 70 metres to my starting position.

So, if the left [centre]-midfielder player takes my place and the left winger takes the midfielder takes the left-midfielders position, then it shortens the distances. If you have to run ten times seventy metres and the same distance back ten times, thats a total of 1400 metres. If you change it so you must only run 1000 metres, you will be 400 metres fresher. That was the philosophy."

Ruud Krol[21]

Rinus Michels' approach is that of players playing freely within a well thought out framework, that of a system of play inside a 1-3-3-3 (or 4-3-3 with a sweeper) formation.

Michels instructed a set of basic tasks for the team for each phase of play: defending, attacking and the build-up play. As well as overall basic tasks or strategies, Michels would propose strict basic tasks for each and every player unique to their playing position and function within his system of play.

It is also true to argue that Michels would employ an approach that would only work if the correct typology of player was available for each and every position.

"In team building, the creed should be that a player must never do a bad job at his basic task. This should not only be a fundamental rule of the coach, but also of the players.

A player can have a bad day, but never due to neglecting his basic task. This will hurt the team, the team's organisation...the ground rule should be that you first take care of your basic task before you try to do more if the situation in the match allows for this to happen."

Rinus Michels[22]

"You must never choose to play 4-3-3 if you do not have fast defenders who excel in the 1:1 duels and who are exceptional in the positional play to dominate large spaces."

Rinus Michels[23]

"[Total football involves] individuals functioning as a perfectly integrated whole machine."

David Winner[24]

Like Maslov's system, total football was not a philosophy that encouraged individualistic play and meandering runs. Totaal voetbal was instead about finding the simplest solution, with the simple through ball to split open a defence always considered more beautiful than the solo dribble.

"Simple football is the most beautiful. But playing simple football is the hardest thing."

Johan Cruyff[25]

This was a view that impacted not just in the era of totaal voetbal, but still sticks with great Dutch players of today, players like Dennis Bergkamp. Bergkamp, a player considered to be world class in every corner of the globe has marked his place in history with a real sense of class in every touch he took.

19   Michels, R (2013). Team Building: The Road To Success. Reedswain Soccer.
20   Ibid.
21   Winner, D (2001). Brilliant Orange: The Neurotic Genius of Dutch Football . London: Bloomsbury Publishing PLC; New edition edition

22   Michels, R (2013). Team Building: The Road To Success. Reedswain Soccer.
23   Ibid.
24   Winner, D (2001). Brilliant Orange: The Neurotic Genius of Dutch Football . London: Bloomsbury Publishing PLC; New edition edition
25   Moallim, M. (2011). Simply The Greatest. Available: http://jouracule.blogspot.co.uk/2011/03/simply-greatest.html. Last accessed August 2012

"In the later part of my career it wasn't [about] giving the assist, but the perfect assist. Not the assist where [the receiver] still has to do a lot of work. In my head it was like, "ok that player is moving this way, and he is going with the attacking player... but if I pass it just in between at the right pace he can control the ball..." You know? No-one expects it. I'm playing here, but my left eye is there.

I give the ball and everyone is thinking "what's he doing?" And then suddenly he is there, which I have seen. There's a tremendous amount of pleasure you get from that. To do something that someone else couldn't see...That's what I always hoped for.

With one pass, with the right pace on the ball, because that's really important. Sometimes put a curve on it, just bend it away from the goalkeeper, or from the defender or bend it in front of your player so it gives him the extra pace which forces him to speed up... phew!"

Dennis Bergkamp[26]

There is a sense that in totaal-voetbal's rationalised problem solving approach, an objective solution is always the most appropriate. Dennis Bergkamp's take on the issues facing a striker in a one-on-one scenario is as insightful as any:

"Listen, if the goalie is a little bit off his line, how much space do you have on his left or right? It's not a lot. And how much space do you have above him? There is more. It's a question of mathematics. It's fantastic. You have much more space above. So if you get it right, you can't miss. If you've got that certain confidence and ability, then it's the best solution."

Dennis Bergkamp[27]

The gravitational impact of total-football is one that can still be felt on every football pitch, anywhere today. Michels took the concepts to the world stage from Ajax (1965-71; 1975-76) , to Barcelona (1971- 75; 1976-78) and the Netherlands national team (1984-88; 1990-92) , packaged together almost perfectly.

By any stretch of the imagination, without total voetbal's place on this timeline, we would not have tiki-taka today. But more than that, the way we perceive the development of young football players through varied training techniques would not

resemble the Dutch influenced approaches we have at all levels of football today.

It is this concept of educating future and current players with it in mind that they are to play in a very particular system that was born under Michels.

Michels understood that neither he or the rest of the coaching staff could win the football match on the field from the sidelines, and that players win matches.

"He can only 'design' a set of team tactical guidelines. The players will have to come up with the correct solutions on the field...players are the directors. Only they can solve the situations while improvising. We call football a players' sport discipline."

Rinus Michels[28]

---

26   Winner, D (2011) The Blizzard Magazine issue 1. Sunderland: A19.
27   Ibid.

28   Michels, R (2013). Team Building: The Road To Success. Reedswain Soccer.

Coaching The Tiki Taka Style Of Play

10. VALERIY LOBANOVSKYI
The Science of His Pressing Approach

Above all else, like Michels, Valeriy Lobanovskyi had total belief in the implementation plan for his playing system. While Michels considered his style of football to resemble that of a qualitative analysed art and not a quantified analysed science. Lobanovskyi championed his approach as a scientific one founded upon a very particular way of thinking about football.

To Lobanovskyi, players were not students of the game who needed to be educated, but that they evolve into something that fits within his system. Tutoring players through their development was not top of Lobanovskyi's priorities, but that is not to say he did not take these concepts into consideration, rather that Michels' approach differed in these ways most.

Lobanovskyi founded his team progression and tutorship on quantitative statistical analysis.

Objective analysis replaced subjective analysis.

Numbers and data based judgement simply replaced that of personal judgement, an approach that removes the element of human error.

Billy Beane - *the Sabermetric Approach and its Effect on Baseball*

The same umbrella of thinking in sport won Billy Beane the plaudits in 2002 as he took control of baseball's Oakland Athletics as they broke an American League record and won 20 games in succession despite losing their star players the season before. They fielded a team of players written off by almost everyone in baseball including scouts, fans, coaches and beyond.

Beane's success had a secret. Billy Beane and his assistant general manager Paul DePodesta, a Harvard University graduate, employed an analytical evidence based approach to assembling their team, ignoring the advice of the clubs scouts and causing tension along the way.

The Sabermetric approach (Sabermetrics is the analysis of baseball through objective evidence, especially baseball statistics that measure in-game activity) simply highlighted players who were statistically better than others and amongst that list, Beane and DePodesta found players who were otherwise universally undervalued by reputation and professional opinion. The statistical analysis both Beane and DePodesta used to single out appropriate players went beyond the general available statistics such as stolen bases, runs batted in and batting averages (the equivalent of goals scored and assists) and instead, the analysis undertaken supported the notion that the on base percentage and slugging percentage were far better indicators in judging playing ability.

The benefits of this approach allowed the **Oakland Athletics** to build a team who were statistically good enough to win games and within the clubs comparibly tiny 2002 salary budget of $41 million (in comparison to other clubs such as New York Yankees' $125 million).

Beane's approach faced much early criticism and the belief that these 'hidden statistics' were better indicators of ability was met with disbelief and a blinded level of absolute doubt and scepticism.

However, fast forward two years and Beane's approach was employed by the **Boston Red Sox** as they ended their 86 year wait to win their sixth World Championship.

Beane declined a luxurious approach from Boston Red Sox after his 2002 season and remains as Oakland Athletics' general manager today having changed the analysis of baseball for good.[29]

Valeriy Lobanovskyi has arguably had the same impact on football on a number of levels of thought. Lobanovskyi caused controversy when he became manager of Dynamo Kiev in 1974 (which was to become a 16 year stay) and he ordered a computer to record and analyse player performance. In 1974 obtaining a computer was not a trip to the shops kind of thing, so Lobanovskyi had to network with every high level military officer and government office in order to buy one.

The controversial purchase even alerted the Soviet Intelligence who began speculating that Lobanovskyi was leaking political and top secret information to rival countries.

In spite of that, the data collection formed the processes to Lobanobskyi's team building and playing identity, analysing everything from zonal statistics to individual player and team statistics.[30]

The process formulated Lobanovskyi's successful 4-4-2 approach and his view that winning football games was to control space rather than the ball itself in both attack and whilst defending. Football became a quantitative matter of 22 elements in a measured space, two sub-systems of 11 elements constrained by the non-variable laws of the game.

Lobanovskyi believed that the whole is more than the sum of its parts and therefore the team efficiency was not the same as the sum of the 11 individual efficiencies of the team's players.

29   Based on Lewis, M (2004). Moneyball: The Art of Winning an Unfair Game. New York: W. W. Norton & Company; 1st edition.
30   Sengupta, S. (2012). Valeriy Lobanovskyi – One of Football's First Scientists. Available: http://stateofthegame.co.uk/2012/07/04/valeriy-lobanovskyi-one-of-footballsfirst-scientists/. Last accessed August 2012.

Coaching The Tiki Taka Style Of Play

"Football, [Lobanovskyi] concluded, was less about individuals than about coalitions and the connections between them."[31]

Lobanovskyi, similar to Michels, employed an approach that mastered the art (or science!) of collaborative pressing high up the field mercilessly as players pressed in both the opposition's half and their own penalty area.

"To attack, it is necessary to deprive the opponent of the ball. When it is easier to do that with 5 players or with all 11? The most important thing in football is what a player is doing on a pitch when he is not in possession of the ball, not vice-versa."
Valeriy Lobanovskyi[32]

"No other coach ever demanded that I should chase opponents even back into my own penalty area. For example, Oleg Romantsev, both with Russia and Spartak Moscow, told me to work hard, but only in the opponents' half. He told me to do everything in my area, but not to intervene where others should be playing."
Sergei Yuran[33]

Lobanovskyi was a classic authoritarian style coach and believed that the players should fit the manager's system and it is not the job of the system to fit the players.

Lobanovskyi was fortunate enough to play under the great **Viktor Maslov** and there was clearly a lasting influence left upon him. Be that as it may, what is surprising is that the player Lobanovskyi would not agree with the manager Lobanovskyi, a remark he made after journalists questioned him about his approach to management after he himself fell out of Maslov's good books by disagreeing with Maslov's strict approach.

"Tactics are not chosen to suit the best players. Everyone must fulfil the coach's demands first and only then perform individual mastery."
Valeriy Lobanovskyi[34]

While it is obvious that the process and methodology of Lobanovskyi and that of Michels are polar

opposites, the end result and playing styles did not differ beyond recognition.

Both teams passed the ball around at great speeds and at the same time reduced the opposition's possession to that of playing away from a hunting pack of pressing players.

"Like basketball teams which coordinated their movement beautifully and always athletic."
Howard Wilkinson[35]

Lobanovskyi placed a higher value than Michels on physical fitness training drills and preferred his players to focus on playing one particular position and become the master of it rather than be versatile and to play many positions adequately.

"Rapid, simple, devastatingly coordinated, everything Lobanovskyi insisted football should be."[36]

Jonathan Wilson sums up Lobanovskyi's approach in four simple words, but Lobanovskyi was anything but predictable. Lobanovskyi would employ a strategy that reflected this, a continuous changing series of strategies to keep the opposition guessing and struggling to adapt.

"The first thing we have in mind is to strive for new courses of action that will not allow the opponent to adapt to our style of play. If an opponent has adjusted himself to our style of play and found a counter-play, then we need to find new a new strategy. That is the dialectic of the game. You have to go forward in such a way and with such a range of attacking options that it will force the opponent to make a mistake.

In other words, it's necessary to force the opponent into the condition you want them to be in. One of the most important means of doing that is to vary the size of the playing area."
Valeriy Lobanovskyi[37]

If nothing else, the mark left by Lobanovskyi on this particular timeline shows us that the processes of a

31 Ibid.
32 Wilson, J (2006). Behind the Curtain: Football in Eastern Europe: Travels in Eastern European Football. London: Orion; New Ed edition.
33 Ibid.
34 Ibid.

35 Williams, R. (2002). Pioneer coach who believed in the appliance of science. Available: http://www.guardian.co.uk/football/2002/may/15/sport.comment . Last accessed June 2012.
36 Wilson, J. (2008). The end of forward thinking. Available:
37 Lobanovskyi and Zelentsov wrote in their book 'The Methodological Basis of the Development of Training Models' cited in Wilson, J(2006). Behind the Curtain: Football in Eastern Europe: Travels in Eastern European Football. London: Orion; New Ed edition.

Coaching The Tiki Taka Style Of Play

playing style dictate the end product. It needs to be more than just the way players train, but the way they think together as a team.

There is no blueprint to playing with a particular philosophy or style of play, and the differences between Michels and Lobanovskyi make that point evidently clear.

Like Billy Beane of the Oakland Athletics, Lobanovskyi's revolutionary school of thought is one that is present in abundance throughout modern day coaching and has created an everlasting impact on the sport.

11. JOHAN CRUYFF
The Father or Son of Total Football?

No other person in the history of the sport has had such an influential impact on football. As a player, manager and director, everything was always Cruyff's interpretation.

Johan Cruyff the player was the focal point to Rinus Michels' teams and never had a dull moment.

By his own admission Cruyff was the complete player aged just 20 and turned his attention to developing his own tactical understanding of the game under Michels.

"Football consists of different elements: technique, tactics and stamina...You can divide tactics into insight, trust and daring."

Johan Cruyff [38]

38   Barend, F., Van Dorp, H. (1999). Ajax Barcelona Cruyff The ABC An Obstinate Maestro. London: Bloomsbury Publishing PLC; New edition

Johan Cruyff the player certainly left his mark on football worldwide, not least with the sublime and unprecedented 'Cruyff turn,' something that presented itself as the simplest solution to Cruyff in the moment. Cruyff went on to played the majority of his career at Ajax (1964-73) and Barcelona (1973-78) winning European Player of the Year three times (1971, 1973, 1974).

Like Michels, Cruyff's relationship to Ajax and Barcelona seemed to play on a replay loop as he would later return to both as a coach (Ajax 1985-88 and Barcelona 1988-96).

Cruyff's impact on the professional game went far beyond any other football career. Without Cruyff, La Masia, Patrick Kluivert, Clarence Seedorf, Edgar Davids[39] and arguably Xavi and Iniesta would all cease to exist in the form that they do today or possibly would not be in professional football at all.

Cruyff had the firm belief that Ajax should prioritise the development of Dutch players and that Barcelona should do so with Spanish players. As the coach of Barcelona he noticeably stuck by this belief as he refused to bring in players from Ajax, of whom he had found success with in his previous contract of employment.

"If I mention an Ajax player that I'd want [at Barcelona], he has to be better than the three foreigners I have now. So he has to be better than Koeman, Stoichkov and Hagi. Van Der Sar is a very good goalkeeper, but he's a foreigner. If Van Der Sar was Spanish, he would be a candidate."

Johan Cruyff[40]

Judging a footballer's ability to take up his place in Cruyff's system was complex. It was never as simple as a player 'being good enough'. Cruyff offers an insight into his thinking when discussing his belief that Richard Witschge could have become as good as the great Marco Van Basten by placing a high level of judgement on the players' character.

"He can go very far, but he still has to prove himself. He can be as good as Van Basten...Witschge has the same advantage that Van Basten has and that I also had. How do you say it? In Spanish they call it 'fibra' [Temperament] "

Johan Cruyff[41]

The concepts of judging players, selecting players to fit within a system and developing players were well defined under Johan Cruyff and enabled Cruyff his legacy as a coach and director. For all that, what is clear is that the system Cruyff employed was not too distant from that he played within under Michels at Ajax and Barcelona as a player. But some things stay consistent with Cruyff, which are the system, the simplicity and the attacking playing identity.

"Playing simple football is the hardest thing...Simple play is the most beautiful...How often do you see...a one-two in the penalty area when there are seven people around you when a simple wide pass around the seven would be a solution. The solution that seems the simplest is in fact the most difficult one."

Johan Cruyff[42]

"I think everyone should be able to play in all different positions on the field...The left winger can't go to sleep when Michels talks about the right back."

Johan Cruyff[43]

"The special thing about the Dutch team is movement. Everybody moves. That's the basis of it...You can only switch positions if one position is free...if they don't follow me, I'm free...If they follow me, they're one man short in defence."

Johan Cruyff[44]

"If you have a midfielder who comes into the attack and has to run back 80 metres, well he can do that three times and then you may as well forget about him, he has to take a rest. You need to be practical all the time. It's better if the same player only needs to run twenty metres."

Johan Cruyff[45]

Cruyff employed a similar 3-4-3 formation as Michels did with the full backs given marking roles. Nonetheless, he made the minor adjustment of pushing the free central defender in front of the defence to form the midfield diamond.

The emphasis was never the formation, but that of a particular playing identity and he stuck by his belief that you should never change a winning system (not team).

39   All three were scouted first hand by Johan Cruyff for Ajax. ibid.
40   Ibid.
41   Ibid.

42   Ibid.
43   Ibid.
44   Ibid.
45   Ibid.

Cruyff did occasionally experiment, albeit unsuccessfully against PSV, by playing 2 centre forwards at Barcelona: Hristo Stoichkov and Michael Laudrup.

The Ajax Playing System Under Johan Cruyff

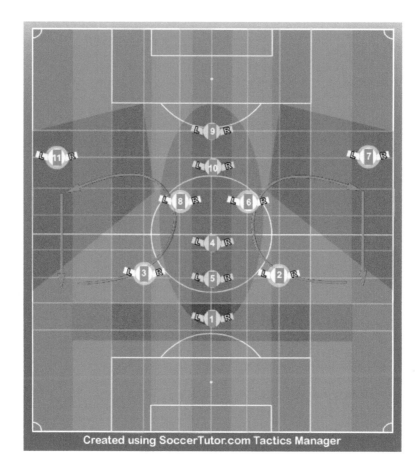

Created using SoccerTutor.com Tactics Manager

The system under Cruyff (see diagram), when in possession, was based around a central nucleus/axis:

The goalkeeper, a central defender, the libero (attacking sweeper), the centre midfielder and striker.

At Ajax the relationship between the libero (Rijkaard - No.4) and striker (Van Basten - No.9) was almost telepathic and described by Van Basten as that of an invisible cord connecting them down the centre of the pitch.

When Rijkaard picked up the ball in the deeper areas of the pitch, Van Basten's job was to make the pitch as long as possible with his off the ball movement, to stretch the play for the more advanced midfielders to exploit higher up the pitch. It was Cruyff's belief that no team should build up play from the back using the 'side-backs' (full backs) because of their inability to use the whole pitch - that is to say, when the right back is on the ball, the left back is no longer in participation. On the other hand, if a central defender or libero is building up the play, he has the entire spectrum of the field to choose from.

The central midfielder (No.10) who finds himself in a more advanced role than the two supporting centre midfielders (No.8 and No.6) should aim to stay within 5 to 10 yards of the centre forward (No.9) to offer support and hold up the play in important advanced areas.

Similarly, the goalkeeper should squeeze the play up as he becomes an outfield sweeper when in possession, offering himself as the 11th outfield player.

Further upfield on the central axis, the libero or free defender-come-midfielder (No.4) acts as the commander of instructions for those further up the pitch when out of possession. This is because he has the advantage of seeing the uncovered and covered spaces in front of him clearly.

"We play space covering. So you cover the space, which means the opposition comes into your space."
Danny Blind[46]

The two flanking centre midfielders (No.8 and No.6) were to act as collectors or supporting players to the system. These two players at Ajax were Jan Wouters and Arnold Muhren; they must be tactically the most consistent and reliable players on the field.

The supporting players are to make up for the mistakes made by others and if they fail to perform their tasks, the system ultimately fails. It is by no means a coincidence that the two players in these roles possess a very particular modest character and sacrifice themselves for the team.

Generally these two players should play behind the phase of play and have the important role of exchanging positions with the pinched in full backs (No.2 and No.3) should they venture into the advanced space on the flanks and in turn, the supporting centre midfield role is then taken up by the relevant winger (7 or 11).

The majority of the positional changes took place away from the central axis of the team. The supporting players on the flanks were often those who needed to make the most dynamic runs and therefore it was here that we saw the art of rotating positions most often.

The wingers are instructed to play extremely wide and hug the touchlines to offer a wide area to find spaces within when in possession and they are occasionally supported by the pinched in full backs.

It was instructed that only one of the two full backs should venture forward at any given time to make sure the defensive balance of the team was maintained. The combination play is enhanced by such coverage and movement, as every player is part of the build up play, attacking play and defensive play (all 3 phases):

"I used to just be a defender. Now I'm part of the team."
Danny Blind[47]

In all cases, Cruyff employed a diamond in midfield wherever he went and all his teams built up play through central players rather than those in the full back positions.

A second variation of the formation that Cruyff used, would be to remove the centre forward and create a flat back four and in doing this you are left with two wide forwards and an attacking midfielder to vacate the space around him.

Cruyff always argued that unless you had a world class centre forward like Van Basten, you should not look to play with a central forward, but rather two wide forwards and midfielders who can get forward when necessary.

If you did possess a Van Basten who was world class in the opposition box, then perhaps you could take away the attacking midfielder and replace him with a central forward. This formation however, would require an exceptional player as Cruyff did not like breaking his midfield diamond format.

Width, depth and a central core are the defining features of Cruyff's model and it takes an exceptional player (Messi, Van Basten etc) for Cruyff to come to the decision of altering such a system. For Cruyff, players do not dictate tactics.

---

46 *Ibid.*

47 *Ibid.*

Coaching The Tiki Taka Style Of Play

12. LOUIS VAN GAAL

While Johan Cruyff and others are strict in their belief that the players should not dictate tactics; rather that the system should dictate what players you select and how they behaved, Louis Van Gaal disagreed. For Van Gaal it was not about the system, but the overarching philosophy and how to match the system, players and the philosophy with a singular pre-agreed output.

"It's a footballing philosophy more than a system. A system depends on the players you have. I played 4-3-3 with Ajax, 2-3-2-3 with Barcelona and I can play 4-4-2 with AZ. I'm flexible. The philosophy stays the same though. I don't think that you can adapt it to every possible situation. You need the right mindset, and it depends on how the players see the coach and vice versa. The coach is the focal point of the team but you need to have an open mind, and so do all the players. Everyone needs to work together to achieve a common goal. Preparing your tactical formation is essential. Each player needs to know where he has to be, and that is why there needs to be mutual understanding because you need absolute discipline. This is a sport played by 22 men, and there are 11 opponents out there playing as a team. Each individual needs to know who he has to beat and be there to support his team-mates."

Louis Van Gaal

Coaching The Tiki Taka Style Of Play

Van Gaal's career like Michels, Cruyff and others' portrays the strong relationship between the Netherlands, Ajax and Barcelona having managed Ajax (1991-97) to Champions League success in 1995 with an unbelievably talented crop of players and then venturing to Barcelona following in the footsteps of the great Sir Bobby Robson (1997-2000 & 2002-2003).

Van Gaal found inspiration in Michels and Cruyff, but was always determined to distance himself from mimicry. It is clear Van Gaal did not employ a strict formational system like his predecessors, as he altered the lenses of which the coach concentrated on spatial coverage and rotation of positions. Instead of player circulation, Van Gaal focused on ball circulation and arguably moved away from the linear thinking of spaces on the field that both Michels and Cruyff exhibited in their systems of play. So long as Van Gaal's team won at least 52% (the magical percentage) of possession and passed the ball better than the opponent, Van Gaal was satisfied with that aspect of the game. It is worth noting that the aggressive pressing element was still a focal point in Van Gaal's philosophy. The emphasis on the individual basic tasks of players was replaced with that of the collective, a functional performance rather than an ideal performance, one could say.

"Everyone needs to work together to achieve a common goal. Preparing your tactical formation is essential. Each player needs to know where he has to be, and that is why there needs to be mutual understanding because you need absolute discipline."
Louis Van Gaal

While the emphasis of Cruyff's methodology was to educate players to make their own decisions within the framework, it can be argued that Van Gaal tipped the balance towards a more militaristic type of Total Football. Marc Overmars, once of Ajax under Van Gaal, was the victim of such an approach as he was instructed not to dribble when faced by two players as this should have alerted Overmars to the fact that one of his teammates was now unmarked. Cruyff clearly set out to educate players to think for themselves, Van Gaal on the other hand wanted players to think in the same way Van Gaal did himself. This was a way of dictating his message for the players to work out for themselves.

Van Gaal's discipline is what unified his whole approach, from culture, tactics and players at the club. Players were to follow a strict set of 'rules', rules that covered being in the changing room 30 minutes before training and banning newspapers while dining with the squad to encourage communication.

"I think it is and advantage that I myself possess a lot of self-discipline. It is part of my character, and that is crucial if you preach self-discipline to others."
Louis Van Gaal[48]

"The second element of my philosophy is communication. Here, too, I first had to create the necessary framework...I engineered situations in which players were obliged, step by step, to communicate with each other and with the coaching staff...Each training session is a form of communication. The drills themselves are not so important, it is more a question of what you do with them. During a training session, the player sees what a coach wants. I often stop the practice games and challenge the players to think about the soccer problems they are facing. Thanks to my eleven years as a teacher, I have enough experience to know whether I need to step in or keep quiet."
Louis Van Gaal[49]

Michels' attitude towards tactical discipline and general thinking would have been different. Player creativity and freedom were the hallmarks of a free passing and fluid side, but once again the evolution of totaal voetbal was one evident as a result of an interpretation difference. Michels, Cruyff and Van Gaal all interpreted the same tactical output in different ways, each altering our understanding of the football philosophy of Total Football.

---

48   Kormelink, H., Seeverens, T. (2003). The Coaching Philosophies of Louis Van Gaal and the Ajax Coaches. Reedswain Incorporated.
49   Ibid.

Coaching The Tiki Taka Style Of Play

13. FRANK RIJKAARD

We cannot disregard the impact of Frank Rijkaard on this linear timeline of tiki-taka's evolution, not least because he was the immediate predecessor to what was about to become Barcelona's most successful ever era and arguably the greatest team to implement tikitaka or any variation of it, but also because of his role as a player and then later his impact as a manager.

The former Ajax and AC Milan forward thinking libero maestro played a significant role in Johan Cruyff's Ajax system in the 1980's and then again with Louis Van Gaal in the 1990's. Therefore Rijkaard experienced the total football philosophy first hand, just like Cruyff had done so himself under Michels, only this time Rijkaard had experienced two different interpretations of the system.

Nevertheless Rijkaard, like Louis Van Gaal, did not set out to mimic the systems he had learnt inside out but rather offer his interpretation of how the philosophy should be played.

"You gain many impressions from the past. You still have it in your mind when you become a coach, and if something happens you can recall how it was dealt with. But I strongly believe that you cannot copy anyone. The decisions that a great coach made years ago will not necessarily work today."

Frank Rijkaard[50]

When Frank Rijkaard left Barcelona in 2008 (2003-08) he became the second longest serving manager since 1924 after Johan Cruyff's eight season run. He won two La Liga titles, two Spanish Super Cup trophies and the UEFA Champions League in 2006. Joan Laporta, former FC Barcelona president, paid tribute to Rijkaard by remarking that he had "made history" in his time as Barcelona manager and re-stabilised the club as one of the world's greatest football clubs by winning what was only their second UEFA Champions League trophy, 14 years after the great Johan Cruyff had done so at Wembley in 1992.

Rijkaard's coaching philosophy represented a continuation of all the great coaches that had gone before him (Michels, Cruyff and Van Gaal).

An attack minded approach was the focal point of Rijkaard's philosophy, one that valued itself on entertaining fans like others had done so before him, but within a contemporary footballing context. By now the concept of a free defender anchoring centrally either in front or behind a defensive line had diminished as a successful strategy. Instead there was a shift of importance to the role of the attacking full backs, a shift that allowed Belletti to break forward and score the winner in the 2006 Champions League final against Arsenal.

By playing a 4-1-2-2-1, Rijkaard offered real width by allowing his full backs to push on forward, enabling the creativity of the attacking players behind the lone forward to be taken out in more damaging central roles, encouraging a centralised approach in the final third and the interplay we see at Barcelona today.

In aid of the short passing game, Rijkaard also imposed a high line for his defenders. With the unit compressed higher up field, the possession could be played deep in the opponents half, patiently waiting for the perfect opportunity to present itself.

Because the emphasis had now been put on a short passing approach deep inside the opponents half, the ability to press aggressively and effectively was aided by the team never being too far away from where the ball had been lost. The tools to press were already present in each situation.

"We favour ball possession games, played in a small area because we like to play our matches in the opponent's half of the field. This means less space and time and if you are better in ball possession in these restricted spaces you have an advantage.

We also like to press in the opponent's territory in order to make it difficult for them to get behind us. We have a lot of exercises for practising this, so that the players know how to position themselves in pressing situations."

Frank Rijkaard[51]

Rijkaard's system was one that allowed players to make their own mark on each role. Who can ask Ronaldinho at his best to only play simply and never take the chance on beating two nearby opponents?

Guily and Deco on the other hand offered a different type of player all together and consequently in Ronaldinho's absence, the team would continue to play the same formation and with the same philosophy but with a different accent; that of the players who stood in the first eleven, there was no value of importance put on symmetry in player roles or playing with a fixed system of roles.

That said, when Messi was finally introduced to the team, it became evident that Rijkaard did impose some restrictions on players as Messi was asked to play in a position that he himself did not enjoy. This was because Rijkaard rejected the notion of a "star system" and instead valued the team performance, that of sacrificing oneself to fulfil the roles of a loose framework, anything offered there after was accepted.[52]

50   Roxburgh, A. (2006). The Technician, no. 31. Nyon: UEFA. 2.

51   Ibid.
52   Radnedge, K. (2002). Frank Rijkaard. Available: http://www.worldsoccer.com/features/frank-rijkaard. Last accessed June 2012.

Coaching The Tiki Taka Style Of Play

Rijkaard would often acknowledge a performance that relied on the brilliance of a single piece of Ronaldinho magic through the context of a team performance, acknowledging player movement elsewhere to create space over a mesmerising dribble with the ball.

Frank Rijkaard furthered the principles put in place by those who had gone before him but with a slight accent on his playing style.

The screening midfielder and full backs were expected to offer different roles to that of a Cruyff philosophy and there was little evidence that Rijkaard opted to include a rotation of positions within his system. Instead Rijkaard had made the interpretation that the modern day footballer no longer needed to take a break and were capable of repeating any 20 run over and over. Having said that, this could not have been possible without adopting such a short passing game, as the attacking players arguably played most of their game through longer periods of aerobic performance and shorter bursts of anaerobic movement.

The screening defensive midfielder simply offered a covering role when the full back broke forward and since possession was rarely overturned at pace, the build up play was slow enough to enable full backs to contribute significantly further forward.

It goes without saying that Frank Rijkaard handed over a Barcelona team to Pep Guardiola with the perfect foundations in place.

These foundations allowed Guardiola to take the current understanding of the system and accelerate the philosophy at an unprecedented rate.

Tiki-taka football was finally the playing identity that brought about success in terms of trophies and league titles and was at a tipping point of boundless greatness.

14. PEP GUARDIOLA
The Great Exhibition

Victor Valdes, Dani Alves, Eric Abidal, Carles Puyol, Gerard Pique, Sergio Busquets, Xavi, Andres Iniesta, Pedro Rodriguez, Leo Messi and David Villa. And Pep Guardiola. No one misses Guardiola off of this list.

Before management, but some time after his playing days were over, Guardiola underwent a period of thorough self discovery as a manager by learning from some of the greatest coaches in the game: Marcelo Bielsa, Sir Alex Ferguson and Juan Manuel Lillo.

There is no doubt however, that Guardiola's employment at FC Barcelona was primarily influenced by the great Johan Cruyff.

When the former Barcelona B manager, La Masia graduate and Barcelona captain finally took charge of the first team he did what all great managers have done throughout history. He used the foundations and remodelled everything to match his interpretation of how football should be played.

Guardiola as a student of the game, understands evolution better than anyone else on this timeline; to never stay static and grow predictable formed the basis of his success. Barcelona went on to win 14 of a possible 19 titles under Guardiola between August 2008 and May 2012, including two more Champions League trophies.

Under Cruyff, Van Gaal and Rijkaard there seems to have been a unity in La Liga performance levels.

- Rijkaard's Barcelona scored an average of 1.95 goals per La Liga game and conceded 0.94 goals per game.

- Van Gaal's Barcelona scored an average of 2.06 goals per game and conceded 1.27 goals per game.

- Cruyff's first five seasons (before the decline) offered fans 2.2 goals scored per game and 0.93 goals against.

- Guardiola smashed these records. His team scored an average of 2.71 goals per game and conceded just 0.72 goals per game.

This was a significant improvement at both ends of the field. Rijkaard's 76 goals scored during the 2007/08 La Liga was met with Guardiola's 105 goals scored the very next season.

Guardiola came into the Barcelona first team management and enforced changes immediately. He sold off stars Ronaldinho and Deco to rebuild the team around La Masia graduates Xavi, Iniesta and Leo Messi.

Guardiola did more than just replace players, as he brought with him an adapted version of the Barcelona philosophy, an adapted version of possession based football. Formation has long become more than the set variable of the numbers of players playing in defence, midfield and attack (i.e. 4-4-2, 4-3-3, 4-1-2-2-1...) to aid the three phases of football: attacking, defending and build up play.

Formations were always zone dependant, but in a Guardiola Barcelona formation was truly space dependant and about a series of smaller spatial scenarios that aimed to outnumber the opposition in particular areas of the field and exploit space in the next. Each space is interrelated to the next, as each player's movement is related to each and every other player on the field.

It is often stated that Barcelona played with a 4-3-3 formation but in truth, while in possession, Barcelona's set up was that of an unsymmetrical, zone dependant 2-1-4-3 formation.

While in a Cruyffian midfield there was a degree of symmetry, with two supporting midfielders either side of a deep lying playmaking libero and a creative attacking midfielder, Guardiola's midfield was far more complex.

In Van Gaal, Cruyff and Michels' teams there was always a sense of a spine in the team's formation, but Guardiola's approach placed no value on perfect symmetry or a rigidity in the spine of the team. The playmaker in Cruyff and Van Gaal's approach was primarily the deep lying playmaker in font of a 'pinched in' defence. In Guardiola's system, one possession based playmaker became two.

Similar to Frank Rijkaard, Guardiola's focus was on a possession based game in the opponents half that consisted of an extremely short passing game and immediate pressing, only this time every player was capable in all aspects of the playing style.

GUARDIOLA'S TRANSITIONAL DIAGRAM
(4-3-3 or the W-W with Full Backs further Forward Turning into a 2-1-4-3 or the M-M)

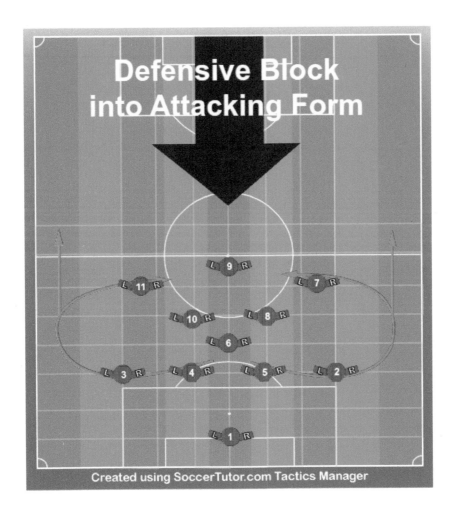

GUARDIOLA'S IN POSSESSION SYSTEM DIAGRAM (2-1-4-3, 3-4-3 or the M-M)

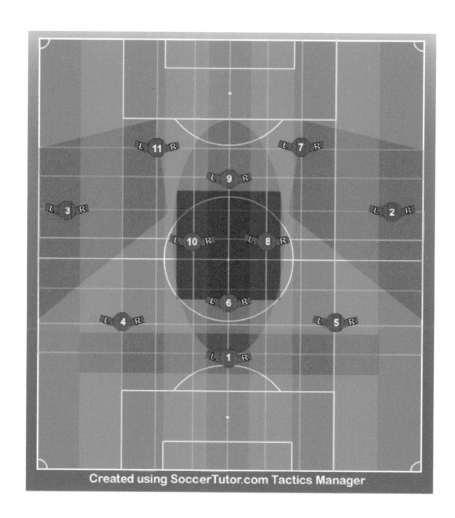

Created using SoccerTutor.com Tactics Manager

*Note: The diagram does not inform us of the whole system. The purpose is to act as an explanation of how Barcelona set about its individual player roles within the system (2008-2011). More information of the 'system' is provided in the following pages.

GUARDIOLA'S TEAM FORMATION:
Players Roles and Responsibilities

The Goalkeeper

Like many of the coaches on this timeline, Guardiola asked for his goalkeeper (Victor Valdes) to play as a sweeper and dominate any space left in behind such a highly pressed line of defence. Without this role being fulfilled, the team are exposed to the long ball over the top and the threat of the quick striker sitting on the last line of defence.

The Centre Backs

The two centre backs (No.4 and No.5) in this system are expected to play significant roles in space creation and ball retention both laterally and vertically on the field. Puyol and Pique push right out onto the flanks to offer width in the defensive half of the build up play, in doing so covering space left by the forward thinking full backs and creating space for Sergio Busquets to anchor in and out of.

The Full Backs

The more advanced wing backs (No.2 and No.3) are expected to become part of the midfield and offer width in the more advanced spaces on the pitch, interlinking play and finding the channels with their dynamic off the ball movement.

The Defensive Midfielder

The third line of play (No.6) has to consist of the most tactically aware player in the team and this has often been the case since Frank Rijkaard played as the free man in the late 1980s and 1990s. **Sergio Busquets** is a player who has received much deserved acknowledgement from his teammates and managers for his role that he plays so well in offering structure to the system. This player's movement covers space perfectly, analyses situations and foresees scenarios that are yet to occur, offers instructions to those further forward when out of possession and plays an integral role in ball retention and the more direct passing that presents itself at times. This player often drops into the central defensive role and plays conscious of space around him in all terms.

The Centre Midfielders

The roles of the two centre midfielders (No.8 and No.10) were set up to offer two unique roles within Guardiola's system. **Xavi** acted as the metronomic possession keeping midfielder and **Iniesta** was allowed to venture further forward and play with a more risk free approach than Xavi.

Xavi is expected to present the team with a responsible level of creativity, one that knows where to pass and move and when to pass and move, the timing of everything here is as important as the playmaking passing ability itself.

The Inside Forwards

The sixth line of play consists of two inside forwards (No.7 and No.11) who venture inside to leave space on the flanks for the two advanced wing backs in the team, but more than that, they are to perform a whole variety of important tasks in the build up play and creating goal scoring opportunities.

Coaching The Tiki Taka Style Of Play

Lionel Messi

When Messi moved centrally and became the seventh line of play (No.9) not many understood the value of Messi offering himself as the false 9, a position we saw Matthias Sindelar playing in the 1930s. As Messi dropped deep, players marked tightly and followed him. As he picked up the ball, he attracted the opposition like flies to a light. This then created space for Iniesta, Pedro and David Villa (or Alexis Sanchez) to roam into and exploit. As Messi's tactical awareness increased with age, so did his ability to create the perfect assist.

These qualities in Messi's play and role in the team are often overlooked as Messi couples this excellence with the ability to score so many goals. Nevertheless, the role of the space creator up front is one that we have seen before, with Van Basten's role to stretch the play and create space for his teammates in more advanced dangerous spaces, and Messi offers the same function but of a different magnitude.

Above all else, Messi's role is in fact to create space for others and find space for himself either via his off the ball movement or ability to pick the ball up in dangerous areas, enough so that it draws the opponents out of position. This is something that comes at great difficulty given the universal opposition's approach to man making such a great talent.

When his team are in possession, Messi covers enough ground for two players in diagram 2 and the 'magnet' effect draws the opposing defenders towards whichever position he chooses to find.

The whole system is related to space domination and creating space when in possession. In both previous diagrams these methods can be depicted through meaningful symbols representative of the basic tasks such as passing focus, movement focus, space creation and analysis of play.

To conclude, in a Guardiola approach to tiki-taka or totaal-voetbal the changes are discreet and packaged in a way we haven't seen before, just like every other manager on this historic timeline.

Position switching exists (albeit in a different area), the false 9 exists, short passing, pressing, the playing identity - none of it was new, but packaged together in the way we saw it grow and evolve was unique and seemingly unplayable at times.

THE FOUNDATIONS OF GUARDIOLA'S PLAYING STYLE: Barcelona's Youth Development System & the Club

It should be said that the foundations to such a successful playing style go far beyond than those mentioned within this linear timeline. In fact, the development of many of the players playing within Guardiola's system is to thank for the ease at which Guardiola's ideas were translated, as the players had been exposed to each element of Guardiola's philosophy for many years. From **Oriol Tort**, **Johan Cruyff** and **Lareano Ruiz**[53] everything was set up before Guardiola had even known he was to be a professional football player.

La Masia was born out of Johan Cruyff's suggestion to remodel the way in which the club develops its youth players and eventually the way the club plays its football. More than that, the philosophy was to become the club's culture.

Ruiz is the man behind the imprinted training methods (such as the famous 'rondo') and playing style of the youth teams. It was under Ruiz's guidance that the youth players began to play with a 3-4-3 formation or a variation of it at every age or ability level within the club.

Barcelona were a club that used to have a very different mentality to the one that lies before us today; there was a strong bias towards the big and strong players, there was even a sign on the wall that once said:

"Turn around if you are here to offer a Juvenil player that is shorter than 1.80m."[54]

Ruiz swiftly had this signed removed, needless to be said.

Many years on and players such as Xavi and Messi have not only found acceptance at the club, but have flourished under such an approach to become two of the game's greatest ever players.

53   Jonson, A. (2012). Laureano Ruiz – the man behind Barça's playing philosophy Read more: http://www.totalbarca.com/2012/history/laureano-ruiz-the-man-behind-barcas-playingphilosophy/#ixzz2cAVEUcUN. Available: http://www.totalbarca.com/2012/history/laureano-ruiz-the-man-behind-barcas-playing-philosophy/. Last accessed August 2012.
54   Ibid.

©SoccerTutor.com   *Coaching The Tiki Taka Style Of Play*

LIFE AFTER PEP GUARDIOLA: Tito Vilanova

So as Pep Guardiola left the club in 2012 and Tito Vilanova succeeded him, there was no expectation on Tito Vilanova to mimic the methods employed by Guardiola, no matter how successful they were. The club has learnt that evolution is brought about through change and that no element of the philosophy should stay still. The most important characteristics required of a Barcelona manager is that he is to understand the principles of the club's philosophy, beyond that of the most recent manager.

"When Pep Guardiola was here, he talked to the players, directed training, analysed videos … Tito was not a leader then, but he is now. [He] is very well-prepared, has clear ideas and understands the Barcelona concepts and philosophy. He's our leader."

Xavi on Tito Vilanova[55]

In the short time that Tito Vilanova was at Barcelona changes were already perceptible. Vilanova instructed his wingers to play with more width under the principles of spatial football and firmly believed that once the first line of the oppositions defence was broken (the midfield line), that the team should not look to go back to the central playmaker (Xavi) in hope that he would find the right pass to open up the opposition.

Instead the players further forward were expected to offer more in this department. Long balls were no longer considered a sin and Victor Valdes then had the option of playing the long ball out to the wide winger should the option have presented itself to him.

Exactly how Vilanova wanted his team to develop is unforeseeable, but no one thing introduced by Vilanova had flown in the face of the overarching concepts of tiki-taka and just as each manager that had gone before him, Vilanova offered his own unique and personal interpretation of how to play, just as Marcelo Bielsa's graduate **Gerardo Martino** will do as he takes over from Vilanova for the foreseeable future.

Fans of the tiki-taka approach need to understand that Guardiola's approach is not the only approach that satisfies the aims and objectives of tiki-taka football and history is not truly linear, but complex. History does not come around to consistently repeat itself but keeps returning to offer a new understanding of how contemporary football can be played. However, one thing is for certain, there is over 100 years of possession based football philosophy development that sits before Guardiola and there will be over 100 more to come if evolution continues to have it's way.

---

55   Tomas, F. (2012). Tito Vilanova: Leading the evolution of the Blaugrana model. Available: http://espnfc.com/blog/_/name/barcelona/ id/319?cc=5739. Last accessed November 2012.

PART 4

TIKI TAKA TACTICAL THEORY

MAKING SENSE OF TIKI TAKA AND THE BASIC PRINCIPLES
What Are the Variables of Tiki Taka Football?

Throughout history, 2 things have become unclouded:

1. Football philosophy continues to evolve and what we see is often a result of a personal interpretation of the philosophy itself. Frequently, it is the mistake of the media to portray the current model as the absolute model of tiki-taka football philosophy.

2. Managers who have implemented a tiki-taka playing style, have each individually offered a unique take on how the playing identity should be implemented and in doing so have altered the 'variables' of such an approach.

Summary of Variables in Tiki-Taka Football

Throughout history the tiki-taka philosophy has come in different forms. Below are the 'variables' that have altered with each and every coach implementing such a philosophy of playing style:

- ***The width of which your team plays and where the width comes from***

Some managers have preferred the inside forward to play as more traditional wide players, which of course alters the focus of the attack significantly.

Others on the other hand, prefer to benefit from a slower build up play and push wing backs into more advanced roles.

- ***The positional movement during transitions of play***

Until wing backs were encouraged to push on into more advanced roles, this playing philosophy often asked them to act as "pinched-in" full backs and enable a centralised free defender to marshal the playing line in front or behind the defensive line of play. The move to playing attacking full backs requires the defence to be move involved in ball circulation than before. If the full backs do not move into advanced positions, the team loses an option further forward.

- ***The general formation (as a reference point)***

Throughout history there has been a preference towards playing a variation of 4-3-3 or 3-4-3 for reasons that will be discussed at great length in later parts of this book, but put simply, these formations aim to create as many lines of play as possible to encourage ball circulation.

- ***The symmetry or imbalance of basic tasks instructed to more attacking players***

Traditionally there has been a structured symmetry in the more defensive roles of the team, however depending on the manager's approach to build up speed and overarching approach, the basic tasks should be set to meet. In some cases these have been set to match the key strengths of the playing squad instead of employing a strict system approach.

- ***The level of opportunism in attack***

The manager's approach to creating chances is interlinked with the ability to retain ball circulation in more advanced spaces of the field. While this relationship absolutely must be understood, on mastering the balance, this can be tweaked to meet requirements set from different opponents.

- ***The absolute approach to ball circulation***

All the approaches listed have employed a shorter playing style relative to the long ball game. However, each personal interpretation alters the distance at which the average pass is made and indeed who can and cannot play the long ball in each relevant space. This of course, is directly linked to the concept of opportunism. It is of absolute importance that the coaches and players understand that passing/possession is a tool within the strategy, not a goal within itself.

- ***The attitudes to each of the 4 processes during the game***

(Ball circulation, the block or being out of possession and the 2 transitions - winning/losing the ball).

What Are the "Non-Variables" of Tiki Taka Football?

On the other hand, there have been some aspects of play that have been consistent throughout history.

We should not actually consider these non-variables, but ask ourselves whether these aspects of play are necessary to carry out the implementation of the tikitaka philosophy.

- *All interpretations must possess the foundations of a possession based control game*

To be better than the opposition with the ball in all spaces of the field. To control possession, space and your opponents through possession.

- *While in possession, the objective (for the most part) is to make the pitch as big as possible*

To stretch and open up the opposition and offer space coverage in a wide variety of ways.

- *To aim to outnumber the opposition in key areas*

This may actually result in players condensing a space and then becoming more opportunistic with their passing given that they are now in a better position to immediately press and make the pitch as small as possible.

- *The same principles apply to defending*

The aim is to outnumber the attackers and make the pitch as small as possible for the opposition. This can be achieved through understanding the narrowing of angles, collaborative pressing and compacting a defensive line. In general, the closer the play is to your own goal, the tighter the marking of key spaces should be.

- *Above all, the strategies should aim to benefit the team in all four phases of the game*

Attacking, defending and during the transitions. Each strategy should compliment the next. An example given in this book suggests that there is a strategy employed that both enables ball circulation and the immediate pressing should they lose the ball high up the pitch (this is an idea that will be discussed at greater lengths throughout this part of the book).

- *The simple and pragmatic approach must be employed in appropriate spaces of the field*

An understanding that if you have two players marking you, you have a teammate available in space elsewhere.

- *The playing identity should become the team's ingrained culture and approach to playing or thinking football*

The philosophy has evolved so that players are to be educated into making their own informed decisions, but within a framework of a singular strategy.

- *You must train as you aim to play*

Through specific training methods such as those employed in tactical periodisation[1] and Horst Wein's approach to segmenting particular aspects of the game to create real game-like training scenarios through age appropriate play.

- *Development is almost always a slow and complex process that should always be explained and understood by players through a more simple set of instructions*

The development should occur through a holistic approach to development.

---

1   *Discussed at length within the latter pages of this book.*

Creating Goal Scoring Opportunities

In all cases success should be measured not on the possession or shots on goal statistics, but through the simplistic perception that the playing identity should aim to create more obvious goal scoring opportunities than your opponent, 'obvious' being the key word here.

This notion of an obvious goal scoring opportunity is a difficult concept to define either by quantity or quality, as personal judgement is a far more effective measure.

For example, a shot from 5 yards may not be deemed an obvious goal scoring opportunity as the striker received the ball with the goalkeeper already inches away. Instead the coach should be true to himself and mark each time his team or opponents create an opportunity that the player would have been expected to score from. Everything else can be left under the umbrella of uncontrollable aspects of the game, no philosophy enables absolute control.

Football, at times, is a game of chance and there should always be place for opportunism. Players can score with a shot from 30 yards or take the chance of squeezing in between two closely marking defenders within the box to win a penalty or break free.

There is no right or wrong way to approach football, only ones that you prefer. But in tiki-taka you have the potential to have the most control possible. The ball, the spaces and the opposition all act according to your conscious decisions.

Finding an approach that fits within the framework of tiki-taka is also a subjective matter, even by meeting all the strategic requirements in place you may fail to create more goal scoring opportunities than your opponent.

Much like following the rules of grammar in language, a sentence can be written that follows the structures in place and yet, be completely nonsensical and fail to succeed despite the framework in place:

"Colourless green ideas sleep furiously."[2]

---

2   Chomsky, N. (1957). Syntactic Structures. The Hague/Paris: Mouton. 15.

The sentence above is one composed by Noam Chomsky, the father of modern linguistics[3], in his 1957 book Syntactic Structures. Chomsky analyses the deep structures in language and considers each language to have a near identical set of structural properties in place to form the languages' rules and structures.

The same can be said of football developments made in the tiki-taka philosophy and coaches that have made the attempt to implement the approach. For each success story there have been tales of failure. How many truly took the holistic and 'correct' long-term approach to the playing philosophy is unknown but in a small corner of the globe someone would have perfected the approach, yet failed where it counts on the field.

But without a doubt, in perfecting the holistic approach it is possible to make infinite uses from finite spatial situations, because after all the pitch is only so big and in reality each player has to deal with the lack of space that naturally occurs on the field.

Through coaching in particular ways it is possible to offer players the platform to defy the notion of the pitch being a finite space. Football was never simply 22 bodies on a marked out football field, but 22 minds with infinite solutions to problems that occur over the finite time available to them and in doing so, timeless memories of football will transpire; football is timeless, infinite and truly boundless.

---

3   Thomas Tymoczko, Jim Henle, James M. Henle, Sweet Reason: A Field Guide to Modern Logic, Birkhäuser, 2000, p. 101; Fox, Margalit (December 5, 1998). "A Changed Noam Chomsky Simplifies". New York Times. Retrieved August 2, 2008.

Coaching The Tiki Taka Style Of Play

Themes of the Development History of Tiki Taka

The following nine chapters touch on many of the themes found throughout the developmental history of tikitaka football and aim to offer a comprehensive analysis of really just what constitutes as tiki-taka football, presenting you with the absolute depiction of the framework that exists:

1.   The Spatial Positional System and Concept of 'Formation'

2.   The Transitions Differentials: Regaining Possession, a FC Barcelona Case Study

3.   The Art of Collective Pressing

4.   Ball Circulation

5.   The Attacking Attitudes and off the Ball Movement

6.   Defensive Organisation: The Block

7.   The Conclusion of the Footballing States and Their Relationships

8.   The Individual Basic Tasks

9.   Tactical Solutions and Variations of the Form

10.   Wigan Athletic FC Case Study

Coaching The Tiki Taka Style Of Play

1. THE SPATIAL POSITIONAL SYSTEM AND CONCEPT OF 'FORMATION'

"There is so much depth to this philosophy and I am starting to realise that it is all about 'the system' as they call it. It is not about passing. It is not about pressing. It is not about possession. It is all about positioning!"

Jon Collins[4]

(Former Reading Coach. Now Head Coach with Oxford University Centaurs)

Van Basten often spoke about an invisible cord that connected players within a formation, that one player's movements would directly affect another.

The possession based philosophical approach to football thinks about football in terms of space. How can a team dominate spaces both with or without the ball?

One thing that has become clear, is that those mentioned on the tiki-taka historical timeline moved away from two dimensional formations a long time ago. Long gone are the days of the WM formation, a formation that thinks in terms of a defensive and attacking component in a two dimensional plan.

The positional system should aim to meet particular playing objectives. The system should offer:

- Width and depth to enhance ball circulation

- Both a mobile and fixed structures within the system

- A maximisation of angled passing options (triangles)

- Maximum coverage of the field's spaces by making the pitch as big as possible when in possession

- The ability to retain possession with a forward thinking approach

- The opportunity to outnumber the opposition in defence, attack and during the build up

- The ability to maximise potential of rehearsed play

- The ability to switch quickly from an attacking or build up phrase towards a defensive one

- OVERLOADS in as many areas as possible through player movement and the system

When thinking about formation in a more three dimensional space, we should consider all things: the individual players, the different phases of play and the relationships of players and spaces alike.

The concept should allow for a coach to plan his own solutions, whether he has 7, 9 or 11 players to plot.

---

4   146private interview - Collins has studied alongside Eusebio Sacristán and Carlos Hugo Garcia and is currently researching a PhD inSpanish training methodology - with assistance from the training centres (both Cantera and Pro teams) of Real Madrid, Barca, Bilbao, CF Malaga and others.

148

Coaching The Tiki Taka Style Of Play

Template for Coaches to Plot Out Their Formation

In drawing up a general template for coaches to plot out their systematic formation a number of criteria has been identified.

The field should be divided into 7 horizontal and 7 vertical lines of play[5] (plus 2 wide channels), this in keeping of the concept of space coverage and offer maximisation of triangle creation and forward options.

Through carefully analysing the following general template we can begin to understand why the variations of the 4-3-3 and 3-4-3 have been employed by teams throughout history.

To successfully plot your own formation it should be understood that all things must be taken into consideration in a three dimensional spatial understanding.

The field's spaces in relation to football have been divided into 6 basic spaces:

1. A sweeper/goalkeeper space.

2. The defensive line of either 2 central defenders or 3 (with 2 pinched in full backs).

3. The structural central ball circulation lines of play. These central lines of play are to be given careful consideration as they are not only important in terms of team and midfield balance, but (as we will see later) they offer a variety of solutions to the general ball circulation spatial emphasis.

4 & 5. Spaces 4 and 5 are made up of the two areas on the left and right wide areas of the field. The purposes of this function is to offer width and stretch the opposition when in play by making the pitch as big as possible when in possession. Whether there are just one or two players within each of these zones depends on the accent of play and choices made by the manager.

6. The central attacking creativity space. An option is available to play one striker up front on his own, one withdrawn striker or both in these spaces.

5   White, D. (2012). Brendan Rodgers' playing philosophy could be a success if he transfers it from the Liberty Stadium to Liverpool. Available:http://www.telegraph.co.uk/sport/football/teams/liverpool/9301301/Brendan-Rodgers-playing-philosophy-could-be-asuccess-if-he-transfers-it-from-the-Liberty-Stadium-to-Liverpool.html. Last accessed May 2012. and Juan Luis Delgado Bordonau (ex-Villarreal coach) analysis of the Latin Football Style http://www.slideshare.net/juanluisdelgado/analysis-oflatin-style

Coaching The Tiki Taka Style Of Play

Positional Systems

In the following diagrams, which you should carefully study, there is a lot of three dimensional information depicted through purposeful designed diagrams.

Before you study the template, you are to examine the solutions offered by Ajax under Van Gaal and Barcelona under Guardiola. It becomes clear how the template begins to relate to reality in this way. The positional system then clearly speaks, in many ways, about how the team sets out play.

The basic general template offers the framework for you to design your own systematic positional formation solution, one that achieves desirable outcomes.

The black marker suggests that this player is not optional and the green markers are to indicate available spaces of which you may plot your formation. The more transparent have been deemed inappropriate spaces of which to mark down the players but are available on the 7 x 7 grid. In selecting a formation you should aim to cover as many of the lines of play as possible, to offer as many passing options as possible.

Remember that there are an endless amount of variables when choosing a formation and this should act as part of a much larger structural rationale that enables you to conduct the desirable style of play; this template offers no solutions to unique player profiles and basic tasks in their relation to a playing system.

The template is simply to offer an understanding and reference point as to how the team sets out to achieve particular aspects of play and details how literally hundreds of variations of the general formation are indeed available to plot and plan from.

You are not limited to mimicking Barcelona's 2012 model.

While looking through the following formations, you should consider how they may pair up against a 4-4-2 for the purposes of understanding overloads. While many teams have moved away from 4-4-2, in reality teams still look to set up their defensive block in this formation.

Subsequently, suppose we have a formation of 3-4-3 (like Barcelona's) we are looking at a formation of 3-5-2 when Messi drops in deep meaning we have three defenders and a goalkeeper against their two strikers, three central midfielders against their two when Messi drops in (promoting central build up play) and in all other positions we possess 1 v 1 specialists who are comfortable at terrorising their man time and time again.

"Creating numerical superiority is the key during the four moments of the game - this takes great energy, awareness and positional sense...to play the purest, most aesthetic form of the game requires a system [that promotes overloads through the structure of the team]."

Jon Collins

Coaching The Tiki Taka Style Of Play

The Tiki Taka Positional System Template

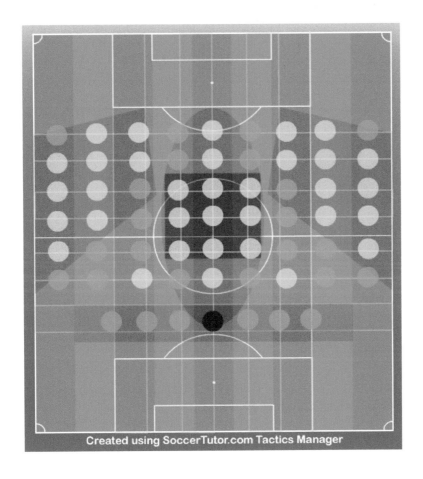

Created using SoccerTutor.com Tactics Manager

Coaching The Tiki Taka Style Of Play

Ajax's Positional System under Van Gaal

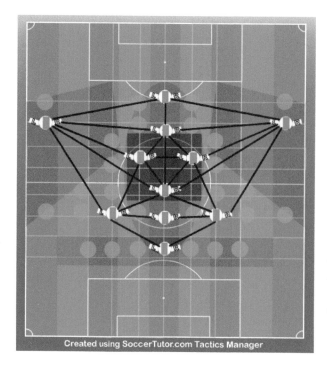

Created using SoccerTutor.com Tactics Manager

The Ajax positional system under Louis Van Gaal suggests that there is an emphasis on two outcomes:

1. The ability of the winger as a target man (either ball to feet or to run onto) and in turn, the wingers ability to connect with the rest of the playing system.

2. The second significant outcome is that of an importance placed on a central core of players within the positional system.

You will have noticed that there are five players placed on the vertical central line of play and this was reflected in the way Van Gaal's Ajax played.

We would often see Rijkaard (placed on the third horizontal line of play) find Marco Van Basten with a direct pass forward to feet in the advanced areas of the field.

The Ajax system therefore, encourages the players to adopt two approaches of playing through the middle and in the wider areas when in advanced positions. Without key players in these areas, the team would become less of a threat when implementing this system. It is imperative that the wingers are selected on a very particular set of attributes and that they are interlaced with the core of the system as well as acting as a threat to the opposition in their own right.

The Ajax approach fills the central lines of play with more players than other studied systems do. This is directly related to the ability for the Ajax system to require less of a physical demand on it's players (as they run a shorter distance).

In keeping with the rationale and theory of position switching, the shorter the distance the players are expected to run, the fresher the players will be. Therefore, as players have run a lesser distance than the opposition, they are able to focus with their full concentration on the more technical aspects of the game.

"Lots of coaches devote their time to wondering how they can ensure that their players are able to do a lot of running during a match. Ajax trains its players to run as little as possible on the field. That is why positional games are always central."

Louis Van Gaal

Barcelona's Positional System under Guardiola

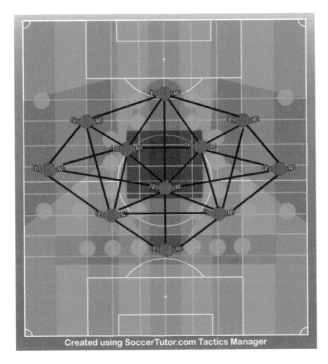

Created using SoccerTutor.com Tactics Manager

[The referenced system of W-W - consider the central overloads should the central forward drop back into the central area. Messi played the false-9 role with this purpose in mind.]

The Barcelona model is essentially built (quite literally) around the central box of players. The passing network best explains the benefits of such an approach to filling space in this way; in every scenario, when one of the 3 players within the central midfield is on the ball, he is faced with a multitude of passing options due to the creation of triangles when in possession.

"Think quickly, look for spaces. That's what I do: look for spaces. All day. I'm always looking. All day, all day. Here? No. There? No. People who haven't played don't always realise how hard that is. Space, space, space. It's like being on the PlayStation. I think shit, the defender's here, play it there. I see the space and pass. That's what I do."

Xavi

Since the Barcelona positional system requires that the players are to run a lot further than those in the Ajax positional system, there is a different requirement placed on players who fill the 'supporting' spaces around the central core.

"When Dani Alves runs up the pitch, he meets himself running back down it."

Jorge Valdano[6]

From analysing the Barcelona system, is it obvious that the Barcelona positional system of play places a higher emphasis on ball circulation over a wider variety of spaces on the football field. The Barcelona positional system is spread out over a 9 x 7 grid, where as the Ajax system was over a 7 x 6 grid and therefore, as mentioned, the Barcelona players are expected to cover a much greater distance.

For these reasons, we can now understand why the Barcelona system requires a slower build up play approach in comparison to that of the Ajax system, which often relied on a longer more direct pass to act as the catalyst for creating goal scoring opportunity.

---

6   Lowe, S. (2012). Dani Alves: 'At Barcelona we are taking football back to its origins'. Available: http://www.theguardian.com/football/2012/apr/16/dani-alves-barcelona-chelsea. Last accessed June 2012.

Coaching The Tiki Taka Style Of Play

Summary of Ajax and Barcelona's Positional System

You will have noticed that in the positional templates, a lot of information has been given in a simplistic diagram.

The passing network, lines of play and key areas have all been highlighted as well as the basic formation. In all possession based systems, the wider areas 'support' that of a central core of players.

The central midfield has 9 possible positions, of which the tendency is to fill this central 'box' with 3 players and an importance placed on the balance of attacking or defensive attitudes of these players. These players in the

Barcelona model are seen as playmakers and the heartbeat of a circulating system.

"Every player has to understand the whole geometry of the whole pitch."
Gerard van der Lem

In both systems, the approach is generally to create a wide opportunity of play in the more advanced systems and the ball circulation is generally played within a midfield centralised core.

In both approaches, space is understood by the players to the highest level of understanding. Space is the defining element to possession based football and space coverage is an imperative element in theorising the approach.

Brendan Rodgers and the Positional System of Play

Brendan Rodgers, the manager of Liverpool Football Club has found success throughout his career utilising the positional system of play. Later on, within this part of the book, we will analyse Brendan Rodgers' tactical variations to the approach and examine the impacts of slight changes to the midfield trio and the resultant differences of the passing network is then made visually clear.

Brendan Rodgers thinks about football in terms of space and lines of play and believes that every player (including the goalkeeper) is to be included in the lines of play, as did Guardiola at Barcelona and Van Gaal at Ajax.

"When we have the football everybody's a player. The difference with us is that when we have the ball we play with 11 men, other teams play with 10 and a goalkeeper."

Brendan Rodgers

The goalkeeper has an important role within the passing network and considerations are given when he is faced with the task of a goal kick. Typically the goal kick within this philosophy of play, is an opportunity to play the short pass to a centre back who has spread wide out onto the flanks or as an alternative to play a central short pass forward to a midfielder who has dropped into the space directly in front of the defence.

On the other hand, when the opposition inevitably presses forward to prevent this pass, the goalkeeper must "hit the second or third line of pass". When the opposition has pressed forward and allowed for little space in these zones, it is then that the long ball is played forward and as a result of the opposition pressing high up the pitch, the forwards are now faced with fewer opponents dominating space around them and more of an opportunity to win the ball and break forward.

The obvious key here is to play where space is available and if space is scarce where you would prefer to pass the ball, you must understand that opportunities have opened up elsewhere. There is always space on a football pitch.

"My template for everything is organisation. With the ball you have to know the movement patterns, the rotation, the fluidity and positioning of the team. Then there's our defensive organisation…so if it is not going well we have a default mechanism which makes us hard to beat and we can pass our way into the game again. Rest with the ball. Then we'll build again."

Brendan Rodgers

Marcelo Bielsa's Positional Play

Positiespel, Joc de posició, Juego de posición, Positional Play. The concept of positional play is the underlying theme throughout this book and it is the understanding of how and where to overload your players (through the system) against the given formation that is a very Marcelo Bielsa way of thinking.

Bielsa used several formations throughout the duration of his spell as Chile's national team manager and his positional play was essentially three fold:

1. How can I outnumber the opponents whilst building up the play from the back?
2. How can I outnumber the opposition in key central areas further forward?
3. How can I look to isolate their defenders to create 1 v 1 situations in the final third?

The diagram above details the positional play of a Chile match under Bielsa, showing how the attacking transition may have been one of two fundamental ideas:

1. To build and probe or to counter attack through the fluid forward movement should the opportunity present itself (typically objectified through a set timed trigger to goal).
2. The team back into their defensive shape.

In the diagram you will see the 'end form' (after an attacking transition) for Bielsa's Chile against a team that played with one forward in 2010.

This was the shape that the team would take up within 8 seconds of having won the ball and having played out of danger to begin the building and probing phase of play. The wing backs cut inside to complete the central diamond as supporting central midfielders, the back 3 spread wide to cover the width of the defensive line, the 2 central midfielders split into an attacking role and a defensive role and the left sided midfielder pushes wide to offer attacking width.

The striker and the right winger would already be positioned in case of a counter attack and the transformation from a 5-3-1-1 to a complex 3-6-1 formation was complete. The defensive transition was one of two choices:

1. To stay in the proactive and attacking positions they have taken up in the diagram and look to press the opposition with the aim of winning the ball back.
2. Look for the first 3 players to press, support and cover while the remainder of the team fell back into their defensive shape within 5 seconds; pressing to delay.

The delaying of this system has been carefully designed as Bielsa expected the left sided midfielder to cover inside to form a midfield 3 while other players were out of position.

That is to say that the lopsidedness of the system is a structure that Bielsa has carefully considered, not one that has been influenced by the players within it.

All the moments of the game are interlined with the considered positional system that Bielsa had designed for that particular set of player profiles against the formation that the opposition choose to play with (in this case it was 4-4-1-1).

The Importance of Positioning to Tiki Taka

We reflect on Jon Collins' quote at the beginning of this chapter:

"There is so much depth to this philosophy and I am starting to realise that it is all about 'the system' as they call it. It is not about passing. It is not about pressing. It is not about possession. It is all about positioning!"

Jon Collins[7]
(Former Reading Coach. Now Head Coach with Oxford University Centaurs)

This is a quote from a Reading coach who has studied alongside Eusebio Sacristán and Carlos Hugo Garcia and is currently researching a PhD in 'Spanish training methodology.' We come to understand why positioning is arguably the most important aspect of tiki-taka football.

But it is not positioning alone that enables such a successful philosophy to flourish and as you read through the remainder of this book you will note, time and time again, the overlaps between each of the pillars that this book suggests.

You simply cannot consider the positional system out of context, not without considering the relationships between each of the pillars.

It is difficult to put a hierarchy on such an approach to football, on what the single most important aspect of tiki-taka football is, but it goes without saying that the positional system considers so much more than formation and forms the foundations for everything else within.

You may well have mapped out a formation on the blank template given within this chapter and in your mind come up with *"a sophisticated design and intelligent system-building team"*[8] but without a comprehensive understanding of all the pillars of tiki-taka football, it is difficult to truly detail a complete positional system in full.

---

7   146private interview - Collins has studied alongside Eusebio Sacristán and Carlos Hugo Garcia and is currently researching a PhD inSpanish training methodology - with assistance from the training centres (both Cantera and Pro teams) of Real Madrid, Barca, Bilbao, CF Malaga and others.
8   Winner, D (2001). Brilliant Orange: The Neurotic Genius of Dutch Football . London: Bloomsbury Publishing PLC; New edition edition

2. THE TRANSITION DIFFERENTIALS
Regaining Possession, a FC Barcelona Case Study

"As you will be aware, during a game, FC Barcelona tend to excel when in 'transition'. However, La Masia coach Sergi Domenech informed me that FC Barcelona try to avoid playing in transition. FC Barcelona see transition as time lost. FC Barcelona are either attacking or defending and are NOT in transition."

Gareth Richards[9]
(Youth team football manager)

Gareth Richards' words best describe how Barcelona think about time in relation to space on a football pitch and reflect how Barcelona coaches approach training for 'lost time phases.'

While it is clear Barcelona take the finite space of a football pitch and impose 2 positional formation states on the field while in possession and when out of possession.

These 2 states aim to meet the 2 polar opposite objectives of:

1. **Making the pitch as big as possible when in possession**

To offer a variety of opportunities to the players involved in ball retention.

2. **Making the pitch as small as possible for the opposition when out of possession**

To squeeze the opponents out of the game and steal the ball back.

Both of these states will be discussed at great lengths through a variety of different perspectives throughout this book. However, what is particularly intriguing is what happens in the 'lost time' between the 2 states;

Firstly, how does Barcelona treat this time in a positional sense?

As we have already seen during the analysis of Guardiola's impact at Barcelona, there are 2 very distinctive states that are interconnected and very different in formation. Barcelona goes from a (almost) traditional 4-3-3 to a 2-1-4-3 or, in more extreme circumstances, the formation resembles something similar to a formation that would not look out of place in the early stages of the 1900's with 5 forwards (as the full backs push on further still - something that can only be described as an unthinkable 2-1-2-5!).

The methodology of a slower and more patient build up play enables for the dramatic changes of formations to successfully take place. The players understand the need and timing of when to perform a slower build up and when to attack in a moment.

The question posed is how exactly Barcelona train for such chaos, how does a team make the transition so seamlessly that in one moment they are defending and the next they are attacking.

"How you play is a product of how you train."
Graham Hunter[10]

The loss or winning of the ball (transitions) while seen as 'lost time' by Barcelona, is often viewed as the most successful phases of Barcelona's play.

When the ball is lost, Barcelona press so effectively (this will be discussed at a great length later in the next chapter) and when the ball is won in those moments of chaos, Barcelona remain relaxed on the ball and ooze class as they transform from state to state so effortlessly, all as a product of successful training methodologies.

So how do Barcelona train for this moment of regaining possession? The resolution for what appears to be a complex phase could not be any more simple.

9   *Personal interview with Gareth Richards, former Chester Football Club Development Manager who was invited to spend some time to study Barcelona's La Masia as well as spending some time at Atletico Madrid, Real Madrid and Espanyol.*

10   *Hunter, G (2012). Barca: The Making of the Greatest Team in the World. Glasgow: BackPage Press Limited; 2nd Revised edition edition.*

Coaching The Tiki Taka Style Of Play

"Playing simple soccer is the most difficult thing of all."
Johan Cruyff[11]

Barcelona's training methodology and solution is for these moments of transition is to make sure the players are exposed to such scenarios in their sessions:

"The coaches encourage sessions of what they call 'Chaotic Football'. This is when they play small sided games with no cones to outline playing area or bibs to differentiate teams. This is done in order to promote free play, expression on the ball and to enhance peripheral vision...when passing the ball, the philosophy is to first and foremost, always try and find players in the line of pass. If this is not possible, players in possession must make it so that the defender has to physically exert himself in order to regain possession. Don't just give possession away. Hold it, use your body as a shield, and your team mates will help."
Gareth Richards[12]

Subsequently it is evidently clear that the 'secret' to Barcelona's success is down to these moments, the treatment of 'lost time'. As you may come to realise in the latter pages of this part of the book, these moments are not treated in isolation, but in a deeply ingrained connection with the task being performed immediately before and immediately after.

Pressing is intertwined with possession and defending is intertwined with attacking. It is this concept of connectivity that explains Gareth Richard's statement of Barcelona either being in attack or defence, as the two polar-opposite states should not be thought of as opposite ends of a linear line. Instead, imagine taking that linear line and bending it into a full circle, the moments of attack and defence are now only degrees apart. It is this relationship that diminishes 'lost time' to moments of genius.

11   Barend, F., Van Dorp, H. (1999). Ajax Barcelona Cruyff The ABC An Obstinate Maestro. London: Bloomsbury Publishing PLC; New edition.
12   Personal Interview.

Coaching The Tiki Taka Style Of Play

Liverpool F.C. Coach Interview:
Regaining Possession

When I had the opportunity to visit Melwood (Liverpool FC's training facility) by private invitation, I arrived hoping to come away with sketches of several training methods used by the coaching staff.

While the excellent Mike Marsh, Liverpool's young first team coach did indeed carry out several eye opening training drills that have influenced those offered in this book, I was pleasantly surprised when Chris Davies joined me for over an hour and spoke passionately and in great detail about the philosophy he had worked with under Brendan Rodgers at both Swansea FC and Liverpool FC, being one of only three of the back room staff that Rodgers took with him from Swansea to Liverpool in 2012.

Chris Davies' role is to watch future opponents and provide Rodgers and the players with a breakdown on how the opposition play and how they may combat the issues tactically; through being employed in this role and his education under Rodgers, Chris Davies has developed a deep understanding in the tactical development and processes of the philosophy.

After speaking with Davies, I left Melwood with an invaluable insight into the mind of someone who I have no doubt will become a fantastic manager within the next 10 to 15 years and has the fortune of continuing his education under Rodgers, who he has a close working relationship with and has even played under at Reading some years before.

Chris Davies dived straight into our deep tactical conversation, covering all corners of every philosophy from transitions to tactical variances, he even confessed his love for Stoke and their own value placed on a polar-opposite philosophy from the one he has expertise in.

Davies stressed throughout our conversation that transitions are one of the most imperative aspects of the philosophy and that there was a pragmatic thought process for developing such a playing identity:

"Transitions are extremely important, for me there are four elements to the game. There's attacking, defending, offensive transitions and defensive transitions. The offensive transition is based around the idea to pass out of the pressure and it's all about building the game and building attacks to get good positions on the field. In order to do that you need to get out of the pressure first and out of the immediate pressing that most teams will attempt."[13]

From this chapter we can confirm that when the ball is won, the formation undergoes a swift transition and Barcelona, like a perfect self sustaining ecosystem, circulate the ball appropriately to enable the central defenders to stretch out wide, for the full backs to become wingers, for the defensive midfielder to anchor the centre of defence and for the forwards to find space through creative concept of off-ball movement.

All in tune with one another, you would be forgiven if you forgot that seconds before the opposition had the ball and it would appear that Barcelona never lost the ball at all. And in complete control Barcelona exchange the ball in a flurry of passes, flirting with the edge of the opposition's 18-yard box before striking ferociously at the heart of the opposition's defence, to feed the ball through for a forward to break free and bear down on goal.

---

13   Chris Davies. Private interview.

3. THE ART OF COLLECTIVE PRESSING

Pressing - A way of slowing down or forcing opponents into areas you desire, keeping the pitch narrow and to win the ball back. A way of control without the ball.

The second solution to FC Barcelona and Sergi Domenech's 'lost time' is that of aggressive collective pressing, a second moment of 'chaos' that fills the transition between attack and defence. This is a methodology that merges the 2 polar opposites of attack and defence in its entirety, an approach that completes the circle of polar opposites.

"The purpose of pressurising is to decrease both the time and the space which an attacking player as in which to make his pass or his dribble."

Charles Hughes

A study in 1988 showed that while the ball was won back only 13% of the time in the final third, a staggering 66% of goals were scored from this 13%.

As a result, pressing was a significant resource for goals scored and in this sense defending deep in the opponents half is the best form of attack.

"You win the ball back when there are 30 metres to their goal not 80."

Pep Guardiola

The concept of pressing aggressively without the ball was first brought to the world scene of football by Viktor Maslov in the 1960s and quickly became a dominant feature of the possession based philosophy there after, as Rinus Michels and Valeriy Lobanovskyi took the art of pressing forward.

Rinus Michels once said that journalist's entitled his coaching philosophy as 'totaal voetbal' (total football), where as he called it 'pressing football' and believed the interchanging of positions was to keep up the high tempo of aggressive pressing first and foremost.

Valeriy Lobanovskyi's book *'The Methodological Basis of the Development of Training Models'* (written with his assistant Zelentsov) examined pressing on a

variety of different scales and verified that within the tactical approach of pressing there were several inner-tactical options.

Pressing, as Lobanovskyi states, presented the team with 3 options:

1. **The Full Press**
2. **The Half Press**
3. **The False Press**

Lobanovskyi believed that a successful team should employ all 3 states of pressing within their tactical approach to winning the ball back from the opposition.

The Full Press

Full pressing promotes this idea of a full pitch aggressive press and demands that players (or components as Lobanovskyi would have referred to them) harass the opponents in all areas of the field, but in coordination with one another.

Half Pressing

This takes inspiration from the tactical employments found in Basketball. The half press simply states that the team is to immediately drop off to the halfway line into a pre-determined formation (preferably into 3 lines of defence) and only attempt to harass the opposition when they enter the pressed territory, which of course does not have to physically be half the pitch, it could only be the final 30 yards.

This concept is based on the principles that the opponents are invited to play but are then prevented from entering more dangerous areas of the pitch. In a full press it is more likely that the opponents break in behind your team and into these spaces.

The False Press

Interestingly, this coincides with the full pressing approach and tricks the opposition into rushing their play out from the back and often returning possession to the pressing side. Put simply, the false press is the pressing of only 1 or 2 players, while the rest of the team drops off and does not join in with the high line of pressing.

Conclusions

Lobanovskyi would often instruct his side to cycle on and off of all 3 phases of pressing during a game.

They would use the full press immediately after kick off and then after 'x' amount of time shift to a false press or half press and still induce an error from the opposition to regain possession.

"The first thing we have in mind is to strive for new courses of action that will not allow the opponent to adapt to our style of play. If an opponent has adjusted himself to our style of play and found a counter-play, then we need to find new a new strategy.

That is the dialectic of the game. You have to go forward in such a way and with such a range of attacking options that it will force the opponent to make a mistake. In other words, it's necessary to force the opponent into the condition you want them to be in. One of the most important means of doing that is to vary the size of the playing area."

Valeriy Lobanovskyi

It has therefore become obvious that pressing offers something more than any statistic can measure, it offers more than just the opportunity to win the ball and score a goal as a result of such an approach.

The concept of pressing forces the opposition to play in a very particular way and enables the pressing team to be in control of the game despite not being in control of possession.

While a team might choose to press only in the final 30 yards and the opposition cannot break through the lines of defence, the statistics will portray the team in possession has a side that have controlled the game.

In truth, the half pressing team have controlled the oppositions location of possession and disabled their ability to create clear cut opportunities within the penalty area.

Pressing is entirely in tune with the concept of reducing the size of the pitch when the opposition is in possession. pressing can be used to delay opponents as well and this is often a more useful and successful application of pressing to allow your teammates to fall back into place.

Thus the most significant benefit of pressing is that of forcing the opponents into making an error and regaining possession. While the approach of half pressing for a full game has it's own situational advantages, the possession based philosophy will recognise the benefits of the full and false press over that of the half press.

The rationale for this is two-fold approach:

Winning the ball back closer to the opponents goal is more likely to result in a goal scored and secondly, the ability to realise the benefits of immediately regaining possession after losing control of possession within the opponents final third.

The 6 Second Rule

Pep Guardiola at Barcelona employed the 6 second rule to pressing in the final third. The notion was that in the scenario that the ball is lost in the opposition half, the team is most likely to win the ball back within the immediate 6 seconds that followed, the 6 seconds of chaos and 'lost time.' Again, there is no transition period.

In these 6 seconds, there are a series of 'triggers' that enable the team to collaborate in perfect harmony, triggers that send out messages to the players about when and where to press together.

This is most often done in threes at first where the 3 roles would be to 'press', 'support' and 'cover. 'This can be put into a language that is age appropriate - 'chasers, hunters and ball winners'.

"You cannot go (press) on your own…You work on zonal pressure, so that when it is in your zone, you have the capacity to press. That ability to press immediately, within five or six seconds to get the ball, is important. But you also have to understand when you can't and what the triggers are then to go for it again because you can't run about like a madman."

Brendan Rodgers

Aiding the ability to smother the ball and space within 6 seconds in such a devastatingly coordinated way are the following triggers:

1. When the opponent wins the ball and is forced to turn back to face his own goal

In doing so, the opponent has narrowed down his vision of play and options to only pass back or out of play.

The pass backwards is therefore predicted and as players smother the player on the ball, other players limit his options and prepare to pounce on the back pass to the goalkeeper when appropriate.

Thus either regaining possession in a 1 v 1 situation or forcing the goalkeeper to rush his clearance either out of play or into the heart of your defence. Therefore, the press results in you regaining possession or scoring a goal.

2. The second trigger is that of the opponent taking a poor touch of the ball

This results in the opponents having to look down to relocate the ball and regain control of the ball. In these precious milliseconds, your team has pounced on the error and reduced the opponents space significantly.

3. Other pressing triggers can be predetermined as a tactical input

The ultimate key to pressing high up the field is to do so coordinating with all other teammates.

4. There is a fourth trigger that occurs while still in possession

This will be discussed in the immediate following paragraphs.

Coaching The Tiki Taka Style Of Play

Liverpool F.C. Coach Interview: Pressing

The secret to pressing as many claim, is the positioning of players before you lose the ball.

"Do you know how Barcelona win the ball back so quickly? It's because they don't have to run back more than 10 metres as they never pass the ball more than 10 metres."

Johan Cruyff

When structuring a pressing approach to football, each of your players will be given specific functions that come together to form one single function of pressing.

Chris Davies of Liverpool FC revealed just how Brendan Rodgers and his coaching team approach instructing the front 3 players to work together:

"There are very specific functions for the front three to press. For example, for the left winger: when the ball is with the opposition's left sided centre-half and it is about to get transferred to the right side centre-half, that's the trigger for the left winger to leave his right full back and jump to the right-sided centre-half. That's his zone, so you lock that one in and then the full-back jumps on to their right back, and all of a sudden you are swarming."

Chris Davies[14]

It is clear that the positioning of each of the players relative to his teammates, can lead to success in such an approach to regaining possession through covering spaces rather than man marking opponents.

Pressing is not a reactive chain of events but a pro-active method where players take up good starting positions.

"Pressing is about positioning, if you have good positioning, you have good possession and good pressing because you cover the field in zones."

Chris Davies[15]

FC Barcelona find the balance between making the pitch as large as possible when on the ball and when to compact the play to a much smaller zone just before a risky through ball is about to be played.

The element of risk is also a trigger of when to prepare to press as a team (despite being in possession). The team would therefore compress the play and play to their own advantages in extremely valuable positions in attack.

---

14   *Private Interview.*
15   *Ibid.*

Coaching The Tiki Taka Style Of Play

FC Barcelona: Preparing for the Negative Transition while in Possession High Up the Pitch

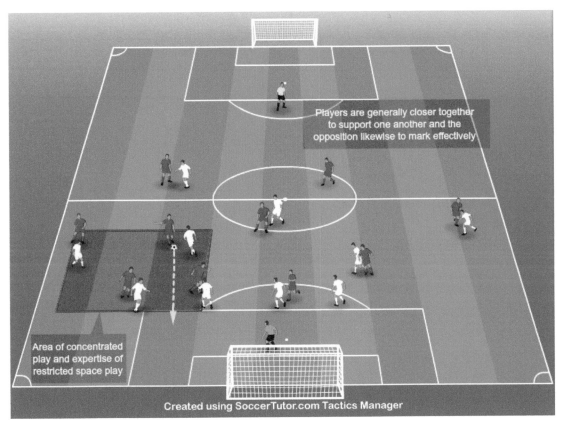

Through compacting the play, Barcelona have manufactured a scenario that the Barcelona players are entirely comfortable with; a densely compacted space which requires the players to play short, quick and technical passes in a tight space.

It is here that the rondo (a short passing training exercise that Barcelona religiously use) comes to benefit the players the most.

Through compacting the play, Barcelona have manufactured a scenario that the players are entirely comfortable with: a densely compacted space which requires the players to play short, quick and technical passes amongst little space.

To find space where there is very little is where the rondo (a short passing training exercise that Barcelona religiously use) comes to benefit Barcelona players the most. If the ball is lost in these moments, the Barcelona players are already in the perfect positions to immediately press the opposition.

FC Barcelona: Effective 6 Second Pressing High Up the Pitch

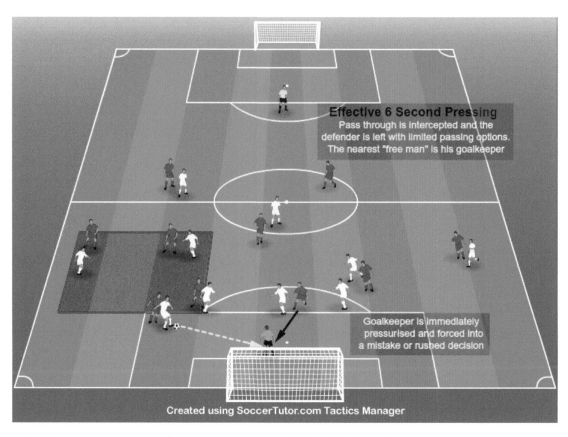

Effective 6 Second Pressing
Pass through is intercepted and the defender is left with limited passing options. The nearest "free man" is his goalkeeper

Goalkeeper is immediately pressurised and forced into a mistake or rushed decision

Created using SoccerTutor.com Tactics Manager

In the diagram we can examine this scenario in process and the left back is reduced to the options of either playing the ball back to his goalkeeper or kicking the ball out of play, if the goalkeeper does receive the ball, he himself is left with a lack of options and therefore possession is returned.

Suitably we can suppose that successful pressing relies on more than its triggers. It relies on the success of the positional system and the possession based ball circulation attitudes. It also relies on the high line of defence to compact the play and reduce the space and it relies on the goalkeeper marshalling the space in behind the highline of defence.

Effective pressing relies on all 9 of the recognised pillars that come together to form successful tiki-taka football.

Once again, you cannot artlessly master one aspect of the game, you must holistically consider the whole for any one of the parts to function successfully.

It should appear obvious now that playing the long ball to a target man from the back, hoping to counter attack and pressing high up the field is a combination that might just be too tall an order for any team, even those with elite levels of fitness.

How 3 Players Can Successfully Press 5

Pressing as we have found out, is a tool of control without possession and should be understood by both players and coaches to successfully implement it without error. The supporting diagrams (below) illustrate just how the nearest man's positioning is essential for the collective press to function as designed.

If the nearest player is compact in the defensive block we have a situation where you have formed the foundations of control without the ball, but the player's job is not done. If the nearest man fails to get close enough to the opposition player, he does not narrow down the ball carrier's options and therefore makes it difficult to control the opponent.

The English FA teach that the most desirable pass in football is that of the forward pass but I would like to add that the forward pass should benefit the team's collective effort and not that of the individual only.

Having understood that the forward pass is the most desirable, pressing should look to reduce the possibility of the pass travelling towards your own goal by forcing the player to play sideways or better still, to turn back towards his own goal.

The key to collective pressing is to make the opposition's play predictable. When the opposition's play becomes predictable, it becomes easier to press aggressively and attempt to intercept any horizontal passes (as the supporting diagram illustrates).

It is even more efficient if you can get your players to work together, by looking to force play down a certain direction through your own defensive body position ('showing him one way') and then offer the defensive support and balance in behind the initial press thereafter, but always remember that often 'delaying' the man on the ball is just as effective as tackling the opponent.

If the nearest man is functioning as designed and the supporting players are both alert and well positioned, it is possible to successfully press when outnumbered. Essentially, pressing comes down to positioning and this is the most important element.

1

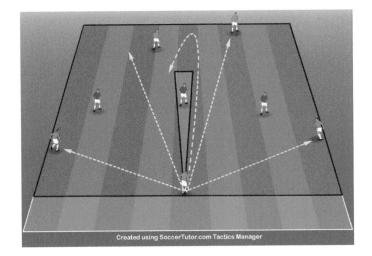

Created using SoccerTutor.com Tactics Manager

Coaching The Tiki Taka Style Of Play

2

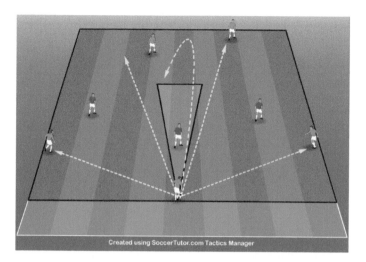

3

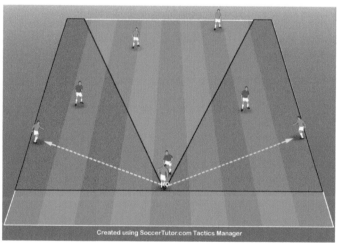

4

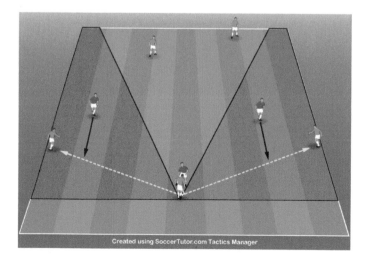

Coaching The Tiki Taka Style Of Play

4. BALL CIRCULATION

Generally speaking, the ball circulation is the first aspect of tiki-taka that a fan and professionals will observe and is employed as a method to maximise the use of space on the field (by making the playing area as big as possible).

We need to be aware that all things are connected and that altering one aspect of the game will impact another.

It is important that when examining the ball circulation of Barcelona, Villarreal, Swansea, Liverpool, Ajax and other possession based teams that we do so not in isolation, but in the context of the bigger picture.

Possession or ball circulation is one of 4 states, the others being:

2. **General pressing when out of possession**
3. **The seconds after winning the ball as the formation transforms**
4. **The moments immediately after losing the ball**

(This is like all other states, an art within itself and requires a more in-depth understanding of why, how and what the team are trying to achieve).

It is imperative to view possession as a tool within football and nothing else. We must not celebrate the statistics of possession alone but the objective of limiting your opponent to a lack of goal scoring opportunities and the ability to maximise your own through possession.

"Ball circulation is a means, not a goal in itself!"

Rinus Michels[16]
(The father of totaal voetbal)

Since ball circulation covers space in a controlled way, it is within the possibilities that a team can return to the same location over and over, faced with variations of the same problem. In this scenario, the opposition should be viewed as problems, ones that can be solved.

---

16   *Michels, R (2013). Team Building: The Road To Success. Reedswain Soccer.*

Coaching The Tiki Taka Style Of Play

Barcelona USA: A Youth Development Success Story

Overview

Barcelona USA coaches Brian and Gary Kleiban are two experts with such an approach to football and have successfully implemented a philosophy while coaching at their club in California after studying FC Barcelona's training methodology for several years.

Youtube footage of the Barcelona USA Under 11 team illustrate just how well the coaches have succeeded in such a relatively short amount of time and the club has gone on to boast victories over the actual FC Barcelona academy teams themselves.

More recently, Barcelona USA have been invited to travel over to Europe and participate in competitions that involve high profile academies such as Barcelona, Manchester United and Ajax. Barcelona USA is an unprecedented success story in the U.S.A that thrives on developing young football players to perform breathtaking flowing football with creativity displayed at its finest.

When I spoke with Brian (head coach) and Gary Kleiban (assistant), I was amazed to find out that the video footage I had seen was that of an under 11 team who had only come under the tutorship of the coaches just one year before and that the majority of the team was inherited.

So how exactly had the coaches set about transforming an ordinary under 10 team from California to overcome some of the elite academies in Europe?

It is by no mistake that the team circulate the ball around the pitch in such a fluid and mature way, one that enables Barcelona USA full control over their opponents and the game itself. The Kleiban brothers had learnt well at La Masia and went about producing an *"almost carbon-copy of what we see at La Masia."[17]*

"The key things are the little details and the little details make all the difference. It's a team-mentality and a singular developmental organism...one

organism: thinking, acting and moving in the same way - everybody is in unison. This way, the collective triumphs the individual easily."*

Gary Kleiban[18]

The Kleiban brothers execute this concept through a strict framework on the field that the young players fit within. It is often seen as controversial, but when we see that at La Masia, tactical training methods are first introduced at under 8 level it is no surprise that Barcelona USA have followed suit in introducing tactical messages early on in the development process.

The way in which the message and the drills are put across to young players is without a doubt the key driving feature of both La Masia and Barcelona USA's developmental approach to the game.

"The delivery of the message that is translated into a language an eight year old can understand is key."

Brian Kleiban

The developmental tools used by Barcelona USA are not long and tedious powerpoint presentations, but simple explanations with the ball and training exercises, often on a personal basis so that no player is left out of the singular organism approach to football.

Through the three 2-hour training sessions and the game on the weekend, Barcelona USA offer their young players 7 hours of strategic and structured play to learn and develop per week, always with the ball at their feet.

The players are also expected to play more freely outside of these hours and expected to complete 'homework' that concentrates on individual aspects of the game. The players are given two team training sessions and one individual focused training session per week and their homework is mixed between focusing on individual basic tasks and techniques or looking for a particular phase of play when watching a professional match at the weekend.

---

17   Brian Kleiban. Private Interview.

18   Ibid.

Put simply, the Barcelona USA youth teams work extremely hard to achieve the results that they do and are given constant feedback on how to improve.

"Hour one is not about talking, it's about showing... basic things like receiving the ball across your body correctly. So if the ball is coming from the right side of the field, you should (if possible) receive the ball with your left foot to open up your body and provide a complete picture of passing options...a simple detail like this aids the overall approach of the possession-based game."

Brian Kleiban

Barcelona USA work tirelessly on spacing and by their own admission choreograph as much of the possession based game as possible. While the Kleiban brothers agree that the game is unpredictable, they also believe that when in possession you are in control and subsequently it is possible to manipulate situations that can occur more than once in a game.

This methodology therefore lends itself to learning set play style movements and functional passing networks that lead to a goal scoring opportunity. A system of pattern recognition and choreographed play is a system where players understand the spaces and the relationships between the components on the field.

"With the young players we break it up into pieces for them that eventually come together: It's about spacing, it's about talking, it's about being aware of your surroundings, it's about deciding what you are going to do with the ball five seconds before you receive it no matter where you are on the field...all these things are ingrained.

At the young ages it's about repetition, it's about creating muscle memory. So we try to break it down and have one objective at a time and only move on when we see it being performed consistently and this may take days or weeks."

Brian Kleiban

Vision and Awareness

Something that Kleiban touches on is the emphasis of importance on players having 'options' and knowing your options before you even receive the ball; knowing two or three options available to you at all times on the field, regardless of where the ball is in relation to you.

"The difference between them and us is we have more players who think before they play, quicker. (...) When you arrive at Barça the first thing they teach you is: think.

Think, think, think. Quickly. [Xavi starts doing the actions, looking around himself.] Lift your head up move, see, think. Look before you get the ball."

Xavi[19]

The scanning of your surroundings before you receive the ball is paramount for midfielders.

Where a midfielder has not explored much before receiving the ball, they would see a forward pass completion rate of 38.2% compared to the 73.2% completion rate where the midfield had done so.

The same research finds that those players who receive the most prestigious awards in world football (FIFA World Player of the Year etc.) explore their surroundings without the ball more frequently than any other players.

The recordings for elite performers show on average one active scan of their surroundings (looking away from the ball) every 3 seconds (0.33 searches per second). The very best players studied on the other hand, scan their surroundings more than once every 2 seconds (0.62 searches per second).[20]

Formation Structure and Phases of Play

The overarching concept for 'ball circulation' and playing as a singular organism is clear but Kleiban goes into far more detail with each of the phases of play and each aspect of the game, far more detail than you would expect at under 11 youth football.

When Barcelona USA are in possession, the two central defenders open out wide and create a 30-40 yard gap between them as the anchor man in midfield drops back to form the third and centralised defender in a 3-4-3 formation.

19 Lowe, S. (2011). I'm a Romantic, says Xavi, Heartbeat of Barcelona and Spain. Available: http://www.theguardian.com/football/2011/feb/11/xavi-barcelona-spaininterview. Last accessed June 2012.
20   Jordet, G (2013). The hidden foundation of field vision in English Premier League (EPL) soccerplayers. Boston: M.I.T Sloan Sports Conference.

Coaching The Tiki Taka Style Of Play

This is a system that encourages the full backs to push on forward and in some part free them of defensive duties when in possession. This is a system we have seen time and time again throughout the theoretical history of the tiki-taka philosophy of football.

Wingers should receive the ball with 5 yards of space on the wing and offer themselves options. When the winger is 1 v 1, the player should have the ability and confidence to go past his defender.

When a 2 v 1 situation occurs or 1 v 2, the player should aim to benefit the phases of play rather than his own ego. A numerical advantage in each situation of the field is the bottom line to 'positioning' on a football field in this philosophy.

Both Gary and Brian Kleiban speak about the field and phases of play in terms of shrinking and expanding space, and they do so in the same way as many great managers have done when advocating this philosophy.

Age Relevant Training

Their secret to coaching successfully under this philosophy however is not done through their own understanding of the space on a field but through their ability to offer an under 11 football player with an under 11 relevant explanation of why, what and how they should be acting in particular scenarios.

The players are the secret to their success, the managers have had to understand them as young developing human beings in order to portray their message in an understandable and simple way.

Choreographed Football

The concept of choreographed football is not a new one. In Simon Kuper's excellent book *'Football Against the Enemy' (1994)* he explains just why through Lobanovskyi's statistical assistant Aleksei Zelentsov:

"Zelentsov worked from the premise that since a fraction of a second's thought can be too long in modern football; a player had to know where to pass before he got the ball. To this end, Dynamo's players had to memorise set plays, as if they were American footballers, and had to run off the ball in set patterns.

According to Zelentsov's calculations, a team that commits an error in less than 18% of a game's key situations is unbeatable. These statistics were the basis for Lobanovskyi's training sessions which were characterised by predetermined patterns of play deeply embedded in the tactical structure of the team. The positional switching of Rinus Michels' Total Football tactics prominently featured as well."[21]

So by choreographing play, the players have the advantage over the opposition of not having to account for the action-reaction timing that the opposition have to. Third man running and the use of a playmaker are some of the tools for such an approach.

"The English don't think until they have the ball at their feet...we don't think about the first man. We think of the third man, the one who has to run. If I get the ball, the third man can run immediately because he knows I will pass to the second man, and he will give it to him. If I delay, the third man has to delay his run and the moment is over. It is that special moment, that special pass."

Arnold Muhren[22]

Through rehearsed creativity, many coaches believe that it is possible for particular situations to occur again and again on the field. The advantage only comes into place when the team has rehearsed plays to offer solutions to the problems (the opposition) on the field and create goal scoring opportunities.

There are not many teams at any level who organise themselves in a way that 3, 4 or more players at any one time are all in tune with each other and come together with such a flurry of interchanges and perfect knowledge.

21 Kuper, S (2003). Football Against The Enemy. London: Orion.
22 Winner, D (2001). Brilliant Orange: The Neurotic Genius of Dutch Football. London: Bloomsbury Publishing PLC; New edition edition.

Training to Create Habits

Through repetition of particular movements, actions or skills, players begin to learn the 'inner-architecture' of each activity and begin to perform these actions without much of the decision making process, without having to think, simply through habit. Habit formation is an area of great complexity and is a new area of literature that is covered by the likes of **Charles Duhigg** in the book **'The Power of Habit.'** In the book Duhigg writes about an American football coach, Tony Dungy, whose coaching philosophy revolves around the concept of habit transformation, by taking the existing habits of players and making alterations.

Dungy believes that if we can get players to perform out of habit to particular cues before an action, we can prevent players from thinking about their actions and instead, lead players to perform their actions habitually. With players responding to particular cues, Dungy could take away the time it takes for a player to think about the reaction to a situation (the milliseconds count in sport).

As a result, Dungy decided not to go down the conventional approach of practicing hundreds of set plays to win American football matches, but to just to coach a handful of plays and educate them to pay attention to particular cues.

In a footballing context we can think about habits in terms of how a player may choose to beat his man in a 1 v 1 situation for example. If we take a right footed winger who receives the ball out on the right hand side, turns with the ball into space and his opponent is 5 yards away 45-degrees to the left, positioned to show him inside, we have a situation where it is possible to encourage habitual action if the player has received effective coaching in how to beat his man.

The winger can pick up the ball and use this space and angle as his cue to perform the roulette by dribbling with the ball at pace directly at the player ahead of him. Whilst dribbling the ball, the winger should look to run just past the right shoulder of the defender and deliberately entice the defender into trying to tackle him by dribbling using his right foot (keeping the ball underneath his own right shoulder) and 'showing the defender the ball.'

As the defender falls into the trap of trying to take the ball from the attacker, your winger is in a winning position by performing a habitually learnt he roulette, rolling the defender away with his body and accelerating into the space behind the defender.

In this example we have a skill that has been performed out of habit rather than through a series of on going decision making points from a simple cue.

Inspired by Duhigg's diagrammatic habit formation cycles in his excellent book 'The Power of Habit', a simple visual explanation has been drawn to detail the habit formation described above through repetitiveness of the skill in training sessions, learning each and every detail by heart (rehearsing play).

It is the idea of cutting 'thinking time' during actions that leads many great coaches to believe that pattern play is an effective solution to translating key messages about pressing or passing networks into a language that players can comprehend.

Habits are also encouraged in coaching players to continually scan the field around them and in player movement through formation related training exercises.

It is for these reasons listed above that certain elite football players will continue to re-use the same skill time and time again on a football pitch and arguably why it may be better to learn 4 or 5 skills inside out to particular cues than it may be to try and learn every type of skill out there.

The idea is to remove choices that can be made 'in the moment' by the player and instead allow the player to focus on looking for cues and performing one or two skills that they have habitually learnt, reducing the reaction time or 'thinking time in a situation where the milliseconds matter.

Habits are formed from 3 components **(1) a cue, (2) a routine and (3) a reward**. Having said that, it is a more complex cycle of learning as 'externalities' such as player belief are involved in reality.

Key Habit Components: A Complex Cycle

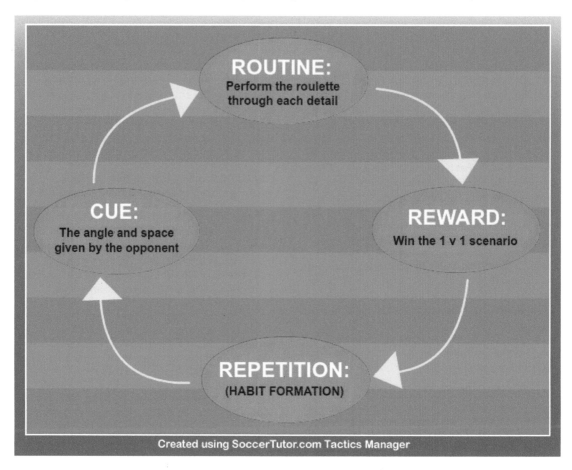

Created using SoccerTutor.com Tactics Manager

The Playmaker

The use of a playmaker is another semi-rehearsed and controlled concept within the possession based philosophy. Through switching positions and an array of players with an excellent ability to pass and use vision, the use of a playmaker is often more complex than using one key player as the focal point of possession.

Take Argentina and Juan Roman Riquelme at the World Cup 2006 for example. Argentina were perceived by many as the tournaments best team and scored a marvellous goal that consisted of 25consecutive passes before Cambiasso finished off the move and ran away in celebration.

Throughout the tournament Riquelme saw the ball more often that any other player and was often the springboard for Argentina's change of tempo when in possession, a way of returning to a reference point and replaying a learnt pattern play through a series of cues and routines.

This use of a playmaker can be argued to be one dimensional and offers a singular outlet for the team to play through. This book on the other hand, suggests a number of other solutions to playing through particular zones in order to achieve the desired outcomes.

Ball Circulation:
4 Possession Based Phases

When we talk about ball circulation we talk of 4 possession based phases.

Phase 1: The construction from behind. This phase is often about the defensive movement when in possession and includes the spreading wide of the central defenders that many teams use to make the field as big as possible.

Phase 2: The preparation in midfield, where the full backs often move forward to provide width.

Phase 3: This is about creation and getting in between the lines of play.

Phase 4: The penetration and breaking of the opposition's defensive lines or as Juan Luis Delgado would put it - *"identifying the moment of disruption."*[23]

Of course, the separation of phases like this is unclear and all the phases overlap into one philosophy.

Nevertheless, each phase will have it's own 'playmakers' and solutions. When constructing the play from behind, the anchor man who drops back in and out of the central void often acts as a linking player for phase one. Further forward, a traditional 'number 10' will become the heart beat of the play, a reference point for possession and always working himself into available spaces on the field.

Building Up Play

It is important to understand that it is desirable for the building up of play and playmaking to be done centrally rather than with full backs or wingers. If you build up play through wide players you effectively shut yourself off from using the entire spectrum of the football field as passing options, i.e. if you have the ball out on the left, you can pass into the centre but it becomes difficult to use the right hand side of the pitch when you have 'made the pitch as big as possible'. You should therefore look to build up from the back in key central areas.

One method of building up a necessary way of playing would be to challenge your players to make 50

23   Delgado. (2011). *Tactical Training Model Presentation*. Available: http://www.slideshare.net/juanluisdelgado/tactical-training-modelpresentation-juandelgado. Last accessed January 2012.

passes from the first third into the middle third. This is the method used by one possession based Premier League manager and forms the foundations of his footballing philosophy.

After a team has successfully learnt to feel comfortable in playing 50 passes into the middle third, you can then move on and focus on the number of passes into the final third the team can achieve during a match. Once you can successfully manage the expectations, then you can begin to coach ball circulation and the decision making processes of when to play the ball and where.

"Good ball circulation puts high demands on the quality of positional play, the mastering of the tempo and the speed of action."

Brendan Rodgers

A number of tactical problems and solutions are offered later in this book under the tactical variations chapter. These solutions directly tackle issues of ball circulation and how to adjust your approach to possession with the objective of creating as many goal scoring opportunities as possible and reducing the opposition's ability to do the same. In every scenario however, the focus is always on retaining possession and controlling the game by using possession as a tool:

"For us when we get the ball, it should be 11 vs. 10... When you've got the ball 60-70% of the time, it's a football death-field...it's death by football."

Brendan Rodgers

The Importance to Implement
all Aspects of Tiki Taka

The single biggest criticism facing the tiki-taka philosophy from the media today exists because of the misconception that tiki-taka entails pass after pass with little or no meaningful direction in terms of chance creation.

Now, in reality it should be understood that tiki-taka is not to be confined to just 'passing'. Passing is, as we have seen, one of many components and is arguably not the most important part of tiki-taka that enables total control of the game, if there can be such a thing.

Since all components overlap and cannot be taken apart without referring to all other aspects of

Coaching The Tiki Taka Style Of Play

the philosophy, we should not aim to draw up a hierarchy of importance that would place a higher value on pressing, positioning, passing or the transitional moments.

Nonetheless, one of the key faults with teams aiming to mimic such an approach is the inability in phases 3 and 4 to create goal scoring opportunities. At the other end of the spectrum, there can be a complete inability to understand that patience is required so the team play in unison, as a single organism.

There are clearly different attitudes to different areas of the field. Team's playing tiki-taka are less likely to cross the ball from deep or play a long ball compared to a more direct counter attacking team. The tempo, direction of pass, length of pass and opportune level of pass are all related to each given space on the field and the scenario the players find themselves in.

The further forward the play is based, the more creative and opportune a pass may become and as with Lobanovskyi's approach to unpredictable pressing (remember - full, half and false pressing), the level of opportunism in passing should also be as unpredictable for the opposition.

This way you keep the opponent guessing and you are far more likely to catch the opponent out of position.

Invite the team out of position and you are in control, but allow the opposition to sit deep and block the final two phases of play and they are the team in control of the game, with or without the ball.

"Opportunism...There needs to remain space in football for a surprising action in the build-up and the attack."
Rinus Michels

Encouraging Natural Elements

It is therefore important to ensure unpredictability is an aspect of your team's play. Instructing young players to always receive the ball across their body for example, is not necessarily the best way to coach. Instead, it may be better to encourage the use of more 'natural' passing methods in congested zones and methods that may have been used in games of street football, such as a quick flick with the outside of the boot.

As a coach, you should look to create players who are able to adjust and be tactically flexible when in possession and not aim to create 'predictable machines' who are able to circulate the ball without player personal creativity.

176

5. THE ATTACKING ATTITUDES

Under the ball circulation chapter of this section an exploration was made into the rehearsal of creativity and attitudes towards retaining possession. However, there must be an understanding of the impacts that occur through different attacking attitudes: to play wider or with more risk (opportunistic) etc.

In this chapter, an exploration is made into how the smallest of alterations to an attacking attitude can have huge implications. For you to manage a team tactically and playing with this possession based philosophy, you must understand why a team is failing to create goal scoring opportunities.

One of the objectives of play that is mentioned over and over throughout the text is this notion that a successful tactical philosophy is one that can create as many goal scoring opportunities as possible and reduce the number that the opposition are able to create.

For a comprehensive analysis of such an approach, we must determine just what a goal scoring opportunity is, or at least the kind that should be considered worthy of a goal scoring opportunity.

In an event to prove to you as the reader that particular areas are more dangerous than others, I conducted a study of every goal scored during the 2011/12 English Premier League season.[24]

The two following diagrams aim to summarise the findings of the study and conclude that the 'zone 14' notion that we often hear coaches talk about is in fact true; zone 14 refers to the centralised region right outside the penalty area.

In this particular study I designed for the greater amount of zones (30) to achieve a higher accuracy of where goals are scored from.

---

24   All statistics used in this study are OPTA owned.

Coaching The Tiki Taka Style Of Play

PREMIER LEAGUE ANALYSIS: Location of Goals Scored 2011/12 (%) Diagram

General Summary:

81.05% of goals scored are from within the penalty area

18.01% of goals scored are from between the penalty area and the 36-yard zone

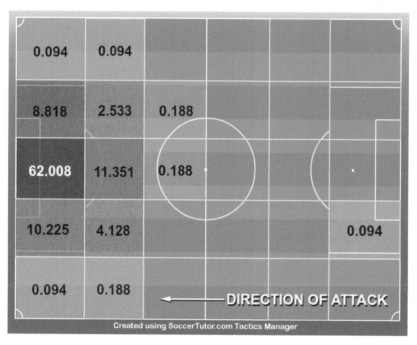

The diagram supports the notion of the 'zone 14' danger that the majority of goals are scored from within a centralised area within the penalty box.

In fact, from the 1066 goals scored during the 2011/12 season in the English Premier League, we can conclude that the objective of tactics should be to get the ball to a teammate who has a clear shot at goal within the central zone penalty area.

The study also shows that a team will find more success shooting from the central area outside of the box compared to the wider areas within the box. It is no coincidence that Manchester City scored the most goals from open play and had the most shots from within the penalty area during the 2011/12 season.

The defensive outcomes would suggest that you should compact the central areas and focus on preventing the opposition shooting from within these zones.

Nonetheless, a further study is required to inform a tactical outcome about how to defend or attack.

Where are goals assisted from?

In answering this question we can arrive at a number of conclusions about how to defend and how we should attack.

Coaching The Tiki Taka Style Of Play

PREMIER LEAGUE ANALYSIS: Location of the Assists 2011/12 (%) Diagram

General Summary:

30.3% of assists were assisted from a central location (18 yard line to halfway line)

25.8% of goals were from set plays (penalties, free-kicks, corners, solo etc.)

24.49% of goals were assisted from within the penalty area

15.76% of assists were from blue highlighted areas

10.04% of assist were from the byline

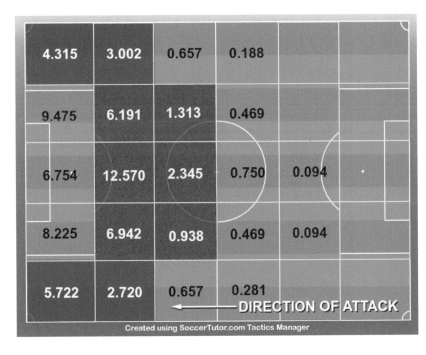

The study reveals a number of interesting facts in how goals are scored in the English Premier League. While it would appear conclusive that crosses are a successful method of assisting goals (15.76%), nearly 65% of these assisted crosses have come from the byline in wider positions.

We can presume that on these statistics, it is better to allow the opposition to have space on the wings compared to space in the more central areas.

Crosses are in fact far more successful when used in a counter attacking situation. When a team is allowed to construct their defence, the success in crossing is diminished.

The average number of crosses per goal during the 2011/12 season was 79. Since the average number of crosses per game from teams was 22 crosses per game, this concludes that relying on crossing alone during the 2011/12 season would result in 1 goal scored in every 4 games. Therefore we can conclude that crossing is not a successful attacking approach to focus on in modern day football, even in a counter attacking division like the English Premier League.

Coaching The Tiki Taka Style Of Play

Assessing the Statistics

Teams that were more successful, like Manchester United, would break on the counter attack and outnumber or match the opposition within the penalty area.

Subsequently in an approach that opts for a slower build up play and a construction from the back, crossing is not seen as a viable way of attacking as the opposition is able to steady their defensive line within the 18-yard box.

In some circumstances, teams will invite you to cross as they are confident that they will win any headers coming into the box, an approach that West Brom successfully employed against Wigan during their 2012/13 fixture in November. West Brom understood that Wigan would be better in possession, but as long as they were kept to the wider areas of the field, West Brom were truly in control of the game despite not being in control of possession.

While it may appear obvious from the data that teams should play through the middle and shoot only when within the central areas of the penalty box, this book highly recommends that a team should not take this approach as a sole solution.

The element of unpredictability often aids a team in their quest of crafting goal scoring opportunities.

However, a team should always aim to stretch the opposition to unsettle their back line and produce the assist that they see fit, so if a cross becomes the best option then a cross should be attempted.

A number of coaches I have spoken to have arrived at their own conclusions that a cross is seen as an opportunity to turn over possession and welcome the opposition's attempt to cross over combination play outside their own penalty area.

These outcomes have significant outputs on a team's tactical approach in both their attitudes towards defending and attacking.

Villarreal: A Case Study

One interesting case study that offers a variety of different conclusions into how wide a team should play is that of Villarreal 2010/11 vs. 2011/12. These two seasons resulted in two polar opposite performances in the league, but both with a seemingly identical 'tiki-taka' identity of play.

While Villarreal qualified for the Champions League in 2010/11 by finishing fourth in La Liga and reached the quarter finals of the Copa del Rey, on the other hand, the 2011/12 season ended in tears as Villarreal were eventually relegated, a result that shocked the footballing world.

How could a team that played such wonderful football achieve the heights they did one season and fall into disaster the next? Was it simply that the pressure of performing in the Champions League was too much or did Villarreal alter the way they played?

In reality the answer is probably a mixture of both but by examining how Villarreal played differently offers an invaluable insight into how altering the smallest of details can result in the biggest impacts.

In an excellent study conducted by football analyst Ravi Ramineni,[25] the two seasons were analysed in terms of tactical differentials.

The study confirms that Villarreal's passing completion rate in the final third went down from 72.6% in 2010 to 69.6% in 2011. There was also a 21% reduction in the number of passes completed in the central zone of the final third.

There was a considerable increase in wide play and a suggestion that Villarreal played with a more risk free (opportunistic) methodology and an increasing dependancy on crossing as an approach for assisting goals.

The Villarreal of 2011 employed an approach whereby wing-backs become heavily involved high up the pitch in the wider areas and the midfield would look to pass wide early on in the build-up play. This lack of penetration can be, in part, put down to the loss of Santi Carzola (sold to Malaga) who would thrive in the 'number 10' role and find space freely in front of a controlling midfield.

Without Carzola's movement, the midfield were left with fewer options to play forwards and get in behind the oppositions lines of play.

Furthermore, Giuseppe Rossi was kept out of much of the 2011 season through injury, a player whose movement would also find space in between the defensive lines of play high up the field. As a result of this, the strikers received the ball an average five metres further away from goal in 2011, meaning the entire zone of play was five metres further away from goal.

While the 2010 midfield of Borja Valero, Bruno Soriano, Santi Carzola and Cani is only one player different compared to the 2011 midfield (replacing Carzola with Senna), the midfield completed far fewer forward passes in 2011, especially through the middle of the field where the most assists are made.

Simply put, Villarreal made subtle differences in player profile (2 players) and thus made conscious decisions to play more in the wider regions of the field. The diagram following this text[26] illustrates graphically the differential's between the 2 seasons and highlights many of the critical points made within this text. The following diagram analyses the number of passes and their accuracy in relation to zones within the attacking third between Villarreal's 2010/11 and 2011/12 seasons.

25   Ramineni, R. (2012). Villarreal 2011-12 – Breaking down a failed season. Available: http://onfooty.com/2012/08/villarreal-2011-12-breaking-down-a-failed-season.html. Last accessed September 2012.

26   Ibid.

Coaching The Tiki Taka Style Of Play

Number of Passes and Their Accuracy in Relation to Zones within the Attacking Third between Villarreal's 2010/11 and 2011/12 Seasons

Direction of Attack ➡️

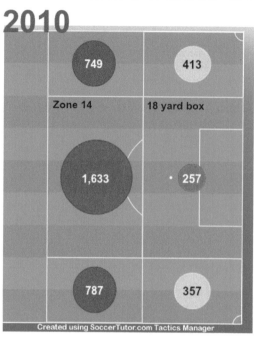

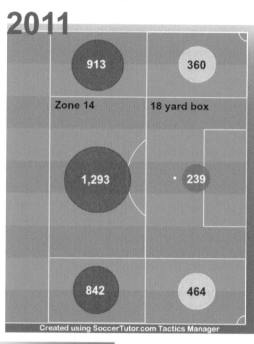

Completion %

44.35   78.20

The data suggests that Villarreal attempted just **12%** more passes in the wider areas per game and **19%** fewer passes in central areas of the field. This therefore leaves a **7%** negative difference between those passes in the attacking third and those not, and this ultimately comes down to the increase in lateral passing in the middle third.

In conclusion, there should be a significant value of importance placed upon the subtle differences made in attacking attitudes. A balance needs to be found on how to stretch the play and approach assisting goals. Patience and knowing how to *"identify the moment of disruption"* are key.

Comparing Swansea City and FC Barcelona's Possession Based Philosophies

The Swansea team of 2011/12 under Brendan Rodgers received much praise from the English media in their first season in the Premier League and they even drew comparisons to Barcelona under Guardiola. While it would not surprise anyone that Barcelona dominated play much higher up the field, according to one study[27] 29% of Barcelona's play consisted of possession in the final third compared to Swansea's 13%.

Both teams actually boasted a similar percentage of the ball in the middle third of the field **(61% Barcelona; 54% Swansea)** however, Swansea gained much of their possession based dominance in their own third **(33%)** and Barcelona simply skipped over this first phase of possession **(10%)**. This evidently details that you can dominate possession in a number of different ways and that the profile of players has a significant impact as to how you decide to maintain possession tactically.

While you might be reading this and thinking 'what is the point of possession if you aren't going to get forward?' I would like to remind you that possession is a tool of dominance and can be used either as an attacking tactical approach or a defensive one as used by Swansea here and Scotland in the 1800s! The desired outcome of the tool of possession is to dominate the game, whether it be defensively or in a bid to score as many goals as possible.

It is without a doubt a more positive outcome and approach if the profile of players you possess is able to play against the opponents faced with possession higher up the field, since this also reduces the possibility of the opposition from scoring. The attitude while in possession is everything.

We must also remember that teams would set up to face Barcelona knowing of their dominance and quality of player in each position. Therefore teams would sit deep and allow Barcelona possession

27   Anon. (2012). Much Ado About Nothing. Available: https://blog. statdna.com/post/2012/02/21/Much-Ado-About-Swansea.aspx. Last accessed November 2012.

further up the pitch. Whereas Swansea were faced with a different challenge of dominating games against teams that would sit much higher up field and effectively resort Swansea to an altered approach. This can be noticeable in the average position of each team's centre backs while in possession (10 yards further up for Barcelona players).

Barcelona's 'controllers' therefore sat further up the pitch and there is then a reduced need for Busquets to fall in as a central defender (compared to Swansea's reliance on this tactic).

Of course Swansea would have preferred to control games 'the Barca way', but as any knowledgeable football fan will know, each and every team is different and you simply cannot replicate the final product of another team, even if the philosophy and process of development are remarkably similar.

The most intriguing difference between Swansea and Barcelona however was their use of wide play. Swansea dictated play in the majority of their games and 70% of their possession was played on either flanks compared to Barcelona's 57%. This is a result of Swansea sitting further back while in possession and using more counter attacks.

The ability to cross is most effective when employing the counter attack and having the ability to get three or more players in the box as the cross comes in.

Swansea achieved this by allowing the opposite winger to come in as a forward and getting the 'number 10' in midfield arriving in the box at the same time.

These are all the components of a team that has the capabilities to use the rare ability to counter attack when the opposition does decide to push on and press high up field. This is a luxury that Barcelona would not be offered as often as teams sat back and invited Barcelona to play out from the back, the opposition would invite Barcelona to play and remove the threat of a Barcelona counter attack as well as they could.

Coaching The Tiki Taka Style Of Play

A good team on the other hand, would invite Barcelona to play in the areas they least desired, out on the flanks. The ability to sit back and be well prepared for a cross coming in allowed the opponents to shift the control of the game in their favour somewhat, even if Barcelona were in control of the ball.

Of course, Barcelona would become experts at pulling the opponents out of position and using the dribble as a tool to draw players out of position, rather than as a tool to travel from A to B. This is a concept that will be spoken about at greater lengths in the tactical variances section of this book.

The attacking attitudes can dramatically alter the way in which we view the philosophy being executed. While Swansea and Barcelona drew many comparisons, these comparisons were often laughed off by fans who misunderstood the rationale of why Swansea played the way they did and why they could not play the Barca-way. But equally, why Barcelona were unable to break in ways they would like to have done so from occasion to occasion (ref: Chelsea vs. Barcelona semi-final of the Champions League).

Ajax would often counter this problematic scenario of being unable to break a team down by opting to play long but diagonal balls in the dying moments out to the advanced wide players. The emphasis on this approach is that the long ball was not played up to a target man but into space on the flanks or to the wide man's feet. The ability to do just this is taken from Barcelona due to the positional formation difference to the Ajax team of the 1990s.

Put short, you cannot have everything. You are unable to effectively cross with the combination of a counter attack and dominate possession in the final third, you cannot play the long diagonal ball out wide with the counter attack and press high up field. The attacking differentials are a matter of choices and compromise. These differences can be as a result of player profiles, formation choices, the opposition's tactical set-up, the moment of the game and so on.

The choices a coach makes tactically, no matter how small can bring about an unsuccessful execution of such a tactical philosophy.

Do not for a moment forget that no component of this system of play should be treated in isolation and that the system is one of Aristotelian holism: the whole is greater than the sum of its components. But more than that, the whole is affected by each and every part, no matter how insignificant or inconsequential that part may seem at first.

The importance of Busquets silently working behind the scenes and off loading the ball to Xavi can no longer be overlooked as an integral component of an attacking system.

The importance of player profile (Carzola and Rossi for example) can make all the difference. It is for these reasons that the Barcelona system cannot be mimicked entirely, as each and every scenario asks a set of different design problems.

Gary Kleiban put it perfectly:

"It's the little details that make all the difference."

6. DEFENSIVE ORGANISATION: THE BLOCK

The defensive organisation is inevitably interlinked with the attacking attitudes of your approach, this is certainly seen from the Swansea/Barcelona examples given in the previous chapter.

This chapter will directly discuss the differences of the medium, low and high block approaches and their relationship with pressing (transition of losing the ball).

"Our instruction has always been to win the ball back as quickly as possible; to try and win the ball back in six seconds. If you can't, then set up your block. There are three types of block: low, medium and high. Usually, after these six seconds you can set up a your block after not winning it high. The key to pressing is covering your zones and the system of 4-3-3 gives you good coverage on the pitch, allowing you to press in the right zones of the pitch rather than just chasing around."

Chris Davies, Liverpool FC

Valeriy Lobanovskyi often spoke about the variations of the 3 types of pressing in a similar way. Lobanovskyi would often employ all 3 types of pressing (see - 4. The Art of Collective Pressing) as a tactical approach and tool for attacking without the ball. Nonetheless, the 3 blocks are seen in a slightly different light.

They are not tools to regain the ball, but tools to control the opponents use of possession and therefore control the game without the ball.

In an ideal world, the high block is used successfully against a team that try to play out from the back. The low block on the contrary would be used when the desired attacking approach of your team is to counter attack and break forward in numbers.

The 3 blocks also detail a variance in how the team should mark opponents and (again, in the ideal world) the closer the opponent is to your goal, the tighter your team should aim to mark the opponents, to 'make the pitch as small as possible.'

The key concept in all 3 cases however, (whether with a **low, medium or high block**) is for the whole team to act as one. If the defensive line sits deep and yet the remainder of his team sit higher up field, you are left with the problem that Rodgers and Liverpool FC faced against Arsenal (2012/13 first meeting) where 3 simple passes can open up the whole defence and open up space for an attacker to score.

The diagrams to follow on the next page emphasise the importance of reducing the space available to the opposition in such a way.

The Defensive Line Sits Deep and with the Midfield High up the Pitch

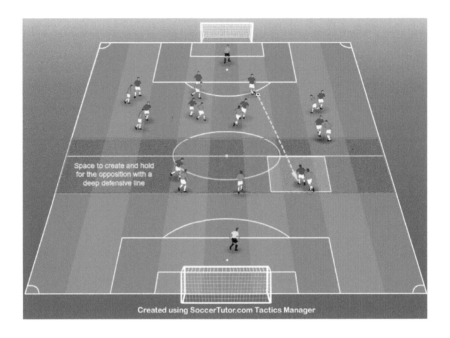

The Defensive Line Is Pushed Higher up the Pitch: Reducing the Space

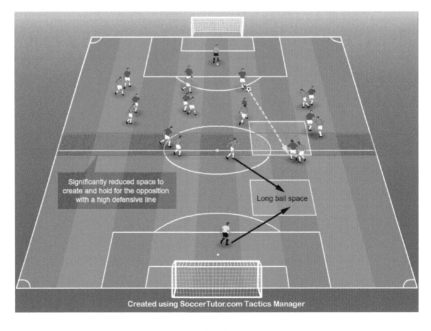

The 3 Types of 'Block'

The High Block

Through high compaction you enable your sweeper goalkeeper and spare central defender the ability to cover space in behind and you significantly reduce the possibilities for the opposition's target man to bring the ball down and invite his players into the play higher up the field.

The simplicity of moving the defensive line up to play in unity brings about a successful approach to regaining possession in the event of the long ball from the opposition (more often than before) and at the same time enables a successful situation for your team to press extremely high up pitch.

Where the design problem does come in to play however, is when you possess a pool of players that consist of slow defenders and the opposition is then enabled to play a long ball and out pace your defensive players to the ball and into a 1 v 1 situation with ease. Therefore, it is not only vital that players have excellent positioning, awareness and the ability to read the game, but also that they are not significantly disadvantaged because of a lack of pace.

The Lower Block

A design solution to this problem may be to play with a lower block. This has implications to the transitions (pressing and location of winning the ball back) and the phases of play.

You are more likely to adopt the Swansea approach of playing out from defence if you have slower players.

Remind yourself at this point, that possession is fundamentally a tool to create more 'obvious' goal scoring opportunities than the opposition. The controlled approach of tiki-taka is not an all out attacking approach but one that is nothing more than control.

The Medium Block

The third option of a medium block offers a middle ground but is often one that is more difficult to execute as the understanding between players needs to be perfected into what exactly constitutes as a 'medium block'. As long as all the players and the coach come to an agreement and understand the implications on ball circulation locations, attacking attitudes and transitions (all the other components), it is then that the medium block can be executed as effectively as the other two (lower and higher). It is a system of agreement between all the components and details.

Conclusion

It is important to consider the act of any 3 of these 'blocks' as a block of the whole team and not just the midfield or defence etc.

The best approach to date is to agree on the amount of space that the team should cover during a block.

Using the relevant case studies, the appropriate distance between the last man and the first man should, while in a block scenario, be fixed at distances that suit the fitness of the team. Barcelona manage to reduce the area of play for the opponents into less than the third of a playing field in length.

It should be noted that this extreme reduction of space should be considered the distance promoted by the most elite performers in the philosophy of tiki taka.

Liverpool FC have taken measures to combat this during the opening months of the 2012/13 season and the inability to perform in unison partially resulted in the alteration on formation and in doing so, clearly employed two clean lines of block with one player feeding in and out of the space in between (see tactical variances chapter).

The block is not to be confused with a defensive approach or to be considered as 'parking the bus' - this is at the extreme level of the block. Instead the block should be considered as a tool to reduce an opposition with the ability to play and in turn, to increase your ability to regain possession through error. The bottom line here is that if the ball is not

regained in the first 6 seconds, the team should fall back into a structural set up of rehearsed positional play, a more rigid structure.

Consider this phase of play as the state between losing the ball and unsuccessfully winning the ball back immediately and the state of winning the ball back playing through 'chaotic moments'; the opposite of 'ball circulation'. You are to break out of this state and into the more aggressive state of pressing when one of the many agreed triggers comes into play.

The fundamental requirement of a successful block is to force your opponents to where you want them to be in possession and to force your opponents into error in vulnerable positions either to counter or to rebuild possession through the chaos of regaining the ball (transition).

The variations of such an approach are explored in the tactical variations section of this book.

7. THE CONCLUSION OF THE FOOTBALLING STATES AND THEIR RELATIONSHIPS

It should now be apparent that the tiki-taka philosophy is anything but linear and simplistic. The states can be divided and described in the pragmatic way in which this book does and there are explicit relations between each of the states. It is the understanding of these states, the relationships between them and creating an appropriate approach to each state that positively impacts the next.

Nevertheless, even with a clear understanding of this tactical design solution, you cannot draw up such an approach without considering the profile of players available to you and the variations (plan B, C and so on) in given scenarios. Those who say a tiki-taka team needs a plan B overlook the fact that within the philosophy here are a number of different approaches or solutions to a number of problem scenarios.

Throughout this text, I have been mindful about directly imposing any suggestion of a 'correct formation'. While those inside the game have promoted the spatial coverage of the 3-4-3 and 4-3-3 formation, It is the aim of this book to enable evolution to continue and I believe it to be formation changes that will inevitably lead to significant evolution of tiki-taka football as it has done so often historically.

It is hoped that a coach may perfect such a philosophy via a less traditional methodology and drive the evolution of the tiki-taka philosophy into the successful unknown, beyond the foreseeable horizon.

The concept I propose is no longer "form follows function". In football terms, the functions are to defend and to attack through particular ideas, like utilising a fast player in attack by playing through balls. Instead I propose that it is line with my favourite architect Mick Pearce's notion of 'form follows process'. The concept that form is to follow process is favoured because when we use function as the aim, we start by having fixed ideas and objectifying players into specific functions. This leads you to having a non-adaptive approach to football in which the player(s) becomes the agent of change, i.e. players performing in isolation and not in collaboration/unison.

The proposal of 'form follows process' enables the tactics and formation to become the agent of change and the team of players to fit within. The supporting diagrams that follow this text provide us with a visual mechanism of states and processes, highlighting a simplistic view of their relationships.

The positional formations selected to harbour the processes and more specifically, the attitude to each of the processes are a result of the process rather than the individual functions (isolated player typologies or a team build around one player's ability).

Above all, the processes result in a singular organism of play. It is worth noting that in Mick Pearce's form follows process approach, they are always carried out to a 'design problem,' such as 'the diurnal shift,' the shift of 2 extreme temperatures between night and day (see the Eastgate Centre designed by Mick Pearce), which in footballing terms translates to a number of developmental and tactical problems (see tactical variances).

It is said that Pep Guardiola would spend the first 10 to 15 minutes only observing the opposition and not the performance of his own players to achieve a true analysis of the opponent's process of play (if they were having a negative impact on the success of Barcelona's tactics).

After analysing Guardiola would quickly respond with an appropriate form that responds to the processes of the game, an adjustment of his default theoretically perfect tactics. Guardiola would plan for every possible outcome and know the exact adjustment to form he would make as he would spend days playing out the game in his head over and over again, with each and every possibility occurring.

Through 'form follows process' in football you arrive at the same conclusion that my friend Mick Pearce arrived at in architectural design: a system that is the agent of change, rather than the persons within it. A way of 'perfect football' within an adaptive structure that responds to tactical issues experienced throughout the duration of a football match.

Coaching The Tiki Taka Style Of Play

Liverpool FC Ecosystem of Play

The following diagrams detail the inter-relationships that you are required to understand and explain simply to your team of players. I have used an example of Liverpool FC's ecosystem of play during a Premier League match in the 2012/13 season.

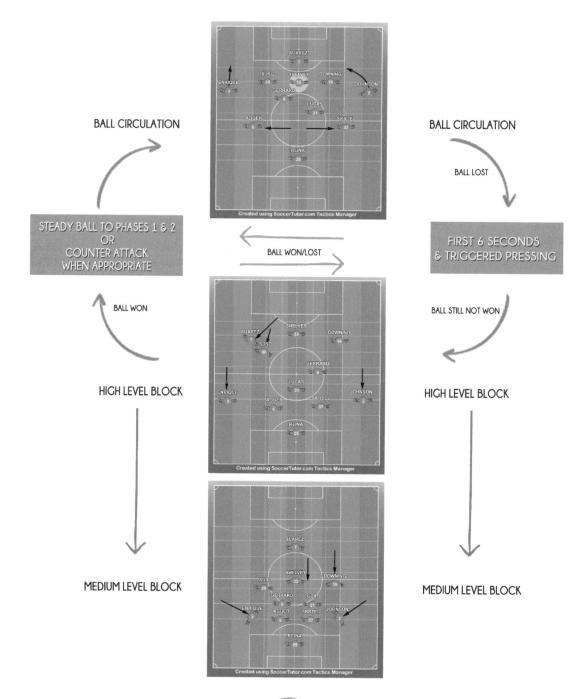

BALL CIRCULATION

BALL CIRCULATION

BALL LOST

STEADY BALL TO PHASES 1 & 2
OR
COUNTER ATTACK
WHEN APPROPRIATE

BALL WON/LOST

FIRST 6 SECONDS
& TRIGGERED PRESSING

BALL WON

BALL STILL NOT WON

HIGH LEVEL BLOCK

HIGH LEVEL BLOCK

MEDIUM LEVEL BLOCK

MEDIUM LEVEL BLOCK

Coaching The Tiki Taka Style Of Play

8. THE INDIVIDUAL BASIC TASKS

It was put to you in the previous chapters that in the concept of 'form follows process', 'form' was to mean formation. In truth 'form' is a much more complex than that as form also refers to the tactical strategies that are employed by the team (whether default or as a result of a tactical problem).

Should a team decide to sit deeper and circulate the ball in a more defensive manner and rely on a more 'loose' number 10 sitting further forward, this is replicated in both formation and in the tactical strategy on controlling the game deeper, perhaps due to a lack of space further up field.

This result is that the opposition are left with a choice, do they allow their defensive midfielder to push on and still man mark the now deeper sitting second midfielder (which would then allow the 'loose' number 10 a 1 v 1 with his marker) or do they allow the deeper sitting midfielder to dictate possession in a deeper role? The change therefore asks a number of new questions of the opposition.

The point that is made here, is that it is not the person playing that position that is the agent of change, but the formation and tactical strategy with the same players. It is this 'adaptability' to tactical problems that the system strives for.

Nevertheless, in all 'forms', players will undertake a set of specific basic tasks within a very particular 'form' (strategy and formation). Of course the pool of players available will have a significant impact on the form you set as the default system, but the philosophy principles will never be lost.

Case Study: A Typical 4-3-3 into a 3-4-3

The following explanation given in this chapter is not comprehensive but provides a brief example of how basic player tasks may come together to create a whole, alongside the tactical solutions to each of the states.

The basic tasks given to players in set positions should reflect both the ability of players available to you (and their characteristics) and the complimentary tactical solutions to each of states of play.

"If certain players do not carry out their tasks properly on the pitch, then their colleagues will suffer."

Louis Van Gaal

4-3-3 / 3-4-3: An Interchangeable Positional System

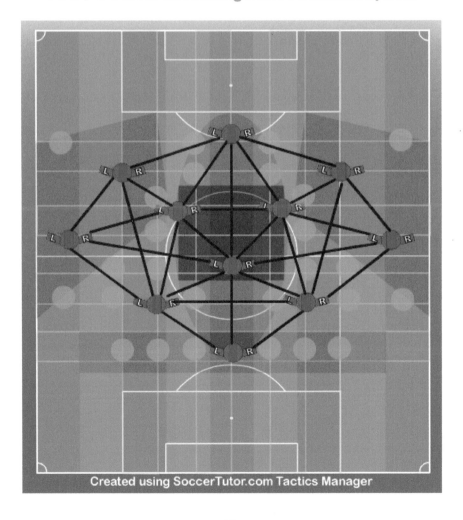

Coaching The Tiki Taka Style Of Play

(1) The Sweeper Goalkeeper

In all positional formations, the goalkeeper in the tiki-taka philosophy is expected to play as a sweeper who has the secondary role as a goalkeeper, 'secondary' as it is expected he will play the majority of the game distributing the ball with his feet.

Throughout history this has been a consistent feature of possession based teams since the reign of Total Football in the 1970s. The goalkeeper is responsible for starting phase one of play, that of building the game up from the back through the two central defenders who have pushed wide and the 'controller(s)' who drops deep.

As a secondary approach to distribution, the goalkeeper should be able to recognise the opposition's strategy in terms of pressing. If the opponents are pressing high and pose a threat to him his short distribution, he must look for alternative methods.

This alternative typically involves looking for the second or third line of pass, i.e. a lofted accurate pass to those who are unmarked further up the pitch (should those nearby be marked). This is something I witnessed Pepe Reina and the reserve team goalkeeper practising after general training at Melwood as they would loft the ball out over a dummy figure and into a marked out square wide on the halfway line. If all the team-mates are marked, this typically means that those furthest forward have less opponents around them and this option should be exploited where necessary. The straight long ball forward is avoided throughout and an angled pass to feet is preferred when possible.

The ball may return to the goalkeeper over and over, and this should not be seen as a problematic situation but an opportunity to continue to circulate the ball. The goalkeeper is not expected to act as a Rene Higuita 'all risk taking' type of player, but he is expected to be consistent and reliable, and a player that the defenders can trust when they pass the ball back to his feet.

Characteristics for the ideal profile of player in this role include composure, the ability to pass, the recognition of when to come out and sweep balls from behind and the ability to recognise the opposition's tactical approach quickly and communicate his analysis effectively.

Essentially the goalkeeper's 3 main roles in this position are:

1. Distribution (first phase of play)
2. To act as a pressure relief for his under pressure teammates (through a side to side calculated movement)
3. The ability to analyse the situations developing in front of them

Of course, a goalkeeper should also be able to satisfy requirements of a typical goalkeeper too, but there is an emphasis on these additional characteristics since these aspects of play are more likely to occur in a successful team employing this philosophy of play.

(2 & 3) The Wing Backs

The full back has evolved to become one of the most important aspects of a team that wishes to build up from deep and offer width through essentially unmarked channels. Dennis Bergkamp once picked up on the ability of Ashley Cole to break forward and commented that no winger has the capacity or attention to track as far back as Cole pushed on forward so consistently.

In a system of play that asks so much of the full back, the profile of player that fits in this role has to display an array of footballing characteristics.

When the team is in the block phase of play, this player is first and foremost a traditional full back, tucked inside to work alongside the central defenders. Guardiola from time to time singled out Dani Alves for criticism in that he struggled to drop back in time to perform this vital role asked of him.

In an ideal scenario, after possession is lost, the full back participates immediately to press if appropriate and then drops back to his position in the block. In this phase of block, we should view this full back role as one that supports the line of defence.

In the phase of ball circulation this player advances to a less rigid support player for the midfield and attacks further forward and this is why the profile of this player should have not only a great understanding of defensive positioning, but a great engine to drive up field and back into position. More than that however, the player is to play a key role in ball circulation and aim to get to the byline should the team look to cross as a strategy. And let us not forget that the full back has a vital role in pressing in more advanced areas of the pitch, often pushing on to cover for the wider attacking players as they move inwards.

One of the key roles of this player is to understand his role in defence. For example, imagine a scenario where an attacker has the ball in the middle third of the field on one of the flanks, the defender would do well to force the attacker further out towards the touchline rather than infield. This would significantly reduce the

number of options available to the attacker.

However, when the opposition has the ball in their own defensive third, it can be beneficial to force the attacker inwards as a ball won here is more likely to result in a counter attacking goal.

The return risk is therefore calculated by the player himself and decision making is key. In any circumstance, the player should consider the wider implications of his approach in defending.

Manipulating a scenario where you can create a defensive situation that can outnumber the opponent is often an ideal scenario if into an area that does not put your team at danger elsewhere.

2 v 2 Situations

In a 2 v 2 situation, the defender is obligated to stay with his attacker unless one of the following events occurs:

- The attacker's position is no longer considered dangerous

- Another defender comes over and takes over the marking responsibilities

- The opponent that has the ball has beaten your teammate and takes up a more dangerous position

- The opponent who may still be marked has taken up a position so dangerous that it requires you to take action to aid the block

It is therefore self-evident that as a player with a vast number of decisions to make in a flexible role in this system, the profile of the player must be able to read the game consistently well in defence and attack while acting as a support to all four moments of the game (all four states).

Coaching The Tiki Taka Style Of Play

(4 & 5) The Central Defenders

The typical central defender is not asked to participate in ball circulation as often as they are in this philosophy of play, however in order to support the goalkeeper's distribution and act as a pressure relief for players further forward, it is necessary that these players are comfortable at using the ball under high pressures where a mistake is often punished.

A lot of defenders struggle with this notion of being composed under the pressure of knowing that if they make a mistake, it is likely that they will be at fault for a goal. This is not an environment experienced at the same pressure anywhere else on the pitch.

The defenders are asked to almost become defensively minded full backs, on a far more advanced line of play These two players are also key when communicating the compaction of the entire team by pushing the line up to the necessary area.

Ashley Williams of Swansea was noted to have played the most direct 'long' balls in the English Premier League under Brendan Rodgers in 2011/12. However, the type of 'long ball' was often one drilled along the floor into vertical lines of play that players in more advanced roles moved into.

Similarly, Van Basten and Rijkaard often spoke about the invisible chord that exists between the last line of defence and the front line. It is for these purposes that at least one of the two central defenders boasts an excellent ability to not only pass the ball, but to have a good vision for movement ahead of him.

While the defensive roles of the central defenders are imperative, the ability to be able to participate in ball circulation is as important in this system of play. They play a vital role in the early phases of the build up play.

THE MIDFIELD TRIO (6, 8, 10):
(6) The Controller (Defensive Midfielder)

Typically, the player in this role is perceived as someone with a limited technical ability. However, in the more successful advocators of this philosophy, this player is just the opposite and is someone with a fantastic technical ability. More importantly, the profile of the player should be one that can read the game tactically better than any other on the field. Some of Sergio Busquet's best moments are those where he does not even touch the ball, but instead lets the ball run on towards Xavi.

This player is asked to drop in and out of the void left in between the two widely positioned central defenders to receive the ball and be available to those in possession.

However, Chris Davies and Brendan Rodgers see this player as a 'controller' and someone who dictates play from deep while linking the phases of play. This is the ideal position in terms of not being under the same extreme pressures as the central defenders and yet not typically surrounded by opponents who have a great ability to mark or tackle.

In the Champions League final (2008), Wayne Rooney was asked to drop deep to mark the controller and reduce the ability for Barcelona to build up play. However, Pep Guardiola saw this as an opportunity to drop a second controller in and ask Xavi to play deeper. From that moment on Barcelona regained the control of possession and went on to win the final.

The profile of this player can vary from someone who is restricted to short and simple passes but asked to break up the opposition and support teammates who are in possession, to someone who dictates the game from a deeper role. This may be a decision made because of tactical rationale or the ability of the available players.

Coaching The Tiki Taka Style Of Play

(8) The Second Controller or Central Midfield Playmaker

"A sumptuous scythe of dexterous pleasure, to deduce the length no eye could measure. Crystalline, perfect, to within a hair, he hit the pass that wasn't there."
Dan Leydon[28]

28   Leydon, D. (2011). Playmaker. Available: http://hotfootynews. blogspot.co.uk/2011/06/playmaker. html. Last accessed June 2013.

Coaching The Tiki Taka Style Of Play

As mentioned earlier in the Xavi scenario, this is a position of much flexibility tactically. This player typically is asked to act as a traditional playmaker and make key passes.

In the situation where this strategy is not being maximised, it is often effective to drop this player back into a deeper role. This therefore asks a variety of questions of the opposition's approach to closing down his new found space and has an array of implications.

In the scenario where this player becomes a second controller in the deeper role, it is imperative for the second more advanced midfielder to take full advantage of the space around him. This 'No.10' should thrive in the space he now finds as a solo advanced midfielder.

The ideal example for such a player in this position, a player who alters between controlling the ball in the central midfield position and a deeper position is that of Barcelona's Xavi, who is nicknamed 'Maki' which is short for maquina or 'machine' in English. This industrial nickname for such a creative and inventive player seems odd but the consistency and discipline that Xavi displays when in possession is superhuman.

This player should be one who understands the impacts of his approach to passing when given the ball and patience at times is dictated by the playmakers tempo of passing in particular areas of the field.

There needs to be an ability to understand that just because a player is free in a more advanced position on the field, that it does not mean you should pass it to him as he may not have the immediate support around should he receive the pass. It is this foresight and planned approach to passing that completes a successful playmaker, not just the ability to pass well.

(10) The Box to Box or Advanced Central Midfielder

The relationship between the midfield trio (6, 8 and 10) is one that is extremely important to the overall approach to the system of play. Should the midfield consist of two deeper midfielders and one more advanced this player is given more freedom. On the other hand, if the midfield is made up on one controller and two midfielders further forward in a partnership, then a new set of requirements is put on this player all together. The partnership is just that, an intimate and positional relative relationship that results in both players having the engine to get forward to support when in the more advanced areas of the field, but then to get back in for the block.

The quick thinking of the midfield is often key to dropping out of the block and winning the ball back during a triggered press, therefore there is a lot of unspoken communication between these players that only comes through experience of playing together.

For these three midfield roles it is easy to point at Busquets, Xavi and Iniesta and say 'those are the role models and the profile of the players we need', however you must understand that the Barcelona model of those three is just one solution to the profile's available to Barcelona.

This is best understood when examining the struggle of Brendan Rodgers at Liverpool who has varied between the two systems of a '2-1' and a '1-2' midfield, both systems which at the time of writing is yet to fully flourish into the level of understanding needed between the three to function successfully.

It is the system that the manager chooses that details the basic tasks for each of these three players in midfield and the characteristics and typology of player profile that is then required.

Perhaps you have a player who would thrive in the more solitude number 10 role and therefore it benefits the team to play with two controllers as a default system, but of course for the most part this is an often unnoticed tactical decision in the most successful teams.

In all three roles there is a level of technical ability expected that results in the players being able to play confidently in congested zones and Xavi often speaks about the positive impact of the Rondo or concept of 'a mig toc' (half a touch) to give an idea of the importance of quick passing and the ability to circulate the ball with freedom despite the pressure.

This partly explains the Swansea approach on converting wingers into central midfielders (Britton and Gower) as they would have possessed a typical winger's ability to dribble and keep the ball away from their opponents.

It is also often the role of each of these players to dribble with a different purpose of getting from AB, but to draw players out of position in front of them and in doing so open up the spaces for the more advanced players.

Coaching The Tiki Taka Style Of Play

THE ATTACKING TRIO (7, 11 & 9):
(7 & 11) The Inside Forwards

This position is one that has gradually evolved for Barcelona over Pep Guardiola's era of management. Sure the inside forward existed long before then in football, but for Barcelona it was a case of trying to accommodate great players into a system of play. Thierry Henry, Messi, Iniesta, Samuel Eto'o, Pedro, Cuenca, Afellay, Sanchez and many more have played this role over the last five years for Barcelona and each of them has brought with them their own unique take on how the position should be played.

Subsequently we can only conclude that this player's basic tasks are that of support and dynamic movement in the attacking third when in ball circulation, and the attitude of the player on the ball varies from one player profile to another.

In all cases, this is a player who can dribble with the ball, has a dynamic approach to off the ball movement and can both assist and score goals from the most unlikely circumstances. To say that these two players should be wingers converted to inside forwards (Sanchez, Cuenca etc) is to undermine the success found using strikers converted to inside forwards (Eto'o and Henry) in the year that Barcelona won everything!

It goes without saying that this role belongs to a very particular type of player (Swansea - Dyer, Routledge, Sinclair, Sterling etc). In all cases, this player is to play a huge role in both the transitional phases of play as part of an immediate press or finding space to offer themselves on a counter attack in threatening spaces.

With the growing conclusion that the ideal is to have the player playing in the more central role in attack is to drop off into deeper positions (Suarez, Messi etc) it would be an expectation on this player to have the ability to get in behind the more advanced line of play and into any gaps left in defence.

Lastly, should one inside forward have the ball in a crossing situation, it is a requirement for the other inside forward to find space inside the box and add numbers to the attackers inside the box to outnumber the opposition in particular areas inside the box.

Coaching The Tiki Taka Style Of Play

(9) The False 9 or Central Striker

The False 9 is a role widely covered in the media with the attention that Messi receives at Barcelona and the intrigue caused by Spain playing Fabregas in this role during the 2012 European Cup.

Simply, this should be a player that can win matches through creativity and confidence. The level of risk taken by this player is considered much higher than others in the team during ball circulation. Messi gave the ball away more than any other player in Europe (bar 4 others) in the top five leagues (2011).

This does not indicate that Messi is unable to hold on to the ball in any way, but that he is expected to attempt passes and dribbles that are considered riskier than those that others would take elsewhere.

This is both accepted and expected when a player plays this role of chance creation.

This player should attract attention and cause headaches for opposition defenders. If they should choose to follow him out of position, the defenders would leave gaps for the inside forwards to exploit and at the same time become vulnerable to being left 1 v 1 against the false 9, who typically would be the most skilful player on the team.

Should the opposition choose not to follow the player, they are then defeated in allowing the player to pick up the ball in the dangerous centralised zones to create with freedom. However, if the wrong type of player profile is selected to play this 'false 9' role, the player becomes ineffective and the approach to attacking falls to pieces. There are not too many players in the mould of Messi and Suarez in the world and therefore it is more likely that a team employing this philosophy finds a solution in other ways.

The bottom line is that this player needs to win games through being effective and by creating space for others, being a link-up player who relies on an excellent level of technical ability to do so (rather than aerial ability). This perception of such a player explains why Cesc Fabregas was considered the ideal candidate for such a role for Spain in the 2012 European

Championship. There are a number of examples of the variety of players who could fit this role as a 'technical number 9' (often viewed as a traditional number 10) such as Bergkamp, Cassano, Raul etc. On the other hand, it seems to be a position within the team that is entirely determined by the strengths of the players available (Eto'o for Barcelona 2008 for example).

Aside from the ability to create and link during ball circulation, the player should also play a key role in the pressing transition and become a team player rather than 'just a striker.'

Team

What has become apparent is that there is much flexibility in the player profile of the selected players and that each component (player) is considered in relation to another. The key message of this text is that while the player profiles are important and you must seek suitable players for the philosophy, it is the form of the team that is most important, particularly as you are to select the more attacking players in the team.

It is an adaptable approach to football that should solve a number of tactical problems rather than an approach that harbours 11 world class individuals: *'The whole is greater than the sum of its parts.'*

9. TACTICAL SOLUTIONS AND VARIATIONS OF THE FORM

This particular chapter is arguably the most significant chapter offered in this book and the purpose is to offer a variety of different solutions to the 5 most reoccurring tactical problems. Pep Guardiola often analysed the opposition's tactics and nothing else in the first 10 to 15 minutes of a game to arrive at conclusions about tactical responses and he would have imagined every scenario before the game to quickly arrive at a decision. He would adjust the processes that make up the team's form and arrive at an alternative form that was appropriate to the particular opposition being faced.

While this book does not claim to offer the solution to every single problem that exists or necessarily the correct solution to every problem, it does draw on a wealth of professional experience of those interviewed in the making of this book. From Barcelona and Liverpool to significant others involved with the professional game, a great value of importance was placed on coming away with a comprehensive set of solutions for tactical problems.

It is hoped that with a deep understanding of a complex approach to football developed throughout reading this book, you may arrive at a few alternative solutions yourself and no other idea excites me more than watching a football game and arriving at well founded opinions on how a team should respond tactically to particular problems listed in this chapter.

There are direct relationships found between particular processes within the philosophy that work. For example, the interlinked relationship of playing with a short passing approach to ball circulation and that of players being positioned perfectly for immediate pressing are conducive of one another.

Whereas, any other combination of approaches to these two processes would result in a dramatic impact differential in the success of one or the other.

Many of the following tactical problems arrive at solutions through understanding the relationships between the processes and through a consideration of the foreseeable impacts.

Tactical Problem 1:

Struggling to Control Possession and Build up from the Back from a Goal Kick

One of the most familiar scenarios on a football field is that of a goal kick and realising the potential to use this scenario to your advantage is key to controlling possession in games. A team that struggles to play the ball out from the back and hold on to possession may face a number of problems that limit your level of control.

This scenario assumes that you are looking to play with width and depth through your central defenders positioning themselves out wide, the full backs pushing on and one controller (defensive midfielder) dropping into the central space. Let us take the example of a goal kick, a reoccurring scenario that can be practiced in training sessions and recreated realistically.

One of the ways in which you can successfully coach these scenarios is to employ a 'starting point' in your training sessions and treat goal kicks as just that and not a quick 'kick back into play'. By forcing your players to set up properly for a goal kick in training sessions, they will recognise this scenarios in match situations.

Nothing is gained by quickly kicking the ball back into play through a short pass.

The first understanding required from the players and the goalkeeper in particular is the hierarchy of options. Should the opposition be positioned in a way that does not allow the first option to be carried out successfully, the goalkeeper should look to option 2, 3 and so on.

Passing Options from a Goal Kick

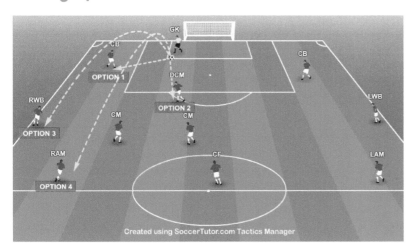

Created using SoccerTutor.com Tactics Manager

If the opposition are pressing high up the field, this should not be seen as a 'problem' but an opportunity to play the ball further forward. The longer goal kicks should never be seen as 'how far the goalkeeper can kick the ball' but as a lofted and controlled pass to the player in space. In truth, although the diagram labels option 1 as the shortest pass to a central defender, this is in fact the most common option.

The most desirable option would be to play the ball forward into the more advanced areas of play. The trick is to force the opposition into thinking your options are as in the supporting diagram.

Playing From The Defence Through To The Midfield

Beyond the goal kick, you may experience difficulty in playing the ball out from a defensive line into the midfield and attack. This may occur if the opposition allows the defenders to dwell on the ball but blocks off any passes further forward and in some circumstances the opposition may identify the defender who is weaker on the ball and allow him time on the ball.

A Liverpool FC coach highlighted that in this circumstance, it may be effective to bring on a ball playing midfielder who is equally able to play in central defence. In doing just this, you have taken the problem of the opposition 'letting your defenders play' (players who we can assume aren't as comfortable with their range of passing as your central midfielders) and turned this problem into an opportunity to bring on a player who is particularly comfortable at playing through the lines.

At Swansea City under Brendan Rodgers of 2011/12 and in particular against West Bromwich Albion FC in the away fixture, we saw games where Leon Britton would fall back into a central defence role and actually stay there for the remainder of the game. This solution does not require a change of formation but a change in attitude of the player on the ball (and perhaps a change of player to achieve this).

A similar problem may be that your controller is being allowed time on the ball but the opposition are marking the supporting central midfielders out of the game. In this scenario, there is an opportunity to really test the decision making of the opposition by playing with two deep controllers and only one supporting midfielder further forward. In doing this, you have asked the opposition whether they are going to allow two controllers the time and space to dictate play or push on further forward and continue to mark the midfielder who has fallen into a deeper position. If the marking opponent decides to follow your deep midfielder into this position, the opposition are now left with a one vs. one situation with your more advanced midfielder - it is therefore beneficial for you if you have a player who can really dominate in these circumstances. Although this change may appear

to be one of minor details, you have really created a situation that will test the opposition far more than you currently are if they have marked your advanced midfielders man-to-man and are not allowing your midfield any space to receive the ball.

Brendan Rodgers often alternates between playing with two controllers and one central midfielder more advanced and using only one controller and two players further forward (like Barcelona do). The function of the controller is to simply control both the ball and the opposition through being tactically aware of spaces to fill when out of possession, while the player further forward needs to have the ability to break forward and get back in position to keep up with the area of action in play. The relationship between the three is key to the systematic play within the system and it's processes; with the wrong balance in the core of the midfield against a dangerous opposition, the whole philosophy and way of playing can be torn apart and appear weak.

In all solutions, you must know your own players' strengths and weaknesses. If you're able to identify a player who is better technically with the ball in confined spaces than another, a player who can demonstrate an array of passing options and a player who is able to dominate in one vs. one scenarios, then you are in a position to solve the problems listed above through simple, yet effective, positional adjustments.

204

Tactical Problem 2:

The opposition are sitting in a deep low block (also known as *"Parking the Bus"*)
and it has become increasingly difficult to find spaces to penetrate further forward.

If the opponents have the discipline to control your possession by forcing you to play in the space they have left in the wider areas of the field and in the middle third of the pitch, you will need to find a solution that allows you to break beyond the opposition block and test their discipline. Anthony Hudson recalled the Chelsea vs. Barcelona semi-final in the Champions League 2012 and suggested that Barcelona played into Chelsea's hands by not being able to break beyond Chelsea's extremely low-block. Hudson believes that if Barcelona allowed Chelsea to play the ball out from the back and inviting Chelsea to come forward with the ball, Barcelona would then be able to steal the ball and break beyond Chelsea's defensive block, particularly at Stamford Bridge where Chelsea would have been urged on by their home support to play the ball more often than they would have at Camp Nou.

Away from the Chelsea vs. Barcelona game, the solutions are found while in possession of the ball. If you can play well with a playmaker (often the controller in a deep position), you can attempt to pick apart the disciplined deep and narrow block by using the dribble as a way to provoke or tease the opposition forward to try and steal the ball.

By taking a touch that could be perceived as a 'poor touch' by the opposition, the opponent may attempt to break from his position to win the ball. In this scenario, the balance of power is in the hands of the player who has purposefully 'mis-controlled' the ball as he is not in the position of needing to deal with the action-reaction time delay. One of the best solutions that Barcelona demonstrate on a weekly basis is just this, the ability to run with the ball to provoke or to tease and not to dribble or beat their man in a 1 v 1 scenario.

When Liverpool FC signed Daniel Sturridge in January 2013, they attempted to tackle the problem of being able to penetrate in the final third (particularly when the opposition would sit back in a deep, low and disciplined block). Liverpool were now able to play Luis Suarez in a slightly deeper role in the 'zone 14' (of 18

equal zones) and central area; by doing this, Liverpool would no longer allow the opposition to control their play and would often resort to doing just what the opposition wanted them to do, to play the ball into the wider areas of the field and look to attempt crosses as a means of creating goals despite being set up as a team to want to play through the central areas.

Rodgers would have preferred his Liverpool to use the wider areas as a way of stretching the opposition from left to right to bring about gaps in a now decompact and narrow defensive block (see the theoretical 'attacking pitch view' diagram on the next page).

Coaching The Tiki Taka Style Of Play

Theoretical Attacking Pitch View Diagram

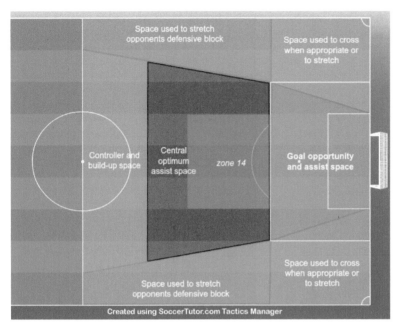

There are a number of options that a team can explore when faced with the situation of the opposition sitting deep and preventing any penetration.

The use of a playmaker offers arguably one of the most effective solutions that fits within the philosophy, a solution that avoids shooting from distance and handing the ball back to the opposition to frustrate you further.

By understanding that the opponents are looking to counter attack and pounce on any mistakes, but allow you to pass the ball freely in the first 2 phases of play, you can look to find solutions within this problematic situation. The opposition are sitting deep and your deep lying playmaker or 'controller' (as Chris Davies and Brendan Rodgers call the role), is able to receive the ball time and time again under little pressure as players sit off and block the space in front of him and man mark many of the controller's passing options out of the game. You, as the team in possession, are left with 2 real options:

1. To continue to pass the ball horizontally to test the organisation of the oppositions deep block and man marking capabilities. This way you hope to stretch the opponents and play through the gaps left vertically.

"You have to test the organisation, move the game, move the ball...once you keep moving them side to side in order to penetrate, someone losing their concentration."

Brendan Rodgers

2. If the opposition is tightly compact and does not offer any opportunities to play forward effectively, your controller needs to begin to function more creatively. This does not mean to play with an excessive amount of opportunism, but to pull players out of position further forward using other methods. One of these methods is called the 'false touch' and involves the controller taking a touch that leads the opposition to believe they can win the ball and counter, consequently breaking forward to try and win the ball. As the opponent leaves his space to challenge for the ball, the controller is now able to play the ball into the newly vacant space further forward and in turn, as each of the players further forward moves, the opposition is now more stretched and prone to an effective penetration through the deep block.

One of the best solutions that Barcelona demonstrate on a weekly basis is the ability to run with the ball to provoke or to tease (and not to just dribble or beat their man) in a 1 v 1 scenario. This solution and the 'false touch' go hand in hand as solutions to such a problem.

'The False Touch' - Example

1

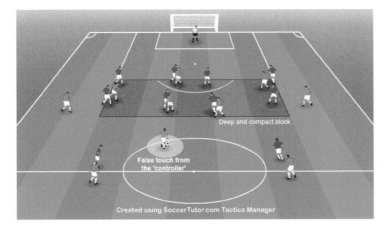

The 'controller' is in possession just inside the opposition half.

The opposition have 8 players in to deep compact lines ahead of him.

He makes a 'false touch' with the intention of drawing one of the players out.

2

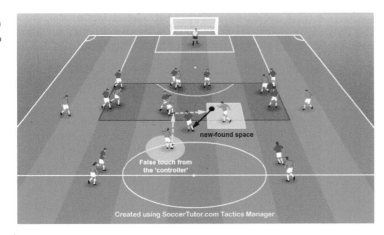

The centre midfielder is drawn out of position to try and win the ball.

This provides space for a teammate to receive the ball.

A player receives the ball in the newfound space after 2 passes (as shown).

The objective of the 'false touch' is to enable simple football and offer the players in the final phases of the play more space and therefore the ability to penetrate effectively.

"Playing simple soccer is the most difficult thing of all."
Johan Cruyff[29]

In the scenario's above, the importance of the controller to the team is obvious. Nonetheless, there are also a number of solutions for other problems on the field when tactically things are not going to plan.

---

29 *Barend, F., Van Dorp, H. (1999). Ajax Barcelona Cruyff The ABC An Obstinate Maestro. London: Bloomsbury Publishing PLC; New edition. 22.*

Coaching The Tiki Taka Style Of Play

Tactical Problem 3:

The profile of players available to you make it increasingly difficult to control the games through the theoretical 4-3-3 (3-4-3) and requires a positional system that still provides the options both in attack and to play out from the back.

This scenario is one that Brendan Rodgers faced during his earlier stages as the new Liverpool manager (2012/13) and required him to rethink his preferred system. Rodgers demonstrated that this particular philosophy of football is not bound by its traditional formation as many would believe. He played with a 5-1-4 formation where the 2 full backs would push into advanced positions and become wingers when in possession.

The change of formation in reality alters very little for the 'in possession' positional system of the 3-4-3 formation (see supporting images) and requires a similar system of positional interchanges.

The team still played with 3 at the back (seen as 2 wide central defenders and 1 controller in a central defence area). In midfield, Rodgers looked for a central midfield duo to complete the triangles of passing options while in possession and the 2 full backs that have pushed on to support them in the wider advanced positions.

Liverpool's 5-4-1 without Possession

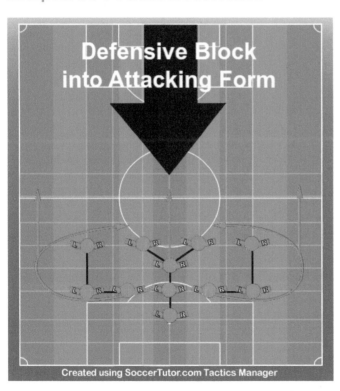

The original 2 players placed on the flanks of the midfield 4 are to push on into the final third and support the lone striker and despite being reported to play 5-4-1, Liverpool played a 3-5-2 while in possession and a 5-1-4 without possession.

But it was not the formations that intrigued most, rather the transitional positional shifts that took place as Liverpool gained possession and progressed further forward with the ball.

This is the Liverpool eco-system of play (temporarily employed late 2012).

Liverpool's 3-5-2 in Possession

Attacking Form

While Liverpool did not find any significant success when employing this formation, theoretically it would be possible to succeed with such a formation if your rotational players possessed the fitness and speed required to succeed in the attacking third.

Secondly, the striker and player that fills the void behind the striker would be required to defend in the defensive block and therefore any opportunity to succeed in the counter attack would be unlikely.

It is for this reason that I believe this formation would struggle as a solution in the English Premier League, where the counter attack is currently a significant source of goal scoring and would need to be considered as a method of goal scoring.

Throughout the 2012/13 season Liverpool explored their own eco-system of play further still as they attempted to find a system of play that allowed for them to flourish during the 4 processes of the game and find the right balance of width and central play specific to the Premier League:

1. Ball circulation (attacking)

2. The defensive block

3 &4. The 2 transitions

It is imperative however, that the coach who is assisting the team playing should be able to identify why a team's eco-system is not successfully functioning. This may be that the opposition are able to counter attack too quickly and that in response the coach identifies positioning, pressing and the advantages of such a scenario.

Underpinning this philosophy is the element of control. Control is to be considered as something much more than ball circulation alone but to include the control of a defensive block and the remainder of the eco-system of play, to control with and without the ball.

Coaching The Tiki Taka Style Of Play

Tactical Problem 4:

You have set your midfield up with 2 controllers and 1 number 10 further forward. Your team have a lot of possession but are struggling to play passes forward and control possession in the final third.

When you employ a system of play that includes 2 deeper controllers and 1 central midfielder in a more advanced position, you alter the general passing network. While you may have decided to use 2 controllers to control the game and keep possession, you have taken away a passing option further forward and in doing so affected the whole system of play. In the supporting images (below) the passing network clearly illustrates the significant alterations made between the two alternative system in midfield (contrast the two images).

4-2-3-1 with 2 Controllers

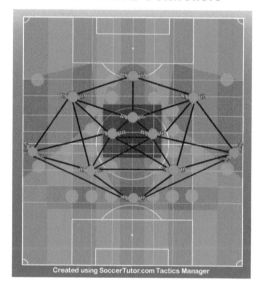

4-1-4-1 with 1 Controller

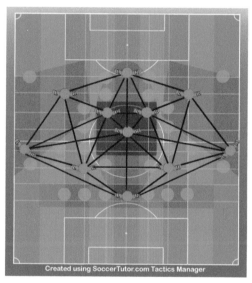

By changing to a system with 1 controller and 2 advanced central midfielders (4-1-4-1 diagram) you pass on some of the playmaking responsibilities to the central defenders and improve the chances of finding a player in a more advanced area of the field.

More than that, you have increased the passing network in the final third and therefore you have brought about the desirable change required.

However, you must be aware that you may be compromising the level of control you previously had as the opposition are unlikely to allow the advanced midfielders the same space and time that they would have found in the deeper role.

To emphasise the impact that this change may have, you should consider the change to the average positioning of the full back. The full back will now find more support centrally in more advanced positions and will therefore (if instructed) be able to support the play in the final third more often as passing options are less horizontal than before. This is a point that Brendan Rodgers highlighted in press conferences throughout the 2012/13 season.

Tactical Problem 5:

You find that your defensive line is too slow to play with the high line necessary for the theoretical system of play and is suffering under the pressure of quicker strikers.

As identified earlier in the book (the chapter on the Defensive Organisation) the theoretical system requires the defensive line to squeeze up and significantly reduce any space for the opposition to utilise their target man. However, if you are presented with a playing squad that does not offer the right player profile for such a system, you must look to adapt your approach and eco-system of play.

Swansea City FC under Brendan Rodgers (2011/12) controlled games through retaining possession as Barcelona do, but did so with the ball in deeper positions. Brendan Rodgers would have analysed the strengths and weaknesses of the players available before looking to stamp his twist on the Swansea philosophy. Swansea did not possess the fitness levels or athleticism that Barcelona found much success with but did have players in advanced positions that would flourish with space to run with the ball into (Sinclair, Dyer and Routledge).

To turn the 'tactical problem' into a tactical opportunity Swansea City put a greater emphasis on ball playing defenders and handed an even greater responsibility to the deep lying controller (Leon Britton). By looking to control the opposition through their dominance of deep possession, Swansea would invite the opposition to defend higher up the field and allowed the explosive inside forwards/wingers to take advantage of the space to run with the ball into, which would typically be where the defensive block would be set up if they had employed the theoretical system of play that Barcelona advocate.

Liverpool FC under Brendan Rodgers have looked to push on into more advanced playmaking positions and employ the pressing rules outlined earlier in this book to slow down the opposition's counter attacks.

Swansea, positioned in deeper positions, were better placed to deal with such counter attacks.

In short, if you are experiencing the tactical problem of being caught out at the back by holding a high line, it may be better to sit deeper and invite the opposition into a more advanced defensive shape. In order to realise the potential of this alternative approach, the defending players need to be comfortable on the ball, patient and unfazed by high pressure situations. This particular method of play may also benefit teams that do not possess players who can look to create opportunities in the final third amongst a compact deep defensive block. Perhaps you do not possess the high levels of technical abilities in the final third (advanced midfielders and the striker) to create goal scoring opportunities by controlling possession in and around the zone 14 and central areas.

Throughout this book a number of theoretical tactical components have been pieced together, it is however imperative that you understand the inter-relationships and impacts of changing any one component on others. Brendan Rodgers has shown time and time again that he is willing to adjust major details that existed at Barcelona under Guardiola but in all cases

Rodgers will look to compete by controlling possession and employing an effective defensive mechanism that allows for the quickest and most consistent transitions. But none of this came without understanding the basic principles of play, being open minded to change and experimentation in game situations.

Coaching The Tiki Taka Style Of Play

10. WIGAN ATHLETIC FC CASE STUDY
Developing a Possession Game

"Players aged 16-18 need more than just being able to demonstrate technical ability, psychological composure and freedom to be able to make mistakes; in possession, I would say that displaying problem solving tactical intelligence and flexibility within the game is absolutely vital."

Tim Lees[30]
(Wigan Athletic Football Club)

Roberto Martinez is a manager who has found success at both Swansea City FC and Wigan Athletic by implementing a very technical possession based game. Martinez's career highlight to date will most certainly be winning the English FA Cup with a Wigan side whose first XI cost just £11.5 million in transfer fees, compared to the £187 million Manchester City first XI they faced in the 2012/13 FA Cup final.

At less than 10 times the cost of the Manchester side, Martinez's Wigan side controlled the game at Wembley on the 11th of May through brilliant tactical solutions that allowed for the likes of Callum McManaman to isolate the Manchester City left back time and time again.

Martinez is a firm believer that players win matches, not tactics, but the manager and the coaching staff should prepare the players in the best way that they can.

"The players have to find the answers to tactical problems but with guidance from coaches. Players have to be able to recognise numerical situations within games and know exactly where and when to overload.

Overloading is such a vital part of a possession based game...as soon as I say overload, most coaches will see this as your obvious full back overlap thus creating 2v1's out wide or midfielders going 3v2 or 4v3 centrally; 4-3-3 vs 4-4-2 or 4-3-3 vs. a diamond, respectively. But, overloading is much more complex than that."

Lees went on to detail the complexities of 'overloading.' There are 2 different types of overload which are explained on the following pages.

---

30 All quotes in this chapter are those of Tim Lees, Wigan Athletic FC, Youth Development Manager U12-16.

1. Through the Coach:

The setup, principles and system that the coach asks the team to have and implement

If the opposition play 4-4-2 against your 3-5-2, then in general terms we have a 3 v 2 to play the ball out from the back; your 3 defenders against the opposition's 2 forwards. Moving forward you have a 3 v 2 scenario in your favour in central midfield and then a 4 v 4 scenario in the high zones. This means your wingers and attackers are in a position to act on their years of 1 v 1 skill practices.

To further add to this overloading approach, you would have an attacking midfielder who will join in the attacks to create a 5 v 4 scenario in the attacking areas.

3-5-2 (or 4-3-3) vs the 4-4-2:
Positioning & Movement Within the Zones on the Pitch

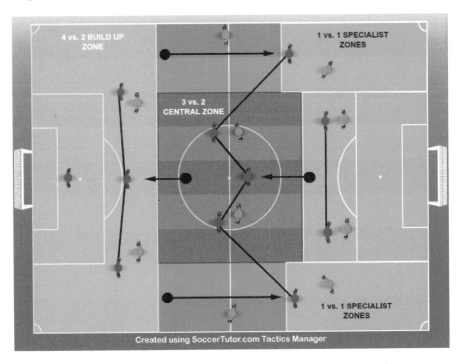

In the above diagram you could see the 3-5-2 that Tim Lees speaks of depicted and you can also see the relationship between the 3-5-2 and the more traditional 4-3-3 formation (retrace players back to movement arrow starting points).

The fundamental message to take from this overloading through system image is to consider how the 3 thirds of the pitch may require particular movement for these overloads to take place. We need to work out whether this is through a more static 3-5-2 formation or through the fluid movement of the 4-3-3 formation which involves a false 9 dropping into midfield and an anchor man in midfield falling back into central defence. Neither is right as all that matters is the overloading of spaces that is key.

Coaching The Tiki Taka Style Of Play

If you analyse the movements of most possession based teams, you will begin to see this particular pattern of central overloads occurring time and time again. These particular principles can be traced back through training exercise 12 in the practices part of this book.

The unmarked opposition wingers in the diagram do not provide a threat during the possession moment of the game. In the event that possession is given back to the opposition and they counter attack effectively, it is the job of the nearest man to delay the opponent for the team's defensive shape to be regained (whatever that may be).

The second key message from this system and Roberto Martinez's philosophy is the concept of creating unpredictable 1 v 1 specialists for particular areas of the field (in this diagram that is the roles of the wingers and 2 central forwards).

While Roberto Martinez has varied this theoretically balanced structure in recent years, the basic elements and structure of how the pitch is viewed still remains vital to his philosophy.

2. Through the Player:

The tactical intelligence of the players within the system

Players must know how to create 2 v 1 and 3 v 2 scenarios all over the pitch as these are the most frequent overload situations in top possession based teams. These overload numbers can be created in virtually any scenario through clever movement and understanding.

While explaining the tactical overloads **Tim Lees'** becomes visibly animated, his enthusiasm fills the room and he begins to paint the picture for me:

"Now where you have a full-back in possession and he is being pressed by the opposition's winger: the 2 vs. 1 scenario can be created in many different ways - your winger offering an angle or dropping deep, a deep lying playmaker (controller) breaking free and offering an option inside or a central defender giving depth in behind the full-back. Once players start to understand the pitch to be a series of mini numerical situations in order to retain and progress then they will develop a possession based game."

Such scenarios can be practiced in training over and over. You can easily mark out a 20 x 20 yard area and play a skill based game of 3 v 2 or 4 v 2. Good players who are comfortable in possession would keep the ball all day long, thus players need to understand the link between the basic principles and the match scenarios. However, if the players just try to keep the ball and have no real context, it becomes a pointless exercise of possession with no purpose and can lead to vulnerability in quick transitions.

Lees is quick to break the optimism for such a mechanic perception of the game:

"Overloads though, cannot be created by the same players with the same movements in the same ways (for example, a false 9 dropping in centrally), they need to be unpredictable, they need to come from the players' own creative input. At any good level, managers will spot predictability, rhythms, patterns and ways that teams try to create overloads thus players must be taught how to be tactically flexible within the system from 16-18yrs. Johan Cruyff is a pioneer in these principles."

Unpredictability was a key theme at Wigan under Roberto Martinez. Martinez does not want 2 players to be the same, 2 players so mechanically trained that they are dictated by a system of play. The same theme flows through to Wigan's attitude towards wing play or crossing.

"At Wigan, we really put our wing play under the microscope with 'unpredictability' being the most important factor."

Unpredictability as Lees tells me, *"is created through coaching, which sounds a complete contradiction but the environment and principles of our sessions create it. Our first team under Roberto are notorious for developing 1 vs. 1 specialists who can deliver in the final third (Moses, Valencia, Maloney and McManaman to name a few). If the opposition play with a low block (very likely against a possession based team) and have recovered well behind the ball then we look to build and probe showing patience in circulation until the killer or vertical pass is on. However, if we can play through the lines quickly and isolate 1 vs. 1 or 2 vs. 1 scenarios in wide areas then we ask our players to have just one focus: find a way, within the next five seconds, of delivering an appropriate cross."*

Wide Players: 1 v1 Situations and Crossing

The concept of educating players to come out on top in 1 v 1 situations is a feature that flows throughout the whole club at Wigan. *"This may be going on the inside, on the outside, executing a skill/trick, a change of speed or a change of direction. The type of cross will depend on both the positioning of the defenders and movement of attacking player(s)."*

From a technical point of view, the cross will be any 1 of the following 4 types of crosses:

1. Delivered early from a deeper area if the full back has not engaged; the best example being Beckham
2. A whipped cross in the corridor between the keeper and defenders (usually the 'second 6 yard box')
3. A pull back or a stand up for a late runner but with disguise and minimal follow through (vital)
4. A drilled cross with the instep which predominantly stays at one height

"At Wigan, our wingers have set-targets of getting four crosses in each half. Although we will speak to them about their delivery, their job is to hit a good area depending on the situation they have managed to create for themselves. By having a two way approach to final third attacks out wide (both build and probe and delivering crosses), I believe that it is very difficult for defenders to predict our play. Regardless of how much the game changes throughout the years, crossing from wide areas will always be problematic if done effectively."

The following parts of this chapter give an account of Wigan FC's philosophy under Roberto Martinez according to Lees, a coach who has worked closely with Martinez to develop such principles throughout the youth teams at Wigan FC. Lees lists off each of the processes and the expectations under each heading.

The Process of Possession (Ball Circulation)

- Play with as much width and depth as possible and look for various ways to create this ("making the pitch as big as possible")

- Play from the back with expansive shape at every possibility but only do so if we have an overload or time/space to play. We play from the back to drag opposing players out of their shape at some point, whenever that may be

- Show a good understanding of how to deal with every defensive strategy the opposition setup with

- Play a patient, possession based passing style through the thirds isolating overloads everywhere at every opportunity

- Play on as many different receiving lines as possible

- Receive the ball in between the lines at every opportunity and look to turn

- View getting in space and not turning to play forward as criminal

- Play with rotation, interchange and unpredictability with regards to movement

- Get product from wide areas and deliveries into the box

- Show intelligent movement in the final third

- Isolate 1 v 1 opportunities in wide areas

The Process of Being Out of Possession (Defensive Block)

- Win possession as high up the pitch as possible

- Show an understanding of how to press high in every situation that the opposition setup

- If opponents have good possession and we may risk being played through/around, we press then immediately drop to be positioned as a narrow and compact unit

- Work off a trigger point and press aggressively when appropriate in 1 v 1 situations

- Show an understanding of which passing lines to cut off when pressing high

- Have the knowledge that it is not often the first man that wins possession but the second or third. The first man's job is to force the opposition into rushing a decision

- Establish whether we show inside or outside and in what areas (body positioning of the defenders)

- The back line must understand when to press, drop and slide

The Attacking Transition

- Upon winning possession, counter attacking has to be the immediate priority

- 7 seconds to score a goal, otherwise build and probe

- Play farthest pass forward

- Cross runs, forward runs, forward passes, dribbling and clever movement are key features

- Team has good shape behind the ball, thus playing forward pass is not a risk

The Defensive Transition

- 4 seconds to recover shape

- Dropping and delaying are key features as opposed to pressing

- Good attitude, work rate and desire are imperative

- Square and/or slow passes are a major risk for the opponents and this should be understood (triggers)

Conclusion

Tim Lees concludes that the specifics of each of these 4 processes are dependant on the opposition and the way in which they play.

"The details of each specific, changes from game to game and within games too. For example, if the opposition setup in a modern version of 4-3-3 then in the moment of the turnover, our immediate thought should be to exploit the space their full backs have left. How we execute the specifics will depend on both the coach's instructions and the player's ability to problem solve in the moment."

"A book containing the tactical details of these four processes would take years to write and would constantly evolve depending on the coaches' exposure, experience and ability to think creatively in the moment."

And with that last quote from Tim Lees, I wish you all the success in the world with your very own personal journey and development as a football coach.

Drawing up a book that includes all aspects of your coaching and playing philosophy is always meant to be a personal journey and this book is not made up of words composed by just myself, but by drawing together the many great minds of those who have found time to tutor and educate not just myself but offered their words as an educational tool for each and every coach, player or parent reading this.

FINAL THOUGHTS:
A SHORT REFLECTIVE MESSAGE

This book throws up many ideas that have been formed over a century and more, ideas that come together to help create the modern day possession orientated control philosophy, but what ties together all the great thinkers in a football related history is the ability to further the existing model.

When I am asked what my philosophy is, I know that the question asked expects me to answer with a simple sentence summing up how I wish to see football played, which would probably run along the lines of "I like to control football matches through keeping possession", but in reality having a football philosophy is far more complex than that. I prefer to think about my philosophy as a set of ideas, rather than ground rooted beliefs: an idea is easy to change, a belief isn't.

However, the one idea that is repeated throughout this philosophy is the team's ability to "control the important spaces on the football field, with and without the ball." That is to say, sometimes it may be better to allow the opposition into your half from time to time (re: Barcelona vs. Chelsea 2012). Therefore in this sense, tiki-taka football is not about possession or pressing but at the earliest stages of implementation, it is about positioning.

Tiki-taka football and all that goes with it, is therefore concluded as a way of playing that looks to dominate the game through the relationship of possession and spacial control; a way of playing that allows you to alter the dimensions of the playing field through your player positioning that is preset by the ability of your playing squad and that of your opponent's. Everything else is variable and unique from person to person, from team to team and generation to generation.

Football tactics change and evolve and as legendary coach Dick Bate reminds us time and time again, we will continue to see football become even more of a team game in the future and we will continue to see players that are able to go beyond what is currently imaginable on a football field. But for the current model, I applaud all those who have formed not only the tiki-taka philosophy, but shaped football to what it is today:

Pep Guardiola, Marcelo Bielsa, Frank Rijkaard, Louis Van Gaal, Johan Cruyff, Bill Shankly, Rinus Michels, Victor Maslov, Valeriy Lobanovskyi, Gusztáv Sebes & The Magnificent Magyars, La Maquina of River Plate, Vic Buckingham, John Harvey & Alberto Horacio Suppici, Matthias Sindelar, Robert Smyth McColl, Peter McWilliam, Archie McLean and all those who haven't been formally acknowledged in this book and have been lost in history, but not forgotten on a football field.

Thank You

Jed C. Davies

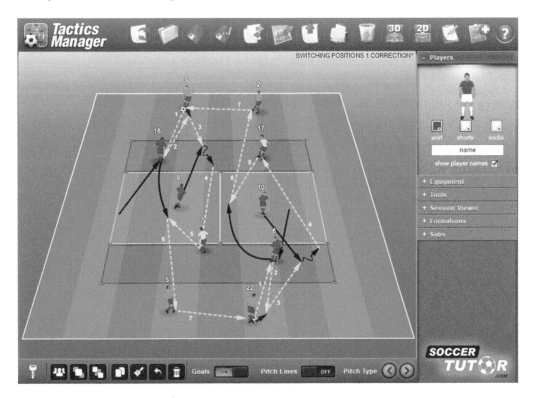